Citizenship, Identity, and Education
in Muslim Communities

Citizenship, Identity, and Education in Muslim Communities

Essays on Attachment and Obligation

Edited by
Michael S. Merry
and
Jeffrey Ayala Milligan

palgrave
macmillan

CITIZENSHIP, IDENTITY, AND EDUCATION IN MUSLIM COMMUNITIES
Copyright © Michael S. Merry and Jeffrey Ayala Milligan, 2010.

First published in 2010 by
PALGRAVE MACMILLAN®
in the United States—a division of St. Martin's Press LLC,
175 Fifth Avenue, New York, NY 10010.

Where this book is distributed in the UK, Europe and the rest of the world,
this is by Palgrave Macmillan, a division of Macmillan Publishers Limited,
registered in England, company number 785998, of Houndmills,
Basingstoke, Hampshire RG21 6XS.

Palgrave Macmillan is the global academic imprint of the above companies
and has companies and representatives throughout the world.

Palgrave® and Macmillan® are registered trademarks in the United States,
the United Kingdom, Europe and other countries.

ISBN: 978–0–230–10454–9

Library of Congress Cataloging-in-Publication Data

  Citizenship, identity, and education in Muslim communities : essays
on attachment and obligation / edited by Michael S. Merry, Jeffrey Ayala
Milligan.
    p. cm.
  Includes bibliographical references and index.
  ISBN 978–0–230–10454–9 (alk. paper)
    1. Citizenship—Islamic countries. 2. Islamic education. 3. Citizenship—
Study and teaching—Islamic countries. 4. Identification (Religion) 5. Political
obligation. I. Merry, Michael S. II. Milligan, Jeffrey Ayala.

JQ1852.A92C58 2010
323.60917′67—dc22   2010019029

A catalogue record of the book is available from the British Library.

Design by Newgen Imaging Systems (P) Ltd., Chennai, India.

First edition: December 2010

10 9 8 7 6 5 4 3 2 1

Printed in the United States of America.

For
Nicholas, Sophia, Peter, Ismael, and Gabrial

CONTENTS

FOREWORD

Scholarship is a calling—a mission-driven endeavor—and its adepts are summoned to tackle serious challenges in the world, and offer reflections, analysis, and visionary ideas in order to move matters forward. It is not a calling to simply report on what is taking place—that is what modern journalism does. Nor is it a calling to constantly be engaged in public debates—that is called politics. Scholarship is a calling to transcend the day-to-day conceptions of what is going in the world—a calling to be unafraid of what *is* to come, and to shape what *may* come.

Scholars have identified a key challenge that faces us today: the interplay between Islam and political liberalism, not only in the West, but also crucially in the Muslim world. When we note "Islam" in this regard, we refer to it as not a set of rituals, but rather as a worldview—a *Weltanschauung* that underpins a legal heritage, a spiritual inheritance, and a theological tradition. In short, what Muslims describe as their *turath* (tradition)—which is the sum of their religious sciences and the cosmology that goes along with it, and are inseparable from it. This volume provides an intriguing contribution as it takes on that interplay from many different angles.

These angles can be addressed through a variety of themes. Can political liberalism, insofar as it is expressed in notions of democratic citizenship, reconcile with the Muslim presence that is now an integral part of the West? This is not an easy question to answer—it begs the primordial question of all societies, "Who are we?" This volume also raises interesting questions about how that question relates to obligations and feelings of belonging. Individualism does not displace the desire for societal cohesion, and that cannot be properly addressed without looking at this issue. Key to this is our understanding of secularism—the question for liberals everywhere is what type of secularism is fundamental and needed for a successful, pragmatic politic.

This line of questioning is not theoretical alone—the absence of a suitable paradigm has already led to a number of crises in Europe in particular. The ban on building minarets in Switzerland in late 2009, and the numerous *hijab*/headscarf controversies are just two examples. We must take this seriously, as our concept of citizenship cannot remain intact without progressing past these problems—the alternative is to allow the populist far right to provide shortsighted, narrow answers that are unsustainable, and ultimately destructive.

Discussions on this point by the contributors to this volume look at both the ramifications of such a question within the West, and within the Muslim world. What arise as issues to be discussed when we consider the interplay between Islam and political liberalism in the Muslim world itself? This leads us to consider the various "Islamization" projects that have been worked on in various parts of the Muslim world. Islamization is a word coined by the contemporary Islamic philosopher, S. M. Naquib al-Attas, whose influence went far beyond his native Malaysia in stimulating Muslims around the world to consider how Islam can become *relevant* to global discourse. [That had to take place by attaching oneself to the concept which underpinned his interpretation of "Islamization"—the view of the world informed by, and defined by, Islam; or, as he put it, the Islamic worldview—a powerful, and unique, philosophical engagement with modernity.] It has not always worked out particularly well—the Islamic world remains deeply affected by being colonized in its recent history, which plays a great role in defining how basic education itself, let alone higher intellectual thought, has developed.

It's important not to overstate these queries, for such queries do not define how the overwhelming majority of Muslim Westerners (or non-Westerners) go about their lives in relating to their societies. Even practicing believers (and there is much evidence to suggest that the overwhelming majority of Muslim Westerners, as well as most Muslims around the world, are not practicing) do not generally trouble themselves with philosophical questions of this nature. They generally exist as most individuals do—affected more by social, economic, and political issues.

Nevertheless, these remain as important questions. In the West, we have so stigmatized the Muslim community in our midst, on account of their connection (even though it may be tenuous) to Islam, that it becomes a virtual necessity, for us as Westerners, to carry out this exercise. The validity of it aside, it may be that we will never recognize the Muslims, whether as individuals or as a community, as part and parcel of our various European collectives, until we are psychologically able to view Islam as a European religion. Whatever can be done to treat that psychological condition in a positive and genuine manner, should be done, and soon. Moreover, within the Muslim world itself, the way that education has developed in recent years indicates that Islam remains a key issue—even if they might not be wholly religious. The empirical analysis that is begun in this volume needs to be intensified and widened, in order to properly understand the experiments that have taken place.

However, in the midst of that, we must consider a question that Muslims are asking themselves: Is the Islam they are attached to a substitute for an ethnic identity, or a call to purpose—an ethical worldview? That needs to be unpackaged, to see if the very questions are correct—as do the incessant and constant fear-mongering about the *ummah*. The concept of the *ummah* has never stopped Muslim communities from becoming indigenous, cultural creationists in the various societies that they inhabit all over the world—and there is no need to think their loyalty is somehow questionable if they maintain that sort of connection now.

For Muslims, Westerners, and Muslim Westerners, therefore, there are a number of interesting queries that should not be avoided and should be engaged. Engagement does not mean compromise, but it does mean being very serious about the depth of our understanding on both sides. Without the deepest type of engagement, we will go nowhere, but with seriousness and genuineness being our twin guides, we may discover things that can lead us to a far more hopeful future for this world and for future generations.

H. A. HELLYER
Fellow, Centre for Research in
Ethnic Relations
University of Warwick

CHAPTER 1

Citizenship as Attachment and Obligation

Michael S. Merry and
Jeffrey Ayala Milligan

Islam and the Crisis of Citizenship

Efforts to address citizenship entail defining, elucidating, and defending the rights, roles, and responsibilities of persons who share a political culture. The discussion encompasses the political rhetoric of freedom and equality on one hand, and decency and social cooperation on the other. Citizenship describes articulated dispositions, entitlements, and actions dictated by governments and constitutions, where cultural, political, and religious differences find common ground. Its virtues remain ideals. Some states manage better than others to deliver on these ideals, while others champion the importance of citizenship in only the thinnest sense. Whatever the case, citizenship entails a reciprocal relationship between individuals and the state, taking in a variety of social, economic, and political virtues, though the ranking of these virtues is unsettled. The contours of citizenship include various and sundry modes of attachment and obligation.

Citizenship is carried out in unique ways. In Europe, each state model differs in important respects; and in Asia, Africa and the Americas no country orients itself to the requirements of citizenship in exactly the same way. This has always been true, and until very recently virtually all notions of citizenship were inextricably linked to dominant religions, languages, and cultural artifacts such as music and literature.

In many places, minority groups have been relegated to second class status, excluded from economic opportunities and public life, or forcibly assimilated by states bent on incorporating their cultural others.

While debates and articulations of attachment and obligation manifest in various ways in different societies vis-à-vis specific minority groups, doubtless no group today is more singled out for scrutiny than Muslims regardless of whether they constitute a majority or minority, and regardless of their doctrinal or ethnic differences. The reasons for the excessive attention paid to Muslims, which seem both obvious and obscure, are difficult to disentangle from ideological, economic, and political interests. Whether advanced by ordinary imams, political pundits, ideologues, or scholars, familiar and well-rehearsed arguments traffic in caricature and hence polarize and distort rather than foster mutual understanding.

Of course Muslims are not the only group for whom occasional disputes arise vis-à-vis the state. Many conservative religious traditions find themselves in conflict with temporal political authority. But Islam's transnational character and the universality of its claims raise a number of questions concerning the primary commitments of Muslim citizens: the nature of their commitments, how they are ranked, and whether they conflict with non-Islamic institutional norms. Whether compliance with a lawful and legitimate government is a requirement for Muslims is not settled simply with appeals to Islamic law. Both personal and collective experiences with discrimination (as well as Western support for monarchical tyrants and controversial wars in, or sanctions against, Muslim countries), have interrupted Muslim loyalties toward the countries in which they reside. Whether Muslims live in majority Islamic societies or not is beside the point. In fact, many Muslims feel alienated by their own societies that often treat them as second class citizens, or worse, as outsiders. While most Muslims ask for public recognition, basic freedoms, and equal treatment, a vocal few grab headlines by denouncing Western or Western-supported governments as morally bankrupt. Membership in the global body of believers *(ummah Islamiyyah)* for many is the paramount form of citizenship from which primary attachments and obligations are derived.

For these and many other reasons, the primary loyalties of Muslims are routinely questioned in the media and the halls of government in a climate of socioeconomic uncertainty and fear. Seen from this perspective—again, majority or minority Muslim society is inconsequential—many simply see Islam as a fanatical religious ideology guided by unsparing and undifferentiated moral dogma. Viewed in this way,

Islam is portrayed as an insidious threat both to noble liberal democratic ideals and to capitalist economic interests (the latter often masquerading as the former). In Europe, for example, talk of the "Islamic threat" is ubiquitous and renewed appeals to "our norms and values" have become a mantra. As if to exacerbate the vulnerable socioeconomic position of Muslim minorities as an immigrant underclass, profiling, discrimination, and mistreatment on one hand, and extremist acts[1] of a radical few on the other, strengthen the politics of fear that sustains the right-wing diatribes of a minority political elite. Both sides of this polarized debate are vocal and visible and attract a disproportionate amount of attention in the media. These patterns continue to play out and thwart mutual understanding; they divide rather than unite persons around common ideals. This unsettling conception of citizenship leads to tensions between dominant groups who are skeptical about the "loyalty" of minority communities and fearful of changes that erode their social position, and minority—and frequently marginalized—groups who are determined to assert their rights to citizenship on their own cultural or religious terms. In a very real sense, then, one may speak of a crisis of citizenship.

The tension caused by cultural heterogeneity and the cultivation of common values and dispositions necessary to produce and sustain national political institutions is particularly acute in postcolonial societies. In many cases (Indonesia, Philippines, Nigeria), states did not exist prior to colonization and often contain, within arbitrarily defined colonial borders, a bewildering variety of cultures, ethnicities, religions, and languages from which newly independent governments have faced the challenge of forging new national identities to buttress newly-won citizenship. Most turned to the same institutional mechanisms—education, for instance—used in the developed world to create Euro-American style nation-states defined by dominant religious, economic, and cultural groups. The emergence of secessionist movements on the peripheries of many of these states has reinforced the experience of many contemporary developed societies: the effort to cultivate forms of identity supportive of democratic citizenship cannot afford to ignore or suppress other forms of attachment and obligation important to the individual and collective identities of a state's citizens.

As societies become increasingly heterogeneous, the values and dispositions necessary to reproduce the political institutions upon which legitimate states rely play a central role in reformulating policy. Some societies have sought to alleviate tensions by experimenting with bicultural arrangements between their dominant groups (Canada, Belgium); though these "experiments" have proven to be difficult to maintain.[2] In some European states this has meant the reassertion[3] of historically repressed languages and cultures (Welsh, Catalan), or an expansion of officially recognized minority religions (Hinduism, Islam) in various forms of institutional support. For more than twenty years Islamic and Hindu schools have received relatively equal treatment in Denmark and the Netherlands.

Of course, demographic changes have not prevented some states from clinging to ideas of citizenship grounded in historically dominant forms of belonging: Japan and China for example. Nor have demographic changes prevented other states, such as some in the former Yugoslavia or Soviet Union, from attempting to reassert traditional forms of nationalism with their conceptions of citizenship. In societies where this debate occurs, there are concerns about social cohesion and stability, particularly in times of economic crisis, mass immigration, and social and political unrest when spikes in unemployment, shrinking state budgets, reactionary politics, and pervasive unease and distrust feed the propensity to circle the wagons around historically dominant groups to the disadvantage of indigenous minorities and recent immigrant arrivals.

Of course this is not the whole story. There is also an undeniable awareness that citizenship cannot afford to be insular. Indeed, perhaps *because* of economic crises, but also climate change, pandemic health risks, and natural disasters, it is no longer possible to consider nation-states as isolated entities with singular requirements—certainly not in this age of the Internet and mass transportation. These facts raise the specter of *global* connectedness, and responsibility and articulations of citizenship, both in political theory and in the halls of government, more often than not assume a cosmopolitan character. Consequently, expanding notions of citizenship have never been more relevant or urgent. In societies spanning the globe there are lively discussions among academics, politicians, and ordinary citizens about its content and requirements.

Yet while a shared political culture is understood by most to mean something roughly coterminous with the nation-state, the idea of a shared political culture is disputed with growing intensity. Indeed, the normativity of so-called "free trade," the importing and exporting of commodities and labor, the globalization of marketing and popular culture, and increasingly, supranational governance, mean that cultural and religious identities, but also social attachments and political allegiances, are increasingly hybrid and in flux. Concurrent with the expansion of inequitable trade practices, the concentration of wealth and influence of multinational corporations, as well as the ever-expanding division between the haves and the have-nots, there emerges a pattern of transnational migration such as the world has never known, which further unsettles established conceptions of national or ethnic identity. Migration from the South to the North in the past quarter century coincides both with a rise in nationalism—and its cousin, xenophobia—as well as a resurgence of religious and cultural distinctions consistent with a politics of recognition. Accordingly, today, on every continent, the invocation of a nation's putative ideals, beliefs, and values operates to exclude at least as many as it manages to include. It is not surprising that many consider *any* state-sanctioned declaration of what it means to be a "good citizen," or to be "integrated," a recent and dubious construction crafted by the engineers of political expedience. While there is much talk nowadays about the "multicultural society," its rhetoric frequently amounts to little more than bare toleration and official expressions of tokenism.

Where these matters bear upon the situation of Muslims and Muslim communities, the meanings of citizenship are not confined to societies where they represent minority populations of fairly recent origin. The meanings attached to citizenship for Muslims in societies—even Islamic ones—in which they count as a strong majority, are not straightforwardly obvious; among other things they are complicated by nationality, ethnicity, immigration policy, and competing interpretations of Islam. The articulations of attachment and obligation in Bosnia or Tunisia will inevitably have to be balanced against a secular constitution but also take into account Serbian and Berber ethnic minorities respectively. Similarly, attachments and obligations for Muslims in Nigeria will inevitably be expressed against a web of complex interlocking concerns: disputes of political and economic power, interpretations of shari'ah, land rights, tribal identities, educational opportunities, and social class. Hence questions of public recognition of minority Muslim groups, defined ethnically, religiously, or otherwise, are equally a challenge for majority Muslim societies.

In majority Muslim societies the relationship between religious identity, ethnic identity, and citizenship presents a varied picture. In some states—Saudi Arabia, for instance—religious identity and citizenship may largely overlap yet not prevent the experience of social exclusion on gendered, economic or cultural grounds. In others, such as Malaysia, citizenship transcends religious identification, which roughly parallels the ethnic differences among Malays, Chinese, and Indians, yet does not prevent a sense of socioeconomic marginalization, especially among Malaysians of Indian ancestry. In Indonesia, citizenship and religious identity transcend ethnic divisions but have not prevented the emergence of ethno-religious nationalisms that trouble dominant conceptions of citizenship.

While the tension between various notions of citizenship and other attachments and obligations is an issue confronted by any multicultural, religiously diverse state, such questions have assumed a greater urgency in a contemporary international climate where proponents of Islamist ideology advocate and carry out acts of political violence against both Muslim and non-Muslim societies while, as a result, proponents of other forms of Muslim identity, in all their diversity, become the object of suspicion and hostility from their fellow citizens. Clearly, then, being a Muslim today means a variety of things depending on the cultural and political context. Further, being a member of the global community of Muslim believers (*ummah Islamiyyah*), articulates a type of belonging that is often perceived either as being in conflict with what it means to be a local citizen, or else a Muslim identity that is indistinguishable from what it means to be a member of an ethnic group or a nation-state. Both forms of misrecognition are a frequent occurrence.

Citizenship, Identity, and Education

It is not surprising that shifting conceptions of citizenship affect educational practices, because states typically consider the promotion of citizenship integral to their educational goals. Yet in order to promote citizenship, states must organize, supply, fund, and govern schools so the requisite knowledge of the workings of political institutions is made available. Schools have long been the institutionalized instruments of the state par excellence to foster identification with one's national or regional identity and to awaken in young people an awareness of certain civic attachments and obligations. And as with nationalist conceptions of citizenship, so too are ethnic and religious identities sometimes promoted through both formal and informal systems of schooling. In the United States, for instance, public schools were explicitly tasked in the late nineteenth and early twentieth century with assimilating European immigrants into the cultural and political "mainstream" of American society, while involuntary, nonwhite subjects of American power—Native Americans, African-Americans, Filipinos, Latinos—were schooled for marginalized and subordinate positions in political and cultural life. Ethnic or religious schooling that attempted to preserve particular identities—German language schooling during World War I or Catholic schooling in the nineteenth century—was actively discouraged as a threat to American civic identity, a fear echoed today in the suspicions of Islamic schooling in many western countries. The early twenty-first century, however, is in the midst of population movements and security threats that, if anything, exceed those of the early twentieth. Therefore, the basis for a shared political culture is an increasingly urgent question in societies around the world. And regardless of how or where this question is addressed, the relationship between education and citizenship is assumed.

But more than mere knowledge of political institutions, educational philosophers (far more often than governments) recognize the need to promote and cultivate the important skills and dispositions necessary for deliberation, among informed citizens, about socially and politically relevant issues. Deliberation entails the ability to reflect upon and communicate one's ideas and interests while engaging generously with the ideas of others. The aim of deliberative citizenship, therefore, is not only to locate shared political needs and interests necessary for the purposes of social stability, but also to possess the dispositions and habits necessary for meaningful recognition and interaction with others within one's shared political space.

Citizenship is a concept that envelops specific political and legal rights, notions of inclusion and exclusion, and intimations of attachment and obligation. Attachments are sometimes, though not always, expressed through patriotic feeling around a set of presumably shared values and norms, or perhaps around a shared language and history. Moreover, attachments frequently garner strength from rituals (war commemorations, national holidays) and emotion-rousing speeches and creeds that extol the lives of political heroes. Yet even the less emotive expressions of citizenship normally point to a general sense of belonging to a particular place with others who share it, even if one expression of civic belonging is political indifference. Put another way, citizenship is the legal expression of how persons *identify* with a particular place.

Persons either are socialized into, or through immigration come to acquire, a particular civic attachment[4]; thus, as with education, citizenship and identity are also mutually reinforcing concepts even if one's primary attachments lie elsewhere. Meanwhile, obligations of various sorts arise owing to one's shared membership in a community whose maintenance requires the (often unremunerated) service of those eligible to fill the requisite roles. Military service and jury duty are examples, but countless *voluntary* manifestations of attachment and obligation may be observed at various times and places. Sometimes these assume a cosmopolitan character but more often articulations of citizenship are expressed at the local level.

As implied by the reference to indifference in the foregoing paragraph, official membership within a nation-state may have little purchase on a person's identity. That is, while citizenship typically refers to political membership, in many instances other memberships simultaneously exist, and often have greater importance and priority. Indeed, conceptions of identity rooted in one's membership in, say, ethnic and/or religious communities more commonly summon one's attention and loyalty. To illustrate: an individual may have been born, raised, and educated in Turkey, possess a Turkish passport, speak fluent Turkish, and travel abroad as a Turkish exchange student yet not *identify with* Turkey per se (but rather with the Kurds). Of course, regardless of how she feels, this may not prevent her from being *identified as* Turkish by others unless, perhaps, she undertakes the formal steps of officially renouncing Turkish citizenship and replacing it with another. The same will be true for deeply religious persons whose faith is the most singular aspect of their identity. Those for whom faith is paramount may even have an antagonistic relationship toward their government (as was witnessed by the world of Buddhist monks in Burma in 2007).

However else identity is construed, it typically speaks to how persons wish to be recognized in the public sphere, but also where their primary attachments are fixed. For most people these attachments shift over the course of one's lifetime, and rankings vary depending on one's present commitments, but also as a direct consequence of how one is perceived by others. Such conceptions of identity do not inevitably contradict the role of citizen in a particular nation-state. For example, Muslim girls who choose to don the headscarf—whether they live in a majority Muslim society or not—may have complicated motives for doing so, regardless of how local and national governments interpret it. In other cases, conceptions of identity more obviously conflict with acceptable forms of citizenship, especially in multi-ethnic postcolonial states where ethnic nationalisms sometimes clash with imposed (and perhaps, artificial) national identities.

Citizenship and Belonging

Debates over citizenship often begin as crude demands employing the language of "integration." Integration is typically confrontational in its connotations; cultural difference remains a "problem" to be solved. In these situations, persons of minority or immigrant backgrounds are not given clear indicators of what being "integrated" means, yet it is assumed that it is their responsibility to integrate themselves. But of course in order for persons—of whatever background—to be "integrated" they must first feel that they are able to accept, and be accepted into, a social and political culture whose price of admission does not require the surrender of other attachments that may be of equal or even more value to them. This sense of belonging denotes not only the feeling one has of being a part of his/her society, but also—and perhaps more important—the conviction on the part of *others* that one belongs. In other words, by belonging we mean that persons do not feel questioned, judged, or discriminated against on the basis of one's appearance, but also one's political opinions, voting record, baseball team preference, language spoken at home, or affiliation with a particular school. Being integrated, then, describes not only one's first language, level of education, employment status, etc. but also the *psychological* condition of feeling oneself a part of the society she inhabits. But feeling oneself to be a part of one's society is just the beginning. For it must also be possible to *contribute* to society, *demonstrate* loyalty to it, and *express* themselves as citizens in a variety of ways. We suggest that this state of affairs describes a healthy pluralism, something that continually appears under threat in all democratic and democratizing societies.

The current climate of mistrust, uncertainty *and* hope demands a careful reappraisal of long-settled notions of democratic citizenship in light of new or heretofore ignored attachments and obligations as well as the collaborative formulation, by both Muslims and non-Muslims, of new conceptions of democratic citizenship that respect Muslims' religious attachments and obligations while legitimately rejecting those attachments, of Muslims and non-Muslims alike, inimical to democratic society. In view of this, we propose in these chapters to explore the tensions inherent in this complexity of belonging in various Muslim communities, the reconsiderations of civic identity it inspires in contemporary Muslim and non-Muslim philosophical discourse, and some of the reforms in educational policy and practice it influences. Carving out an identity—a place of belonging—within these rather different contexts, and the role that education and citizenship play in constructing those identities, is the primary focus of this book. With these essays we contribute to a fuller and more nuanced understanding of the diverse and evolving discourse on citizenship, identity, and education for Muslims in the contemporary world.

Each of the contributions examine the interlocking notions of citizenship, identity, and education from different national and cultural perspectives. Specific case studies inform several of the chapters. Our aim is to capture some of the diversity of orientation and thinking on this complex subject, while also showing points of convergence across the international spectrum. Though various disciplinary backgrounds are represented in this volume, each contribution in its own way critically examines the manner in which different conceptions of citizenship, identity, and education are closely related. These conversations occur both at an abstract and a practical level.

One aim of this book is to show that the tendency to focus solely on political citizenship, or alternatively, membership in the *ummah Islamiyyah*, to the extent that it ignores other attachments and obligations, cannot adequately account for the many tensions that exist within and between Muslim communities and the larger societies they inhabit. The essays gathered in this volume explore some of these shifts in philosophical and educational policy discourses on religious identity, civic identity, and education in a cross-section of the Muslim world, thus emphasizing the creative rather than the destructive responses to the tension between a globalization shaped by Western presuppositions and the demand of many Muslims to have a say in their integration into the global community rather than being assimilated into it on terms set by others. The essays gathered in this volume promise to serve up an engaging international, interdisciplinary conversation with the philosophical rigor such a subject deserves.

Islam and Democratic Citizenship: Theoretical Possibilities

The opening chapter of this volume, Andrew March's "Islamic Foundations for a Social Contract in non-Muslim Liberal Democracies," directly confronts the central question at the heart of concerns about the compatibility of Islam and democracy: Do the teachings of Islam itself militate against the sort of overlapping consensus between Muslims and non-Muslims around the political values that are necessary for the

existence of a liberal democracy?[5] In doing so he avoids the easy plati-
tudes of both those multiculturalists who claim there is no problem at
all as well as those Islamists who argue that the question is settled in
favor of the rejection of Muslims' loyalty to non-Muslim states. Rather,
he carefully and critically examines a range of classical and contemporary Islamic legal discourses on the question of the permissibility
of Muslims' citizenship in non-Muslim states and the nature of their
obligations to such states to "examine the potential for a positive, principled, and stable Islamic affirmation of citizenship in a non-Muslim
liberal democracy."

This includes, crucially, the question of Muslims' obligation to
refrain from participating in efforts to harm the state of one's residence or to actively participate in the defense of the state, issues central
to the widespread concern about "home-grown radicals" such as the
7/7 bombers in London or Major Nidal Malik Hasan, the U.S. Army
officer who murdered thirteen fellow soldiers at Fort Hood, Texas to
avoid fighting fellow Muslims. While March finds that there is a stream
of Islamic legal discourse underwriting the notion that one's obligation to the *ummah Islammiya* trumps one's obligations as a citizen of a
liberal democratic state, there are also interpretations of that discourse
by authoritative Muslim jurists that articulate "firm and culturally
authentic Islamic values...that can ground Islamically a social contract
between Muslims and a non-Muslim liberal democracy." The conditions this discourse places on such a social contract, such as the security
of Muslim citizens, the freedom to practice one's religion without fear
of seduction away from it, and freedom to manifest one's religion, are
conditions, March argues, that political liberalism is quite content to
grant. While none of this guarantees that Muslim citizens and residents
of liberal democracies will choose to interpret their religious obligations in this way, it is doctrinally plausible for them to do so. Thus, an
overlapping consensus between Muslim and non-Muslim citizens on
the shared political values necessary to a liberal democracy is possible,
if not guaranteed.

If Andrew March's chapter asks whether Islam can include liberal-
ism, Lucas Swaine asks the corollary question: Can liberalism include
Islam? Swaine's "Demanding Deliberation: Political Liberalism and the
Inclusion of Islam" identifies reciprocal and inclusive political delib-
eration as a central feature of liberal democracy and asks "whether
Muslims face doctrinal or other religious impediments to becoming
good citizens in pluralistic democracies."[6] His answer, in short, is no.
He finds no doctrinal or religious impediments to Muslim participation

in democratic political deliberation, noting as well the empirical fact that millions of Muslims *do* participate in such deliberation in both Muslim and non-Muslim democratic societies around the world. Swaine goes beyond this observation, however, to argue that Muslim citizens of liberal democracies have "special capacities to renew the vitality of democratic polities" by reintroducing into the political discourse of increasingly secular western—especially European—societies the perspectives of more heteronomous communities. In addition, Swaine asserts that "more liberal-minded Muslims" can, with liberal non-Muslim allies, facilitate a communication between Muslim and non-Muslim communities that translates liberal democratic principles in ways that make sense within the value system of Muslim communities while also translating the values of such communities in ways that resonate with liberal democratic concerns. In this way liberal political deliberation is enhanced by the inclusion of the broader range of voices present within a democratic society.

Despite the doctrinal and philosophical plausibility of an overlapping consensus between Islam and liberal democratic theory, Tariq Modood's "Multiculturalism in the West and Muslim Identity" reminds us that what may be plausible is not necessarily practiced. He describes a "crisis of multiculturalism" that challenges the Muslim minority community in Britain—and by implication minority Muslim communities in other western democracies—to develop a sense of belonging to a British society that is perceived as being at war with Muslims abroad and insensitive to them at home, while at the same time the Muslim identity politics to which such perceptions give rise lead many in the majority to view British Muslims with suspicion, if not outright hostility. Modood argues that some classical liberal conceptions of citizenship ignore the myriad differences of actual citizens in order to assert the fundamental equality of citizens. On the other hand, some conceptions of multiculturalism posit specious distinctions between ascribed and voluntary identities in order to justify relegating religious identities to the private realm and thus preserve a secular public discourse. Both, he argues, are inadequate to meet this crisis. He argues instead for a "multicultural citizenship" that recognizes the political salience of differences—both those asserted by the members of a community as well as those ascribed to it from without—as the ever evolving social reality in which formal citizenship is enacted by actual citizens while at the same time eschewing the all-too-common multiculturalist rejection of the idea of a common identity across differences. A "multicultural nationalism" and a "multicultural citizenship" that recognizes and celebrates difference—religious and otherwise—as part of who "we" are, Modood argues, offers a more hopeful solution to the present tensions between British Muslims and the larger British society. The reassertion of liberal conceptions of citizenship or conceptions of multiculturalism that deny the relevance of the very identity markers—in this case adherence to Islam—that serve to identify the Muslim community to itself and others does not offer such hope. Reconnecting with this form of multiculturalism is, he argues, "the best way to overcome the present state of fear, polarization and ultimately the suicide bombings in our cities." The recognition and celebration of difference Modood calls for necessarily precludes the imposition, either overtly or implicitly, of preordained, authorized forms of identity. There can be no one, right way of being British and/or Muslim.

In their contribution to this volume, "Being Muslim, a Fact or Challenge?" Yedullah Kazmi and Rosnani Hashim argue for just such a notion of identity. They reject the idea of a monolithic Muslim identity in favor of a conception of identity as a dialogical construct between the unique characteristics of any given individual—race, gender, ethnicity, religious belief—and the sociohistorical context in which he or she happens to live. Thus identity is not a preordained fact but rather a challenge, a life project in which the individual has the freedom and the responsibility to ethically construct an identity consonant with her fundamental beliefs and the sociocultural milieu in which she finds herself. For Muslims, Kazmi and Hashim argue, this involves building on the Qur'anic tenets that define what a Muslim believes "in the context of concrete historical and cultural reality" so that an Islamic spiritual expression is given to historical experience. This historical consciousness precludes the mindless acceptance of conceptions of Muslim identity formed in other sociohistorical contexts and demands the thoughtful consideration of what it means to be a Muslim in this particular context. This requires dialogue and deliberation, not only among Muslims as they wrestle with the challenges of living as Muslims in particular contexts and ensuring the Islamic survival of subsequent generations, but between Muslims and the broader societies they inhabit. Thus the conception of Muslim identity outlined by Kazmi and Hashim highlights the necessity of dialogue between Muslims and their non-Muslim fellow citizens over the ways in which the broader society shapes Muslim identity without changing its "Muslimness" and the ways that identity in turn "enriches the repertoire of meaning" available to the broader society.

Kazmi and Hashim argue that Muslim educators all too often ask the wrong questions. Rather than asking *what* should be taught, a question that tends to elicit prescriptive answers, Muslim educators should ask *who* is to be taught. Attending first to the particular needs of actual learners in concrete circumstances foregrounds and celebrates the diversity within the Muslim community and the diverse sociopolitical circumstances in which the members of that community reside. Kazmi and Hashim articulate a concept of Muslim identity potentially consistent with the expectations of democratic citizenship offered by Andrew March and Lucas Swaine as well as the "multicultural citizenship" and "multicultural nationalism" posited by Modood. And they raise the possibility of an approach to education designed to realize that potential.

These first four contributions to this volume lay important theoretical groundwork for the essays that follow. Tariq Modood reminds us of the problem that animates this book; namely, the apparent tensions between Muslim identity and democratic citizenship that manifests itself in Muslim residents of western democratic societies who feel marginalized and singled out for unreasonable scrutiny and the majority populations of these same societies suspicious of Muslims' ability and interest to integrate into the mainstream as full-fledged, loyal citizens, as well as the claim from within some Muslim majority societies that democracy is un-Islamic. Modood offers the provocative concepts of "multicultural citizenship" and "multicultural nationalism" as a framework for bridging this gap and ameliorating these tensions, while Andrew March and Lucas Swaine identify and articulate characteristics required of such citizenship in a liberal democracy. These include a sense of belonging—both in terms of the legitimacy of one's presence in and the capacity for loyalty to a multicultural, multi-religious polity, the willingness to contribute to the defense of such a society or, at the very least, refrain from participating in threats to it, and the capacity for engaging in political deliberation with other members of society who do not share one's religious or other commitments. Yedullah Kazmi and Rosnani Hashim articulate a concept of Muslim identity consistent with both Modood's multicultural citizenship and March's and Swaine's criteria of democratic citizenship. Though four essays cannot possibly cover everything that can or should be said on these topics, they at the very least put to rest the misbegotten arguments of both the "clash of civilizations" advocates and those radical Islamists who posit some fundamental incompatibility between liberal democracy and Islam.

These four essays demonstrate the theoretical *possibility* of a doctrinally plausible overlapping consensus between liberal democracy and Islam and offer some broad outlines of how such a consensus might be achieved. They suggest, in the language of John Dewey (1916), "something to be tried," but they do not offer specific instructions or concrete examples. Such steps are the natural substance of educational experimentation, to which the other contributors turn their attention.

Islamic Education and Democratic Citizenship: Experiments in Practice

Perhaps no country is more consistently invoked to illustrate western fears regarding the purported tensions between Islamic education and democracy than Pakistan. Journalistic analyses of Islamic extremism in Pakistan almost universally locate its intellectual origins in the influence of the *madrasah* in the educational vacuum created by a failed system of government education. Matthew J. Nelson, however, argues in his chapter, "Dealing with Difference: Religious Education and the Challenge of Democracy in Pakistan," that the challenge to democracy in Pakistan from religious education is not the *madaris* per se, which account for only a tiny minority of the overall full-time school enrollment, but rather the approach to difference supported by the large majority of those who choose a mixed—religious and secular—education for their children.[7] Nelson's extensive ethnographic study of the mixed education sector of an increasingly privatized Pakistani educational system reveals a widespread belief that the unity of Islam demands the suppression of sectarian and doctrinal difference in favor of a single, authoritative expression of what it means to be Muslim. Unsurprisingly, this authoritative version typically conforms to the beliefs and practices of the particular religious community questioned. Ignoring difference, or "overcoming" it in favor of a stress on commonalities, is seen by Nelson's respondents as the best way to avoid sectarian conflict.

However, this equation of unity with perfect sameness in the context of a competitive educational market yields monopolistic orientations that, in effect, pit each expression of religious identity against other expressions in an effort to define the terms of unity within its own rather particular set of beliefs and practices. Thus, though Nelson's respondents believe that the suppression of difference in favor of unity will *prevent* sectarian violence, Nelson finds that it is in fact the denial of difference that *contributes* to sectarian violence and undermines the promise of Pakistani democracy. In effect, Nelson's analysis of the nexus of Islam, Islamic education, and democracy in Pakistan recalls Kazmi's and Hashim's thesis that attention to the various expressions of Islamic identity that emerge from the ongoing effort to remain true to Qur'anic values in different sociohistorical circumstances is necessary to the success of democracy in diverse Muslim and non-Muslim societies. Nelson shares Kazmi's and Hashim's implicit concern that the suppression of difference in favor of authoritative commonality is inimical to democracy. He finds a small measure of hope, though, in the minority of his respondents who argued that differences should be respected and celebrated and the larger group of those who, once they recognized the ongoing fact of difference and the necessity to avoid conflict, concluded that respect for diversity must be a component of religious education. The critical educational question for Nelson, then, is how might it be possible to respond to local demands for religious education while countering the language of "unity-as-monopoly" and finding ways to appreciate the terms of religious difference, sectarian diversity, and ongoing political debate?

Robert Hefner's "Islamic Schools, Social Movements, and Democracy in Indonesia" describes one possible response to Nelson's question in the approach to Islamic education taken by a democratizing Indonesia.[8] Hefner describes a contemporary system of Islamic education in Indonesia that is "among the most intellectually dynamic in the entire Muslim world," where girls make up fully one-half of the student population, and where "the overwhelming majority of Muslim educators have concluded that constitutional democracy is compatible with Islam, and is the best form of government for Indonesia."

Within this context, Hefner's chapter focuses on one recent trend in Indonesian Islamic education: the growing prominence of "integrated" schools that self-consciously attempt to infuse Islamic values and precepts into the secular curriculum in order to produce devout, well-educated graduates equipped with the knowledge and skills necessary to engage with and transform the broader society. While these schools are committed to the "Islamization" of society, and a tiny radical minority has been implicated in acts of political violence, it appears that these schools, as well as the broader system of Indonesian Islamic schools may be more open to the conception of Muslim identity described by Kazmi and Hashim and thus more conducive to the respect for difference that Modood, March, and Swaine find so necessary to democracy and the absence of which Nelson reports from Pakistan.

Hefner reports the results of surveys of the general public and Muslim educators in 2004 and 2006 that show overwhelming majorities of both groups support key principles of liberal democracy and shari'a. However, other data show that actual political support for pro-shari'a parties is considerably lower than what these survey results might suggest. This suggests, Hefner argues, an ongoing effort of Indonesian intellectuals and citizens to work out a satisfactory balance between Islamic values and democracy in the world's largest Muslim country. Islamic schools' positive role in this process, Hefner suggests, should "dispel any impression that the Islamic educational establishment is a reactionary drag on an otherwise pluralist public."

Charlene Tan's and Intan Mokhtar's chapter, "Communitarianism and Islamic Social Studies in Singapore," moves the examination of Muslim education from one of the world's largest democracies to one of the smallest. Tan and Mokhtar critique the recently implemented Islamic Social Studies curriculum as a mechanism of a secular, democratic Singapore state intended to create "good" Muslim citizens in line with a distinctively communitarian conception of democratic citizenship. Their description of the Islamic Social Studies curriculum and its aims suggests a concrete experiment in the sort of identity construction described by Kazmi and Hashim coupled with the respect for difference called for by March, Swaine, and Nelson with the explicit purpose of producing multicultural citizens along the lines of that envisioned in this volume by Tariq Modood. Though Tan and Mokhtar are critical of certain aspects of the curriculum; namely its failure to adequately foster critical thinking skills, its superficial treatment of cultural difference, and a relatively uncritical embodiment of the state's nation-building agenda, the curriculum's effort to help "produce a comprehensive, systematic, and integrated educational system for the *madrasahs* in Singapore" represents an educational experiment that promises to shed light on the theoretical possibilities articulated in earlier chapters.

Finally, Rosnani Hashim concludes this volume's brief survey of educational experiments in the reconciliation of Islamic identity and democratic citizenship with a description of educational developments in Malaysia, perhaps the most vibrant Muslim-majority, religiously and ethnically diverse democracies in the world. She describes Malaysia's post-colonial efforts to transform an educational and political system that relegated religious identity to the private sphere into a system that tries to reflect the centrality of Islam to Malay culture and identity while at the same time respecting the rights of other ethnic groups within Malaysia's pluralistic society. Her historical account traces Malaysia's response to the educational agenda promoted in the First World Conference on Muslim Education held in Mecca in 1977 through the implementation of a national philosophy of education in 1987 and subsequent efforts to integrate Islamic values into school curricula at all levels, including key universities such as the International Islamic University of Malaysia. Hashim notes that, while teaching methods have thus far changed very little, the effort to Islamize the curriculum of Malaysian schools and thus support Malay students in the development of a modern Islamic identity has made considerable progress.

One element of these educational reforms crucial to the flourishing of Malaysian democracy is their impact on the rights and freedoms of Malaysia's ethnic minorities, particularly the Chinese and Indian communities that comprise as much as one-third of Malaysia's population. Hashim notes that educational reformers have endeavored to protect minority rights to an education that reflects their culture through the support of Chinese and Indian schools at the elementary level and working to ensure that schools at all levels respect the cultural sensibilities of all Malaysians. The ongoing effort to reintegrate Islamic values into the core of Malaysian education and society has not been without its difficulties. Sporadic violence in response to the recent controversy over the use of the word Allah by some Christian groups to refer to God is but one case in point. Nevertheless, Malaysia's effort to cultivate Islamic identity, celebrate cultural pluralism, and promote democratic governance may well constitute the most successful and promising example of a multicultural Muslim democracy in the world today.

Democracy and Difference

A recurring theme in each of the contributions in this volume is the question of difference. How a community accounts for and responds to difference appears to be at least one critical factor in realizing the potential of democratic citizenship and a democratic society. Is difference tolerated, respected, celebrated? If so, then the sense that one's identity is respected and therefore secure from external threats enables, though it does not guarantee, the sense of belonging that seems so essential to democratic citizenship. Respect for difference underpins the legitimacy of the various participants in democratic deliberation over the nature of the community in which those participants jointly reside. Or is difference denied, delegitimized, or targeted for elimination? If so, then the full citizenship of those marginalized is denied and the citizenship claimed by those who carry out the marginalization is not recognizably democratic. The prospects of social cooperation are enhanced in the first case, while the prospects of social conflict are enhanced in the second.

Another point these chapters drive home is the fact that dealing with difference is a challenge for both Muslim communities and non-Muslim communities. Sectarian differences within Islam as well as differences between Islam and other religions may be denied in ways that mark minority ethnic, racial, or religious groups as illegitimate and thus undercut the possibility of democratic citizenship for minorities and the majority. Comparable forms of marginalization on the basis of gender have similar effects. On the other hand, formal and informal constraints on the expression of difference—such as the ban on the *burka* or *hijab* in French, Belgian or Turkish schools, the refusal in Britain to extend multicultural discourse to religious identity described here by Modood, or the racism and Islamophobia prevalent in so many western societies—also denies full democratic citizenship to those so constrained and undermines the claims of the societies engaging in such practices to be democracies. This does not mean, of course, that any and all forms of difference must be tolerated. It does mean, however, that any truly democratic deliberation over the forms of illegitimate difference *must* include and account for all elements of a society, not just the majority.

Understanding and respecting difference is, fundamentally, a pedagogical problem. Though it is not necessarily a problem to be addressed only by schools—it encompasses of course the civic education of the larger community—schools are nevertheless one important venue for addressing the problem. The contributors to this volume do not offer any recipes for addressing the challenge of difference in democratic society. Indeed any attempt to do so would be self defeating because the imposition of successful practices developed in one sociohistorical context on a different sociohistorical context likely neglects the salient differences of that context and thus fails the test of respecting and accounting for difference. This does not mean, however, that we cannot learn from the successes and failures of others and experiment with their practices, suitably adapted to the particularities of our own context. This is what we attempt to do in these essays, to establish the theoretical possibility of a philosophically and doctrinally plausible overlapping consensus between Islam and democracy, to identify respect for difference as one critical component of that overlapping consensus, and to examine a range of educational practices in various sociohistorical contexts for insight into better ways to educate for difference and democratic citizenship in other contexts. It is our hope that the essays gathered here will further the deliberation and educational experimentation necessary to fully realize the democratic prospects of both minority and majority Muslim communities wherever they may be.

Notes

1. Brazen acts of violence and aggression, frequently carried out against civilian populations, are equated not with fanatical extremists but with Islam itself.
2. As many have noted, the different groups within a single nation-state often are strongly disinclined to learn about, or interact with, each other. This is certainly true of French and Anglophone Canadians as well as the Flemish and Walloons in Belgium, where verbal hostility is commonplace. Switzerland represents another example of a multi-lingual/multi-cultural state where one finds not so much mutual hostility as mutual indifference.
3. This reassertion does not always transpire as one might hope. Indeed, there is often discrimination associated with the newly found freedom to organize one's own institutions on a equal par with other groups. Examples are myriad, but the Quebecois constitutional requirements for French are one example.
4. Of course some individuals possess more than one citizenship owing to complicating factors of birth, parentage, or both.
5. An earlier version of this chapter was published in *The American Political Science Review* Vol. 101, No. 2, pp. 235–252. Reprinted with permission of Cambridge University Press.
6. An earlier version of this chapter was published in *Journal of Islamic Law and Culture* Vol. 11, No. 2 (May 2009), pp. 92–110. Reprinted with permission of Taylor and Francis.
7. An earlier version of this chapter was published in *Modern Asian Studies* Vol. 43, No. 3 (2009), pp. 591–618. Reprinted with permission of Cambridge University Press.
8. An earlier version of this chapter was published in Robert W. Hefner, Ed., *Making Modern Muslims: The Politics of Islamic Education in Southeast Asia* Honolulu: University of Hawaii Press. Reprinted with permission of University of Hawaii Press.

CHAPTER 2

Islamic Foundations for a Social Contract in Non-Muslim Liberal Democracies

Andrew F. March

Islamic Objections to Citizenship in Non-Muslim States

For Islamic doctrine, there are two broad problems with citizenship in non-Muslim liberal states. First, that those states are *liberal* in character; and second, that they are *non-Muslim* in character, both socially and politically. The first challenge of citizenship in liberal democracies for Muslim communities is to endorse the idea of entering into a social contract within a non-Muslim political community.

A minority tradition in Islamic law and ethics maintains that Muslims are not permitted to reside in a non-Muslim state, which is often referred to as *dar al-harb* ("abode of war") or *dar al-kufr* ("abode of unbelief"), both in the sense of states with non-Muslim majority populations and states governed by other than Islamic law. Muslims who find themselves in such situations through conquest are obligated to migrate (perform *hijra*) to the "Abode of Islam" (*dar al-Islam*) (Abou El Fadl 1994). In classical jurisprudence, this position was advanced mostly by the Maliki school of law, predominant in North Africa (e.g., al-Wansharisi 1981, 2: 121–138), but in the modern period it has been advanced by Saudi adherents of the Wahhabi doctrine, which claims derivation from the Hanbali school of law (e.g., al-Shithri n.d.), as well as certain fundamentalist thinkers not adhering to any single school, such as the Egyptian Sayyid Qutb (Qutb 2001, 3: 286).

However, the reasons that have traditionally been advanced as under-lying the prohibition are illuminating for our purposes, and Islamic scholars addressing the problem of Muslims living under non-Muslim political authority often feel the need to begin by raising the question of the permissibility of residence in non-Muslim lands (e.g., Qaradawi 2001a, 25). In addition to the claim that there is a categorical divine command to migrate from spheres of non-Muslim rule based on two Qur'anic verses[1] and a number of reports of prophetic speech (*hadith*),[2] Muslim thinkers who regard residence in a non-Muslim polity as impermissible generally advance six types of rational arguments (Abou El Fadl 1994):

1. Muslims must not be subject to non-Muslim laws (e.g., Sahnun n.d., 3: 278);
2. Islam and Muslims must not be put in a position of inferiority to non-Muslims (e.g., Wansharisi 1981, 2: 132–137);
3. Muslims must avoid aiding or increasing the strength of non-Muslims (e.g. al-Shirazi n.d., 2: 227);
4. Muslims are forbidden from forming bonds of friendship or soli-darity with non-Muslims (e.g. Shithri n.d., 3–4, 28–30);
5. Muslims are required to avoid environments of sin or indecency;
6. in non-Muslim environments it will be more difficult to pre-vent sin or the loss of religiosity in subsequent generations (e.g. Nadwi 1983, 113–4).

It is clear that all of the underlying reasons for prohibiting residence in a non-Muslim polity reveal a desire to avoid precisely the types of relationships with non-Muslims constitutive of both thin and thick conceptions of citizenship: from basic political obligation to deep bonds of solidarity based on values and ends shared with fellow citizens. What is crucial to note here is that while most Islamic scholars have not drawn the conclusion from these arguments that residence in non-Muslim lands is prohibited, many of those who regard it as permissible have nonetheless expressed some sympathy with the underlying argu-ments. Thus, it is common to find both classical and modern Islamic jurists arguing that it is permitted to reside in a non-Muslim polity if Muslims can do so safely and without threat to their religious practices; however, if possible, Muslims should seek to establish their own politi-cal authority (often considered part of what it *means* to enjoy religious freedom), avoid contributing to non-Muslim welfare or strength, and commit themselves to the ultimate Islamization of the non-Muslim society, all of which are conditions incompatible with the spirit and letter of citizenship in a liberal democracy (Abou El Fadl 1994; 'Abd al-Qadir 1998).

Considering that there is a debate among jurists regarding whether Muslims are permitted to reside permanently in non-Muslim states, it follows that rendering loyalty to them will present a more demanding ideological requirement of citizenship. At the most general level there are two basic attitudes within Islamic revelatory texts which challenge the idea of being loyal to a non-Muslim state. First is the idea that Muslims should not ally themselves with non-Muslims or non-Muslim polities. Islamic scholars often point to a number of Qur'anic verses, including 60:1[3], 3:28[4], and 3:118[5], to support the conclusion that political alliances with unbelievers, of which they consider citizenship to be a form, are impermissible. Second, Muslims should not harm individual Muslims and even less so the interests of the Muslim community or polity. A just life for a Muslim does not only consist of worshipping and avoiding sin, but of serving the community of believers in any way required of him, including (perhaps especially[6]) in war for the cause of Islam. This intuitive stance receives authoritative grounding in both the Qur'an[7] and in a few reports of Muhammad's speech (*hadith*) considered to be authentic and accurately transmitted. Two indicative *hadith* reports are the following, found in all of the authoritative collections: "The blood of a Muslim who proclaims that there is no god but God and that I am the Messenger of God may not be legally spilt other than in one of three [instances]: a life for a life, the married person who commits adultery, and one who forsakes his religion and abandons his community"; and "whoever carries arms against us is not one of us" (Bukhari 1997, 9: 20).

A further *hadith* would seem to have implications for even non-combatant service in a non-Muslim army engaged in combat with Muslims: "Whoever assists in killing a believer even by half a word will meet God with no hope of God's mercy written on His face." Finally, Islamic tradition holds that Muhammad's contract with the peoples of Medina ("the Constitution of Medina") included the following article: "A believer shall not slay a believer for the sake of an unbeliever, nor shall he aid an unbeliever against a believer. Believers are friends one to the other to the exclusion of outsiders." (Guillaume 1955, 232)

Muslim jurists and exegetes have, of course, argued from these two basic attitudes for very specific positions contrary to the idea of Muslim loyalty to a non-Muslim liberal democracy. Virtually all Islamic legal scholars from the earliest times of Islam to the present have agreed that serving in a non-Muslim army against Muslim forces is apostasy and, thus potentially punishable by death (surveyed in 'Abd al-Qadir 1998 and Topoljak 1997). Even serving in a non-Muslim army against other non-Muslims has been either strongly discouraged or only permissible if it advances Muslim aims (al-Shaybani 1966, 193; al-Sarakhsi 2001, 10: 106). One finds in juridical sources a frequent antipathy to Muslims helping non-Muslims when it is viewed that the cause is the advancement of a non-Islamic faith or conception of truth. The roots of this antipathy are manifold: not only might such help be seen as directly detracting from the Islamic cause, but even if there is no direct harm to Islam or Muslims, advancing the cause of unbelievers is something prohibited to Muslims. This antipathy thus applies not only during military or political conflict, but often to social and political forms of cooperation as well (Qutb 2001, 2: 62–3).

The preceding section demonstrates that Islam, as a comprehensive ethical doctrine, has the resources to provide believing Muslims with reasons to reject some of the most basic terms of citizenship within a non-Muslim liberal democracy. For the same comprehensive ethical doctrine to give support to an overlapping consensus on the terms of citizenship, it would have to provide reasons for endorsing on principled grounds something like the following positions (I argue for this in March 2006):

1. *It is permissible for Muslims to reside in non-Muslim polities under their legal authority if they enjoy security and the freedom to manifest their religion, even without separate political and legal authority.*
2. *In conflicts when a non-Muslim state in which Muslims live is under attack by a Muslim force, it is nonetheless legitimate for a Muslim to forswear on grounds of principle engaging in activities damaging to their non-Muslim state's activities of self-defense.*
3. *In conflicts when the state in which Muslims live is under attack by a non-Muslim force, it is permissible to contribute directly to the self-defense efforts of the non-Muslim state.*

These three statements are not sufficient to establish a comprehensive doctrine of citizenship in a non-Muslim liberal democracy. For such a doctrine, we would need to examine Islamic foundations for (at least) the following further beliefs: that the classical expansionist doctrine of jihad has been plausibly supplanted by a modern doctrine that allows Muslim citizens to affirm the right of non-Muslim states to permanent recognition; that Muslims may regard non-Muslims as political equals; that Muslims may regard non-Muslims as objects of solidarity in secular matters (possibly including schemes of distributive justice); and that Muslims may participate in certain aspects of non-Muslim political systems. However, the questions addressed in this present inquiry are not only fundamental to the basic idea of a social contract but, as I show below, the answers to them suggest the foundations for affirming the other demands of citizenship that I necessarily neglect here.

Loyalty and Belonging in a Non-Muslim State: Islamic Foundations

The Conditions of Residence in a Non-Muslim Polity

Muslim legal and political thinkers often find it necessary to justify residence within non-Muslim societies and submission to non-Muslim legal and political authority. Scholars permitting residence find it necessary to first show that residence is not, in fact, categorically banned by the authoritative proof-texts (the Qur'an and the *hadith*). For our purposes it is enough to note that most Islamic legal scholars reject on technical grounds the evidence advanced by the minority school: they dispute the interpretation of the two Qur'anic passages cited earlier (4:97–100 and 8:72), arguing that they referred specifically to the Muslim community living in Mecca during Muhammad's exile and offer another series of *hadith* reports where Muhammad or his Companions declare the duty to migrate to the Islamic polity lifted upon the return of Muhammad, victorious, to Mecca (e.g., Abu Dawud 1997, 3: 8).

In addition to rejecting the evidence in favor of a ban on residence on technical grounds, Muslim jurists and exegetes have advanced several arguments for the legitimacy of living permanently in a non-Muslim state. For our purposes, the most interesting argument holds that one may live safely and that it may be possible to fulfill the basic duty to "manifest one's religion" even in the absence of sovereign Muslim political authority (e.g. Qaradawi 2001a, 33–4), The crucial conditions underlying this argument are, of course, the Muslim's security, his lack of fear of seduction (*fitna*) away from Islam, and his freedom to "manifest his religion." In fact, many jurists and exegetes do not see the freedom to practice religion as a mitigating factor on a general ban supposedly implied by Q. 4:97–100, but rather read these verses themselves as only requiring migration because of the oppression experienced in Mecca. The argument is that those verses refer *specifically* to Muslims who were oppressed, harried, and constantly being induced to abandon Islam. Thus, the obligation to migrate is only for those who find themselves in this condition. For all others, jurists arrive at a variety of recommendations. Some argue that residence in non-Muslim lands where one is safe and can "manifest one's religion" is permitted, but that migration is still preferred in order to avoid the negative consequences of such residence (e.g., al-Tabari 1999, 4: 147–151; Ibn Qudama 1990, 13: 151). Other jurists, however, go so far as to argue that residence in non-Muslim lands, given the conditions of security and freedom, is recommended, in rare cases required, or that "if a Muslim is able to manifest his religion in one of the unbeliever's countries, this country becomes a part of the Abode of Islam" (al-Nawawi 2000, 21: 5–7). The argument in these cases is invariably that Muslims residing in non-Muslim lands may be the cause of the eventual return of Islam (in the cases of conquered lands) or of its spread. Given the duty of "calling" (*da'wa*) to Islam, present-day Muslim jurists ask how it could be possible for residence in non-Muslim lands to be forbidden (e.g., Qaradawi 2001a, 33–4; al-Fawzan 1992, 236).

These arguments leave some important questions for comparative ethical purposes, foremost: What do Muslim jurists mean when they refer to freedom from seduction from religion (*al-fitna min al-din*) and the freedom to manifest (*izhar*) or practice/uphold (*iqama*) one's religion? Do these discourses include a conception of practicing one's religion that is consistent with liberal restraints on communal and paternal authority over group and family members, or do they presume some form of communal autonomy within non-Muslim states where certain areas of Islamic law will be applied? (Lewis 1992)

Manifesting one's religion

All Muslim jurists have insisted on the condition of enjoying religious freedom as crucial to justifying residence in a non-Muslim polity. However, the majority of these jurists do not specify what these terms require. Indeed, as Abou El Fadl remarks, "there is no consensus among jurists with regard to the level of freedom necessary for Muslims in a non-Muslim territory. Perhaps the vagueness of their expressions on this point indicates that the jurists did not wish to articulate a fixed, non-negotiable rule that might be difficult to apply to specific situations, especially situations in which Muslim territory is occupied by non-Muslims" (Abou El Fadl 1994, 159). The essential question in Islamic juridical terms is whether the duty to manifest or practice religion is satisfied by the rituals of worship (*'ibadat*) or only by some quasi-political authority applying the laws of social relations (*mu'amalat*).

The concern, for our inquiry into an Islamic doctrine of citizenship in a non-Muslim state compatible with the liberal conception, is that Muslim jurists will insist that religious freedom for Muslim communities entail some form of communal autonomy with sub-state institutions of authority competent to enforce Islamic family, commercial, and certain criminal codes. Indeed, a number of jurists have suggested this more or less explicitly (e.g., Ibn al-Humam n.d., 8: 131; Ibn 'Abidin 1994, 3: 252–3). Helpfully, one of the most preeminent legal scholars of the medieval period, al-Nawawi, distinguishes between levels of religious freedom by contrasting the conditions of self-protection (*al-imtina'*: related to refusal, abstention, forbearance, etc.) and segregation (*al-i'tizal*: related to self-seclusion, withdrawal, disassociation, etc.). For al-Nawawi, the second more demanding condition is clearly analogous to some form of parallel political authority, as demonstrated by his expectation that such a community will be in a position to challenge the wider non-Muslim polity (al-Nawawi 2000, 21: 5). It is al-Nawawi's position on a condition *without* this form of communal autonomy that is interesting for our purposes:

> And if they are capable of self-protection but not [complete] segregation or calling for fighting, then migration is not obligatory. In fact, if one hopes that by remaining Islam might spread in his place of residence, then it is obligatory that he reside there and not migrate, as well as if it is hoped that Islam might prevail there in the future. Yet, if one is weak in the Abode of Unbelief and is not able to manifest one's religion then one's residence there is forbidden (al-Nawawi 2000, 21: 7).

Although the Islamic political imagination certainly can include a call for some communal autonomy within non-Muslim states (such as that enjoyed in countries like India and Israel), modern theorists by and large endorse the weaker condition of a liberal conception of free practice as sufficient. Particularly helpful here is a fatwa by the prominent twentieth-century Syrian jurist and exegete Rashid Rida, which was his response to a questioner from Bosnia inquiring whether migration was required of the Muslims of Bosnia after that territory's incorporation into Hapsburg Austria. This fatwa is important because Rida, unlike most of the classical jurists, specifies what constitutes "seduction away from religion," the condition that virtually all jurists agree mandates emigration. Rida writes, "Migration is not required for those who are able to practice their religion free from seduction away from it, *that is, coerced abandonment of religion or the prohibition on performing religious duties*" (Rida 1980, 2: 773–4). Further on, he denies arguments that worship and marriage are invalid under non-Muslim rule, "There is no difference between the worship and marriage of a Muslim in the Abode of Unbelief and a Muslim in the Abode of Islam but only in the ordinances of political, civil, and military relations." The implication of Rida's justification of life lived in these conditions is that the latter ordinances are not prerequisites for living a just life or securing salvation.

The above discussion contains some important resources for our construction of an Islamic social contract with non-Muslim liberal democracies. The first thing we have established is that not only is it permitted to reside in a non-Muslim polity, but it is permitted to do so *while being subject to and obeying non-Muslim law*. It is true that we have not yet introduced any substantive arguments for the potential justness of non-Islamic law, which would have to occur for a case to be made for a comprehensive Islamic doctrine of citizenship in a non-Muslim liberal democracy. However, given that some Islamic scholars have argued that living under non-Muslim law is a sin, it is surely significant to find some of the most authoritative classical jurists (such as al-Nawawi) refuting this position. Second, it is important that we have encountered reasons for permitting residence in a non-Muslim state that are deeply compatible with liberal aims: namely the possibility that a Muslim may enjoy safety and freedom of religion. These two goods, while not exclusive to liberal polities, might not be enjoyed in *all* non-Muslim societies (or, indeed, all nominally Muslim ones, which is a common theme in the Muslim literature on these questions). Muslim scholars have given us Islamic grounds for arguing that liberal societies that protect individual rights and liberties (including security, freedom of property, and freedom of religion) are *particularly worthy* of loyalty and recognition.

Establishing the permissibility of residing in a non-Muslim state and obeying its laws, however, does not alone make the case for the possibility of a full social contract. How have Muslim jurists conceived of the *status* of Muslims residing in non-Muslim polities? Affirming the legitimacy of one's (potentially permanent) physical presence in such a space does not resolve this. As we will see, some thinkers that are on record permitting residence are explicitly opposed to Muslims fulfilling certain duties of citizenship such as military service, or even adopting the citizenship of these countries in the first place (Topoljak 1997, 79).

The assumption of Muslim jurists was that Muslims would reside under non-Muslim authority under a contractual guarantee of security known as the *aman* (as would non-Muslims visiting or residing in a Muslim polity). In the following section I examine Islamic juridical discussions of what moral obligations the acceptance of the *aman* places on Muslims, focusing in particular on the question of loyalty during wartime. Like the question of migration, the question of contributing to the self-defense of a non-Muslim state relates to the problem of balancing loyalties between a state of residence and the global community of believers, and will thus serve as the complement to the above discussion of residence in a non-Muslim state.

The aman: Foundation for a social contract of civic loyalty

The most prominent contemporary advocate of the notion that Muslims can fully and without contradiction embrace their citizenship in European countries is Tariq Ramadan. He has written that "contracts determine our status, fix our duties and rights and direct the nature and scope of our actions. Once agreed, the terms of a covenant should be respected and if there is a point that seems to work against Muslim rights—or even their conscience as Believers—this has to be discussed and negotiated since Muslims are, unilaterally, not allowed to breach a treaty" (Ramadan 1999, 162). Ramadan argues further that "millions of Muslims have tacitly or explicitly recognized the binding character of the constitution or the laws of the country they enter into and then live in. By signing a work contract or asking for a visa, they acknowledge the validity and authority of the constitution, the laws and the state all at once" (Ramadan 1999, 164).

For most contemporary Islamic scholars, even those less ambitious than Ramadan, the question of general political obligation to a non-Muslim state does indeed fall under the rubric of the duty to uphold contracts. Once a Muslim has accepted the security of a non-Muslim state he is bound to follow all of its laws, including paying taxes that contribute to general social welfare. Crucially, for most scholars this is a moral duty grounded in religion, and not a mere quietest exhortation to avoid punishment or other negative consequences for the Muslim community.

Is loyalty during wartime, however, an obligation of citizenship to which a Muslim may legitimately contract himself? In what follows, I examine in more detail the specific contours of this idea of contract in classical and contemporary juridical works. The question to be addressed here is to what extent the duty to uphold contracts can ground compatible responses to the specific demands of civic loyalty as I characterized them, particularly the second statement. (*In conflicts when a non-Muslim state in which Muslims live is under attack by a Muslim force, even if a Muslim finds it morally impermissible by divine imperative to kill a fellow Muslim, it is nonetheless legitimate for a Muslim to forswear on grounds of principle any active aid to the Muslim force and promise to engage in no activities damaging to their non-Muslim state's activities of self-defense.*)

A well-known series of Qur'anic verses exhort Muslims to honor any contract into which they enter, including:

> "Fulfill God's covenant when you have entered into it and break not your oaths after asserting them, for you thereby make God your guarantor" [Q. 16:91].
> "Fulfill every contract for contracts will be answered for [on the Day of Reckoning]" [Q.17:34].

There is also a famous *hadith* reported through multiple chains and in multiple forms about the sinfulness of breaching contracts, "When God gathers all earlier and later generations of mankind on the Day of Judgment he will raise a flag for every person who betrays a trust so it might be said that this is the perfidy of so-and-so, son of so-and-so" (Muslim 1998, 3: 1094).

In addition to these texts that deal generally with the status of promises and contracts there are a number of revelatory texts that apply this duty to the context of military conflict with non-Muslims. Verse 8:72 speaks of those who failed to join the Islamic community through migration, "If they [Muslims living amongst non-Muslims] seek your aid in religion, it is your duty to help them, *except against a people with whom you have a treaty.*" This verse has been traditionally read to impose upon the Islamic polity a duty of restraint toward non-Muslim states harboring Muslim subjects if there is a treaty between them (e.g., al-Qurtubi 1996, 8: 37; Ibn Kathir 1998, 4: 84–6).

Another *hadith* applies the principle of upholding promises to non-Muslims not to fight them to the level of individual oaths and commitments. A certain Companion of the Prophet is reported to have said:

> nothing prevented me from being present at the Battle of Badr except this incident: I came out with my father Husail to partici-pate in the Battle but we were caught by some Qurayshi unbe-lievers. They said: "Do you intend to go to Muhammad?" We said: "We do not intend to go to him but we wish to go back to Medina." So they took from us a covenant in the name of God that we would turn back to Medina and would not fight on the side of Muhammad. So when we came to the Messenger of God and related the incident to him he said: "Both of you proceed to Medina. We will fulfill the covenant made with them but seek God's help against them" (Muslim 1998, 3: 1129).

Although this episode does not deal with a contract with non-Muslims arising as a consequence of legal residence, it seems a perfect example of the justification of some Muslims refraining from fighting non-believers because of a promise made to them. The fact that the *hadith* is situated during the lifetime of Muhammad (when there can be no question about a Muslim's fealty to the leader of the community and his obligation to participate in jihad) can only add to its potency as a guide for Muslim behavior in non-apostolic times.

Jurists from across the Sunni schools are quite clear that contracts made with non-Muslims, including the *aman*, are as morally binding as those made with Muslims. They are unanimous in holding that the enjoyment of *aman* imposes on the Muslim certain moral and some-times legal obligations to the non-Muslim entity in question ('Abd al-Qadir 1998, 160). Eleventh-century jurist al-Sarakhsi declared that "it is abhorred for a Muslim who requests an *aman* from them [by swear-ing] on his religion to deceive or betray them, for treachery is forbid-den in Islam. The Prophet said, 'He who betrays a trust will have a flag raised for him on the Day of Judgment so that his betrayal may be known'" (al-Sarakhsi 2001, 10: 105). The thirteenth-century jurist Ibn Qudama agrees with, and in fact goes beyond, Sarakhsi's position:

> Whoever enters the land of the enemy under an *aman* shall not cheat them in transactions. [This] is forbidden, because they only gave the *aman* under the condition of refraining from deceit or betrayal, and of his [guarantee of] security to them from him-self. Even if this [contract] is not explicitly pronounced it is still

binding because it is presumed. For this same reason, whoever comes to one of our lands from one of theirs under an *aman* and betrays us thereby violates his contract. So if this is established then it is not permitted [for a Muslim] to betray them, because this is deceit [*ghadr*], which is not permitted in our religion (Ibn Qudama 1990, 13: 152–3).

Note a number of additional elements to this basic position, most importantly: (like many Western doctrines of political obligation) a recognition of tacit agreements, the usage of parity and reciprocity as operative ethical values, as well as the legal point that Muslim authorities may in fact enforce the rights of non-Muslims.

On this section's narrower question of loyalty in wartime Muslim jurists have traditionally spoken in surprisingly precise terms. It is quite clear for the majority that this duty to honor contracts and to abide by conditions freely endorsed overrides for many jurists any general duty to contribute to an Islamic polity's military efforts against a non-Muslim state. Indicative here are the juridical treatments on the behavior of Muslim prisoners. Note how seriously al-Nawawi takes the act of agreeing to conditions even as a prisoner:

If they capture [a Muslim soldier] then he is obligated to flee as soon as he can. If they free him without condition then he is obligated to try and kill them because they are unbelievers with no guarantee of security. But if they free him on the condition that he is under a guarantee of security [*aman*] from them, then they are also under a guarantee of security from him. If they guarantee his security and ask for a guarantee from him then it is forbidden for him to kill them or steal their property on the basis of what the Almighty has said: "O you who have believed! Fulfill all contracts." [5:1] But if they violate their guarantee to him then he may do so as well to them. If they free him under a guarantee of safety but without asking for one themselves, then even in this case the majority say that they are still under such a guarantee on his part because of their placing him under a guarantee (al-Nawawi 2000, 21: 130. Also: 'Abd al-Qadir 1998, 167).

Ibn Qudama advances a similar position with the addendum that even the condition to remain in the country rather than return to the Islamic polity must be honored, again "for the Prophet said, 'Muslims are bound by their conditions'" (Ibn Qudama 1990, 13: 184–185). While the jurists in question do not seem to address directly the obligations of Muslims residing or visiting non-Muslim countries for purposes other than war to the war effort of a Muslim polity, the only reasonable interpretation is that if the above applies to prisoners during wartime then it does *a fortiori* to non-prisoners and non-combatants who reside or enter there willingly under an *aman*. The duty to honor contracts, even tacit ones, is binding on all Muslims, and entering a non-Muslim land is only done under an *aman*, which is regarded as a contract including among its conditions the obligation to do no harm to non-Muslim interests. If a Muslim decides that it is his duty to serve in a jihad or otherwise advance Muslim interests over non-Muslim ones then jurists require that he first renounce his *aman* as a way of advising non-Muslims honorably of his intentions.

This value, articulated deeply and widely in the classical legal tradition, is the most common present-day Islamic justification (in both Sunni and Shi'ite sources) for honoring non-Muslim interests while residing in non-Muslim lands (European Council for Fatwa and Research 1999, 19–20; Fadl Allah 1999, 80–1). The contemporary system of visas and naturalization are commonly referred to as the legal and moral equivalent of the former *aman* and thus fidelity to their terms is exhorted (Mawlawi 1999, 222). Importantly, the most prominent clerics issuing fatwas on these matters, including through their co-chairmanship of the European Council for Fatwa and Research, Faysal Mawlawi and Yusuf Qaradawi, extract from the duty to honor contracts an even more robust position than my original wording, which refers only to a Muslim's behavior when his state of citizenship itself is under attack. They insist that the duty extends to self-restraint during times when one's non-Muslim state of residence is attacking a Muslim state, and when it thus may be held that all Muslims have a duty to resist or oppose this action (Qaradawi 2003; Mawlawi 2003).

Mawlawi, Qaradawi and the European Council for Fatwa and Research represent what we might refer to as the "neoclassical" strand of contemporary Islamic ethical thought, insofar as they seek to articulate their positions as much as possible within the framework of the classical juridical tradition and thus claim a certain conservative authority and authenticity. The articulation of compatible positions from within such conservative or canonical discourses represents particularly strong evidence of a plausible overlapping consensus. In this case it seems quite clear that there are very stable Islamic foundations for a principled, religiously-grounded affirmation of our first statement of loyalty, the abstention from and repudiation of any acts damaging to one's state of citizenship even when it is engaged in conflict with a Muslim force or entity.

Defending a Non-Muslim State

A Muslim could coherently affirm the moral obligation to refrain from harming his state of residence while at the same time asserting that it is impermissible for him to risk his life for a non-Muslim society or to advance non-Muslim communal interests. Such a position was indeed that generally advocated by the classical jurists, who held that it is impermissible to contribute to the military strength of non-Muslims. Yet, because Islamic law does not proclaim a general doctrine of pacifism but rather a duty on the part of individuals to contribute to their society's self-defense, I argue that in the Islamic case a doctrine of refusal in the context of a non-Muslim state may in fact suggest a rejection of the bonds of solidarity characteristic of citizenship and an indifference to the fate of the society in which they live. While recognizing that liberalism has traditionally placed limits on the goals for which a state may demand that its subjects risk their lives, we can assert that "there are likely to be moments when all residents, aliens and citizens alike, are morally obligated to defend the state that defends their everyday social life" (Walzer 1970, 105–6). I thus submit that a doctrine of citizenship in a non-Muslim state would include the justification of direct contribution to self-defense efforts (whether or not in the form of direct military participation), particularly when the aggressing force is a non-Muslim one.

While classical jurists did not argue on principled grounds for a Muslim resident's contribution to a non-Muslim polity's self-defense efforts, it is not rare for contemporary "neoclassical" scholars—some of whom hold that fighting fellow Muslims on behalf of non-Muslims constitutes apostasy—to assert that there is no moral dilemma in serving in non-Muslim armies against other non-Muslim armies. There are three basic categories of argument for permitting this: one, that the revelatory texts do not prohibit such service and, therefore, it is presumed to be permitted; two, that it is undesirable, but there may be certain benefits to Muslims arising as a double-effect of such service; three, what the Qur'an and *hadith* prohibit is serving to advance the "word of unbelief," which is not what service in a modern-day non-Muslim army constitutes. The second two categories are clearly the most interesting for our purposes; indeed, it is the third category that justifies my claim that states proclaiming political liberalism will be more attractive to Muslims than states proclaiming perfectionist forms of liberalism.

Statements permitting military service of the first category are not generally based on *positive* textual evidence of the permissibility of this, and are usually satisfied with noting the various restrictions on such service. In his book devoted entirely to Muslim minority issues, Qaradawi simply remarks "Muslims are confronted with the question of mandatory military service in these countries, and there is no objection to this unless such a country declares war against a Muslim country," before moving on to other questions (Qaradawi 2001a, 25). A typical statement is that of Canadian Muslim Sheikh Ahmad Kutty, who emphasizes not the Muslim or non-Muslim character of the state but the ethical status of the war:

> Muslims who are citizens are definitely allowed to serve in the armies of their own country, regardless of whether it is a Muslim country or predominately non-Muslim country. They are also allowed to fight wars that are legitimate and ethical.[8]

In the case of the positions here, the primary reason for holding that it is permissible to serve in a non-Muslim army is merely that this is not one of the things *specifically* forbidden by the revelatory texts. Thus, one can do whatever is not specifically forbidden, limited here to fighting brother Muslims, contributing to a war of aggression or aggressing within war. Legitimating service in a non-Muslim army simply on the grounds that nothing in Islam forbids it is an acceptable form of the type of argument we are looking for: it is an Islamic argument (rather than public), and it is principled. The only potential question relates to its plausibility: if aware of Islamic arguments against such service that rely on authoritative texts, then the Muslim believer looking for guidance may not be satisfied with anything less than direct refutation of the incompatible positions or at least similar citation of evidence.

An example of the second type of argument, i.e., referring to benefits accruing to Muslims from serving in a non-Muslim army, is Rashid Rida's 1907 fatwa on Russian Muslims participating in the Russo–Japanese War. Rida proclaimed that he did "not consider that fighting on behalf of the Muslims of Russia against Japan is disobedience to God [sin] nor forbidden by shari'a, and in fact may be one of the things rewarded by God if engaged in with the correct intention" (Rida 1980, 2: 565). He proceeds to outline two different rationales for fighting in the Russian army that would qualify as correct intentions.

The first reads, "His obedience to the state [by serving in the army] protects his brothers from amongst the state's subjects from any oppression or evil that may befall them if the state is an oppressive, autocratic one; it makes them equal to any other citizen in rights and privileges if it is a representative, just state; and it benefits them in other ways if the state is in between." The concerns in this statement all relate to benefits that accrue to the Muslim community from participating in the war, and have nothing to do with either the rights or interests of the state of citizenship or the justness of the war in question.

Rida's rationale might be read as implying more problematic positions, including: one, that if none of the benefits here described will in fact accrue to Muslims then there is no justification for aiding non-Muslims; two, that if the benefits accrue then Muslims are permitted to engage in whatever acts secure them, including unjust wars; and, three, that even if Muslims are permitted to join non-Muslim armies to secure benefits for themselves, there is no suggestion that the cause of the non-Muslim state is in itself just or reasonable. Thus, there might be a reading of Rida's first rationale that sees it as either insufficiently principled or principled in the wrong way (i.e., only concerned with the interests of Muslims).

The case for the compatibility of Rida's rationale with a liberal conception of citizenship rests in his recognition of some states as "representative and just." This statement alone constitutes a major step toward an overlapping consensus in its suggestion that states might be at the same time non-Muslim and just, quite a break indeed from the implications of some jurists that equate non-Muslim states' unjustness precisely with their non-Muslimness. More specifically, however, he seems to be accepting the desirability of a social contract in which Muslims enjoy equality with non-Muslims in exchange for sharing the same duties. In terms of our interest in the specifically Islamic grounding of the desirability or acceptability of this type of social contract, we can infer a similar type of "no prohibition" justification discussed above: if there is nothing specifically contrary to Islamic requirements in a given act then it is in that way the object of an overlapping consensus. Note that this argument would also resolve the dilemma of dealing with the fatwa on its utilitarian interpretation from the previous paragraph: it doesn't matter if the jurist is advancing consequentialist reasons for doing something if he does not think that these are reasons for doing something that would otherwise be impermissible or sinful. The utilitarian justification can simply be an added benefit to one's conception of the good, but the legitimation of the act consists in the statement that nothing in the conception of the good contradicts it.

Rida also offers a second rationale for serving in a non-Muslim army that requires separate analysis:

> The knowledge and practice of war remain amongst the most important facets of social life for human beings. Thus, if they are forbidden for a certain people then that people is weakened, and the weak are never but humiliated and degraded. It is thus better for Muslims who are subjects of those states that they participate like the ordinary people of those nations in the basic elements of social life, strengthened and made proud, rather than being weak and degraded by their religion, for Islam does not permit that its adherents chose weakness and subjugation over strength and pride. Thus, if they chose the latter [by not serving in the Russian army] they are incapable of preserving their religion.... [We] advise Muslims to choose pride over humiliation whatever the source of pride and strength may be over weakness and consider that preserving Islam outside of its abode requires this.

The question to be addressed here is whether Rida's emphasis on strength and pride for Muslims, as well as military knowledge, is a questionable justification for discharging a civic duty. By comparison, note the response of Topoljak, which is that "participation in the army of a non-Muslim country with the intention of training and gaining fighting skills for jihad is permitted, even required" (Topoljak 1997, 113). He gives the examples of those Muslims who had been trained in non-Muslim armies but later helped used those skills in the wars in Bosnia and the Caucasus, and in fact cites this fatwa by Rida. What is problematic about Topoljak's argument are the auxiliary beliefs by which they are legitimated: namely, that Muslims ought not be citizens of a non-Muslim country if the Islamic state exists, that there is a duty to prepare for jihad in the classical sense and that Muslims are not supposed to strengthen non-Muslims if they can help it. For Topoljak, serving in a non-Muslim army is justified by the jurisprudential principle of necessity (*darura*) as the only way of acquiring the skills to discharge a duty that is directly hostile to the interests and rights of a non-Muslim state.

For Rida, despite some similar use of language, it appears that the benefit in question is quite different. He speaks generally in terms of "strength" (*quwwa*) and "pride" (*'izza*) without referring, as does Topoljak, to jihad or to the acquisition of these qualities at the expense of non-Muslims or in order to use military skills against them. Thus, his understanding of these qualities does not seem to be incompatible with the aims of a liberal democratic society, if enjoying a status of equality in relation to non-Muslims constitutes "strength" and "pride." It is likely that given his historical context, the alternative for him was a situation of hostility, marginalization and suspicion. Countering this potentially destructive majority-minority dynamic through insisting on full inclusion and full participation is precisely the response that liberalism prefers minority communities to articulate.

Rida's justifications of service in a non-Muslim army are thus presented as beneficial double-effects of the given civic duty in question. Even though the citizen is affirming a civic duty for a different set of reasons than the ones for which it is required by the state, and even though there is no direct consideration of the interests of the non-Muslim community, they must be judged as compatible motivations: All of these goals are themselves consistent with the aims of a liberal society (i.e., a Muslim can both pursue these aims without violating any of the legitimate interests of a non-Muslim society and he can hold these motivations *alongside* a recognition of non-Muslim rights without incoherence or self-contradiction), and they presume the desirability of political integration into the non-Muslim community.

The third path to compatibility on this question is one of great interest for political liberalism's aspirations. I first introduce two positions I previously cited to demonstrate the traditional Islamic rejection of serving in non-Muslim armies:

> I asked: If some Muslims were in the *dar al-harb* (abode of war) under an *aman* and that territory were attacked by people of *another territory of war*, do you think it would be lawful for those Muslims to fight on their side?
>
> He replied: No...because the jurisdiction of the unbelievers prevails there and the *Muslims cannot enforce non-Muslim rulings*.

I asked: If the Muslims were fearful of their own persons from the enemy, should they fight in defense of themselves?

He replied: If the situation were thus, there would be no harm to fight in defense of themselves (al-Shaybani 1966, 193).

If there is a group of Muslims under an *aman* in the abode of war and that country is attacked by another non-Muslim country, then the Muslims are not allowed to fight, for fighting involves exposing oneself to danger which is only allowed for the purpose of exaltation of the Word of God, may He be glorified, and the glorification of religion, which are not present in this case. Because the laws of idolatry are dominant over them Muslims are not able to rule by the laws of Islam, and thus *any fighting on their part would take the form of exaltation of the word of idolatry* and this is not permitted unless they fear for their lives from the invaders, in which case there is no sin incurred in fighting to defend themselves rather than fighting to exalt the word of idolatry (al-Sarakhsi 2001, 10: 106; emphasis added).

A similar view is advanced today by Topoljak, "It is permitted to fight on behalf of non-Muslims against other non-Muslims if they are defending themselves, their families and their property from the same attacking non-Muslims and if the non-Muslim commander respects the Muslims, grants them their rights and if they fear that he may be defeated by someone who will oppress them. If Muslims fear a greater enemy then they can co-operate with a smaller enemy" (Topoljak 1997, 119–21).

There are two possible reasons to think that the views encountered in the above three quotations might be approaching a compatible position. The first reason is that the scholars all implicitly allow for the possibility of identifying Muslim interests with those of the non-Muslim majority, and with the consideration that a Muslim would naturally prefer the state that practices the least oppression toward them. It is, of course, central to liberal justification that the rights it gives citizens, particularly minorities, give those citizens reasons to support and be loyal toward liberal institutions. This is the very idea of a social contract. Furthermore, there are prominent theories of political obligation (from Hobbes to Nozick) that presume that the "citizen" (if he can be so called) will be interested in the fate of his state and fellow citizens no further than it concerns his own safety and welfare. Political liberalism cannot *require* as part of a minimal doctrine of citizenship any robust or emotional attachment to one's community of citizenship, or principled altruism, beyond what is necessary to secure the equal rights of all.

Thus, there is an argument to be made that even if Muslims are fighting an invading force only to defend their *own* property, families and persons, that that is all some theories of citizenship assume *any* citizen is doing.

In the case of these particular scholars, this is probably an optimistic reading. The potential difference between Shaybani's, Sarakhsi's, and Topoljak's reasoning and that of individualist theories of political obligation lies in the distinction between initial motivations for endorsing a social contract and subsequent reasoning in society (and, of course, that fellow citizens are not regarded as "enemies" merely because of their conception of the good). A social contract may appeal to individual (or group) self-interest (whether in the form of appeals to reciprocity or mutual advantage) as a justification for the general structure of rights and duties, but cannot allow that every discrete demand made by the state be accepted or rejected in situ by the individual according to some self-regarding utility calculus. This latter scenario seems to be precisely what Topoljak has in mind: that Muslims residing in non-Muslim states (let us presume that they enjoy both security and religious freedom) can adopt a stance toward a war of aggression against their state depending on whether it *directly* threatens them and their interests or whether they have more to gain by their state preserving itself or being conquered. That is, there is no suggestion of general moral duties toward a state that has fulfilled the needs of protection, respect for rights and welfare provision, nor of the independent rights and interests of non-Muslims except when and where they align narrowly with those of Muslims. There is no question but that this justification of serving a non-Muslim state as it stands in Topoljak's present formulation does not indicate the existence of an overlapping consensus.

However, a believing Muslim could plausibly draw different conclusions on the basis of the same basic reasoning. First, a Muslim could accept that the only justification for fighting is to defend himself and his family without necessarily adopting the auxiliary mistrust and hostility toward non-Muslim polities one finds in Topoljak's reasoning. He could also accept that the only reliable way to defend himself is not alone or in groups selected by him personally (such as sub-state religious communities), but by supporting the institutions of his political community. But then, on this reading, the Muslim's reasoning is no different from that of any other citizen entering into a social contract. The only difference is *for him*, in that he does not feel in this case the *additional* motivations and reasons that he has for defending a

Muslim state. But his reasons, as they stand, are certainly sufficient for the Rawlsian liberal. The question is: *does he have reasons* not to adopt Topoljak's indifference *cum* hostility toward the non-Muslim polity?

Here I would like to draw attention once again to the underlying objection to serving in a non-Muslim army in the views of Shaybani and Sarakhsi, namely that Muslims should not be "enforcing non-Muslim rulings" or "exalting the word of idolatry." I believe that this objection has both a strong and a weak form. The strong form holds that all non-Muslim authority is illegitimate simply in being un-Islamic. Here, a Muslim would have no good reason for making a moral distinction between, say, liberal and communist forms of government. He may have reasons to *prefer* one over the other, but they would be equally illegitimate in their being non-Muslim and he would be equally committed to overturning both.

There is also a weaker form implied in Islamic legal discourses; here that is reflected in Sarakhsi's phrase "any fighting on their part would take the form of exaltation of the word of idolatry." An argument could be made (and here I venture into a stronger form of comparative ethics) that Sarakhsi is assuming that non-Muslim polities will not only be non-Muslim in not applying Islamic conceptions of justice, but that they will be so in applying conceptions of truth that directly contradict Islamic metaphysical claims—the "laws of idolatry." Thus, *this* is what a Muslim is never permitted to do: to uphold or strengthen forces that proclaim the falsity of Islam.

And here is where political liberalism feels it can sincerely and transparently address Muslim citizens in light of Islamic concerns. Of course, the whole project of political liberalism aims at responding to just this kind of objection to a political system: that it is based on the public affirmation of a controversial truth-claim. To the Muslim invoking an argument like Sarakhsi's, the political liberal responds, "But we are not asking you to 'exalt of the word of idolatry.' We are asking you to recognize that at times our interests in security and welfare overlap, for no other reason than that we live in a common state. We, too, prefer a political system that does not ask you to proclaim the truth of anything that contradicts Islam. We, too, are committed to only permitting laws that can be justified based on common civic interests, rather than particular, un-Islamic moral ones." Of course, the Muslim may deny this. He may assert that merely in not affirming Islamic truth-claims, the non-Islamic state in fact rejects and denies them, or that democracy is in fact idolatry in calling for obedience to the will of humans. Here we have no response beyond what we have said. However, what I believe

I have shown is something very important: *that the Muslim might not deny this.* He might look at his authoritative sources and decide that there is a crucial difference between what a Marxist non-Muslim state or another militantly secular republic would demand of him and what a politically liberal regime demands. This distinction may very well determine whether the Muslim feels that he can in good conscience contribute to that society's security and well-being.

Notes

1. Q. 4:97–100: "Those whom the angels gather in death while in a state of sin against themselves they will ask, 'What was your plight?' They reply, 'We were oppressed on earth.' The [angels] will say, 'Was not God's earth vast enough for you to migrate within it?' They will have their refuge in hell and how evil is such a destiny, except for those truly oppressed, those men, women and children who cannot find any means and have not been shown the way. For these there is hope that God will forgive them, for God is Forgiving and Merciful. Anyone who migrates in the path of God will find in the Earth many an abundant refuge. Whoever leaves his home in migration toward God and his Messenger, and death overtakes him, his reward with God is guaranteed, for God is Forgiving and Merciful." And, Q. 8:72, "Those who believed and migrated and struggled in the path of God with their property and their souls and those who sheltered and supported them, and friends and supporters of one another. Those who believed and did not migrate, you have no duty of protection toward them until they migrate. But if they seek your support in religion, you owe them this support, except against a people with whom you have a treaty. God sees all that you do."
2. "The *hijra* [migration to a Muslim polity] will not come to an end until repentance comes to an end and repentance will not come to an end until the sun shall rise from its place of setting." "I am innocent of [I disown] any Muslim who lives with the polytheists. For you will not be able to tell them apart." "Do not live with and associate with the polytheists. Whosoever lives with them and associates with them is like them." These are found in the various authoritative collections of *hadith*, the reported sayings and doings of the Prophet Muhammad.
3. "O you who have believed! Do not take My enemies and your enemies as friends, offering them affection while they have denied what Truth has come unto you, driving away the Messenger of God and yourselves because you believe in God your Lord. If you have gone forth to struggle in my cause and longing for my blessing do you secretly hold affection for them? For I know all that you may conceal as well as what you do openly. And who does so has erred from the path."
4. "Let not the believers take the infidels for their allies in preference to the believers—for who does this has nothing to do with God—unless it be to protect yourselves from them in this way. God warns you about Himself and the final goal is to God."
5. "Oh you who have believed! Do not take for your intimates other than your own kind. They will continually cause you turmoil and love anything that will distress you. Loathing has already come forth from their mouths and what is concealed in their breasts is even greater. We have made the signs clear to you if you will use your reason."
6. Q. 4:95: "Not equal are those believers who sit [at home] and receive no hurt, and those who strive and fight in the cause of God with their goods and their persons. God has granted a grade higher to those who strive and fight with their goods and persons that to those

who sit [at home]. Unto all has God promised good, but those who strive and fight has He distinguished above those who sit [at home] by a special reward."

7. 4:92–93: "Never should a believer kill a believer; but (if it so happens) by mistake (compensation is due)...Whosoever slays a believer intentionally his reward is Hell forever, and the wrath and curse of God are upon him, and a dreadful penalty is prepared for him."

8. This was a response to my request for a fatwa through *Islamonline.net* that was delivered but not publicly posted.

CHAPTER 3

Demanding Deliberation: Political Liberalism and the Inclusion of Islam

LUCAS SWAINE

Introduction

In this chapter, I explore the prospects of political liberalism to include Islam in a principled, moral, and politically auspicious fashion. I lay bare and defend some central principles and values of political liberalism, and consider the extent to which they are compatible with the commitments of Muslim citizens dwelling in pluralistic liberal democracies. I begin by examining normative issues pertaining to democratic citizenship, focusing on the demands of democratic deliberation in particular. I investigate the compatibility of Islam with the desirable procedures and ends of deliberation, and consider the potential of Muslim minorities in liberal democracies to ameliorate some of the deepest, most pressing challenges to citizenship, identity, and the legitimacy of liberal democracy. I argue that Muslims have special capacities to renew the vitality of democratic polities, especially when their efforts are joined with those of more liberal, non-Muslim citizens. Promulgation of cardinal liberal principles can yield transformative, educative effects, bringing devotees of Islam and many others in liberal polities to affirm liberal governance, on grounds they should accept.

Muslim Minorities and Political Deliberation

I turn first to the question of whether Muslims face doctrinal or other religious impediments to becoming good citizens in pluralistic liberal democracies. Joel Fetzer and Christopher Soper note that whereas in the 1990s there was some controversy over "how best to ensure the successful incorporation of Muslims into the values of a liberal democracy," the current debate has spread to the question of whether Islam and liberal democracy are compatible at all (Soper 2005; see Monsma & Soper 2009, pp. 68, 71, 83, 188–89, 219).[1] I believe that nothing in the nature of the Islamic faith is preventative, here, and that, quite to the contrary, there is good reason to think that Muslims can be exemplary citizens of liberal democracies.

As a first step, it serves briefly to consider the values and requirements of liberal-democratic citizenship that political theorists identify and discuss. First of all, capacities to engage in standard forms of political participation presumably count among the requirements of democratic citizenship. But it is clear that Muslims can engage in normal political participation, such as voting, campaigning, letter-writing, pamphleteering, and so forth.[2] One sees this by simple observation. Many Muslims are active in the domestic social and political life of the liberal democracies in which they dwell; and a 2004 Georgetown University survey found 70 percent of American Muslims reporting that being Muslim is a weighty factor in their political decisions, with 86 percent stating that it is important to participate in politics (Abdo 2006, p. 83). Genieve Abdo suggests that whereas the majority of American Muslims had previously preferred to keep a low profile in political matters, the shift "was a direct response to sharp increases in discrimination, harassment by law enforcement, and racist rhetoric against Muslims in America sparked by the so-called War on Terrorism" (Abdo 2006, p. 83).

The naked capacity to participate in political life cannot be what really motivates commentators and critics, therefore, when they worry about Muslims as citizens. Instead, the critics seem to be concerned about Muslims' abilities to take part constructively in political interactions, such as joining in respectful deliberations with others and treating fellow citizens as equals. Perhaps Islam recommends or even requires public behavior on the part of the faithful that grates against liberal-democratic values, practices, or procedures. Alternatively, it could be that Islam requires its members to press for policies or political institutions inimical to liberal democracy or a constitutional order. It is also possible that Muslims are enjoined by doctrine to behave in certain unpalatable ways in public debate, and that their manner of participating is problematic for liberal democracies. Can Muslims in liberal democracies be positive, participating citizens?

The Importance of Political Deliberation

At the center of normative theories of democratic citizenship, one finds a wealth of work on deliberation. Deliberative theorists propose that deliberation has many virtues; and they identify particular aims of deliberation, too, potential benefits resultant from well-oriented democratic discussion and debate. I will outline some of the more prominent aims and goals that deliberative theorists single out, pertaining to broad matters of social and political concern. To be clear, I shall focus on political deliberation instead of small-group deliberations or discussions of a non-political kind. Placing the purported benefits and values of political deliberation clearly in view allows one to distinguish a workable standard for determining how well Muslims fare in public discussion, and whether they are inferior to their fellow citizens in that regard.

For the sake of simplicity, I divide the aims of political deliberation into two kinds: aims for *outcomes* and *procedures*, respectively. Consider first the outcomes of deliberation that deliberative theorists variously promote. Some argue that political deliberation produces efficient outcomes by utilizing aggregative processes in which people's preferences are seen as exogenous and given; but this putatively valuable outcome is often criticized as being insufficiently ambitious and normatively confused (Gutmann & Thompson 2004, p. 13).[3] Deliberative theorists hope for more: when deliberation works well, they suggest, it has the potential to bring about consensus on tough and divisive issues.[4] James Bohman proposes that deliberation aiming at consensus can reduce social fragmentation, contending that it holds promise for overcoming social inequalities (Bohman 1996, pp. 1, 107–49). He joins Amy Gutmann and Dennis Thompson, who argue that political deliberation can yield corrective measures for past errors, injustices, and political or legal mistakes (Gutmann & Thompson 2004, p. 11); and he shows solidarity with Iris Marion Young, who emphasizes that deliberation is capable of lessening or even removing illegitimate manifestations of power in political institutions.[5] What is more, political deliberation is said to have the potential to promote not only mutually respectful processes of decision-making, but a "thicker kind of respect" between citizens, helping them to see the reasonableness of others' views (Gutmann & Thompson 2004, pp. 11, 79). On this point deliberative theorists are quite correct: well-oriented political deliberation can yield justifications for the laws, policies, and procedures that people collectively impose upon each other.[6] Justifications arrived at through dynamic processes of deliberation can indeed provide legitimacy to the decisions that people reach, imperfect though those processes tend to be. In short, political deliberation has the potential to encourage "public-spirited perspectives on issues," as Gutmann and Thompson put it, promoting greater participation as well as a rightful sense of the legitimacy of citizens' procedures, processes, and ultimate determinations (Gutmann & Thompson 2004, pp. 10–11).[7]

Many deliberative democrats wish for political deliberation to include the provision of public reasons, following the enterprising advances of John Rawls,[8] but I shall allow that, as a matter of definition, it may not. This permits the "everyday talk" of Jane Mansbridge to be included under the rubric of political deliberation, discourse in which one finds non-ideal discussion, rhetoric, private reasons, emotional outbursts, browbeating, and power plays (Mansbridge 1999).[9] If deliberative processes often "[fall] significantly short of [the] ideal" of deliberative democracy, as Ian Shapiro suggests they do, it makes sense not to exclude those processes from the broad rubric of political deliberation (Shapiro 1999, p. 29).[10] This allows for a useful, reasonable conception of political deliberation, and it has the benefit of not making some particular normative conception of deliberation true by stipulation. In addition, the characterization I provide permits, but does not require, a wide variety of normative conceptions to count as forms of political deliberation. It allows that debate can and should be normatively well-oriented and helpful, that political deliberation best occurs in the form of discourse and dialogue, and that political deliberation might rightly aim to establish some procedures and outcomes, while working to avoid others.[11]

Because its processes often lead to binding decisions, one understands deliberation's importance and relevance to citizens' pursuits: political deliberation tends to have coercive implications, often touching citizens' lives in personal ways. Deliberative procedures yield decisions and policies on abortion, school vouchers, same-sex marriage, immigration laws, war measures, tax apportionment, legal accommodations for minority groups, and so on. Mansbridge observes that deliberation in public assemblies regularly aims to "[create] a collectively binding decision" (Mansbridge 1999, p. 212) to which Gutmann and Thompson add the normative point that the decisions can and often should be temporary and politically provisional, leaving them open to reconsideration in future (Gutmann & Thompson 2004, pp. 116–19). Nevertheless, deliberation sometimes results in deadlock; and this is to be expected if, as Alan Wertheimer reflects, one does not assume that there is always a "right answer to [the] issue" under discussion (Wertheimer 1999, pp. 171 ff., 180–82). These considerations stand with the normal sense and understanding of deliberation, as Mansbridge suggests (Mansbridge 1999, p. 216), and the elements of provisionality and imperfection reflect the spirit of collective problem-solving that animates democracy (cf. Dewey 1927).

Along with these desired outcomes, deliberative theorists identify procedural values that political deliberation should strive to incorporate, values pertaining to the very methods and practices of deliberation that structure public discourse and decision-making. Procedural values are different than the outcomes of deliberation, although hale and hearty deliberative procedures are often thought to complement and facilitate good outcomes. Outcomes can be made better, even legitimated by procedure, theorists argue, where deliberation is done well. As with the outcomes of deliberation, one observes natural variation from theorist to theorist on just what procedural values political deliberation should embody. However, theorists converge interestingly on the two procedural values of *reciprocity* and *inclusiveness*, in particular.

Gutmann and Thompson emphasize that political deliberation requires reciprocity for constructive and well-oriented processes of public discussion and debate (Gutmann & Thompson 2004, p. 133). As they put it, reciprocity's basic premise is that "citizens owe one another justifications for the institutions, law, and public policies that collectively bind them" (ibid.). Here, they follow Rawls's arguments from *Political Liberalism*. When it functions well, political deliberation not only works to provide justifications for laws and policies, but also includes displays of mutual respect, which is "part of the meaning of reciprocity."[12] Gutmann and Thompson suggest famously that deliberative reciprocity asks people to make claims that others "can accept in principle" (Gutmann & Thompson 1996, p. 55).[13] They are clear on the normative importance of reciprocity,[14] and to that central value they adjoin three additional principles "that provide the content of deliberative democracy": basic liberty, basic opportunity, and fair opportunity (Gutmann & Thompson 2004, p. 137 ff.).[15] Other deliberative theorists generally do not dispute these procedural norms, at least viewing reason-giving as a desideratum of deliberation if not an actual requirement. Bohman shows concordance with the idea, reflecting that illegitimate political decisions fail to reach a level of reciprocity, "they are not addressed to an audience of politically equal citizens."[16] And Mansbridge maintains that Gutmann and Thompson's conception of reciprocity "applies well to everyday talk."[17] That Gutmann and Thompson's conception of reciprocity does not admit all of the chatter in everyday talk seems evident, however, because they wish to exclude discussion of such matters as slavery policies in democratic deliberation on the grounds that slavery is not a moral position (Gutmann & Thompson 2004, p. 70).

A second procedural value that deliberative democrats identify is inclusiveness. Young strongly advocates on behalf of this value.[18] As she puts it, the collective problem-solving that deliberative democracy promotes "depends for its legitimacy and wisdom on the expression and criticism of the diverse opinions of all the members of society" (Young 2000, p. 6). Political discussion and decision-making should include "all those affected" in nontrivial ways by the prospective decision (Young 2006, p. 23). Furthermore, the manner in which people are included matters to deliberation, too. On most accounts, it is not enough to suggest that people only need, say, a formal right to join public discussions, because that does not take seriously the prospects of unequal levels of inclusion. Young advises that deliberations should include concerned parties "equally" in the decision-making process; this is an important qualification on inclusion, she maintains, and one that deliberation should aim to achieve (Young 2006, p. 53).[19] As Young puts it, people should have an "equal right and an effective opportunity to express their interests and concerns," on any appropriate understanding of deliberative democracy.[20] Bohman seems to agree, where he states that people should have equal opportunities to participate (Bohman 1996, p. 16).[21] He proposes that the inclusive element of deliberative democracy should also involve "[reflecting] on the general interest or [the] common good";[22] Young criticizes this notion, but both concur that inclusiveness and broad participation in discussion and debate are important for healthy political deliberation.[23]

It is in this sense that political deliberation should not aim to rebuild ancient Athens: democratic deliberation must actually include people's voices, allowing them to speak for themselves and support representatives of their own choosing, instead of merely proceeding on assumptions about what others think they really desire, or are best suited for in life (Gutmann & Thompson 2004, pp. 42, 57). Young reflects that the conditions of "inclusive decision-making" can help to achieve "more just and wise political judgments" (Young 2000, p. 31), and many advocates of deliberative democracy share the view. However, some take pains to add the capstone argument that the principles of deliberative democracy are themselves contestable: Gutmann and Thompson make this point, contending that deliberative principles are not only subject to change, but are also "self-correcting" (Gutmann & Thompson 2004, pp. 42, 57). They maintain that citizens should "continue to reason together" when faced with disagreement: this is part of the dynamic character of deliberation, as Gutmann and Thompson describe it, at least when it is properly democratic.[24]

Muslim Minorities in Political Deliberation

With these values of political deliberation in plain view, I turn to the question of how well devotees of Islam can achieve or observe the desired outcomes and procedures of deliberation, and whether the teachings and values of Islam prevent Muslims from taking part in deliberation in fruitful and ethical ways. From the outset, it is interesting to note that Muslims seem to be fully able to take part in democratic deliberation, and that they violate no commandments of their faith by so doing. For instance, Mohammad Hashim Kamali points out that it is entirely permissible to express opinions, in Islam (Kamali 1997, pp. 61 ff., 63, 64). He suggests that conscientious reasoning leading to disagreement is not only to be tolerated, but that it even may be beneficial; this, he reflects, is perhaps why "[disagreement] merits a reward" in Islam (Kamali 1997, pp. 45–46). Khaled Abou El Fadl notes, furthermore, that Muslims are permitted to be critical of democratic forms of government and of democratic ideals or their specific implementation (Abou El Fadl 2004, p. 112). Muslims can actively be involved in the constructive criticism and monitoring of government activity, it seems, and may refuse to obey government in cases where officials break the law.[25]

Abou El Fadl supplements these notions with a reminder that the Prophet Mohammed conferred regularly with Muslims and consulted with fellow travelers (Abou El Fadl 2004, pp. 16–17). This provides a foundation for inclusive deliberation, one that can be supplemented by Surah 60, verse 8 of the Koran, "God does not forbid you from being kind and equitable with those who have not fought you about religion and have not driven you out of your homes. God loves the equitable" (Abdo 2006, p. 36). But it is important to note that Islam also encourages rational inquiry and the display of mutual respect, requiring respect where others show it in return.[26] If equitableness, rational inquiry, and mutual respect are encouraged by Islam, then mutual reason-giving seems amenable to the Islamic faith.[27] These notions appear to be easy for Muslims to affirm, at the theological or philosophical level, and so it seems quite fair to say that Muslims can observe important deliberative norms without violating religious demands.

Furthermore, empirical analysis seems to show general consonance between predominantly Islamic polities and democratic values. This does not directly defeat commentators' worries about Muslim minorities and their capacities to engage in healthy political deliberation, but it lends recommendatory support to the view I advance. In their study of religion and politics worldwide, Pippa Norris and Ronald Inglehart included treatment of predominantly Islamic polities, along with postindustrial liberal democracies and former Eastern bloc countries. Interestingly, their cohort analysis revealed that members of Islamic countries do not differ with publics of liberal democracies on the matter of democracy, but, rather, over issues of gender equality and sexual decency. In particular, Norris and Inglehart found no significant differences between Western and Muslim publics regarding: (a) support for practical efficacy and workings of democracy; (b) support for democratic ideals; or (c) approval of strong leadership (Norris & Inglehart 2004, pp. 146–47). While Muslim publics do show greater support for a strong social role for religious authorities, it turns out that the lowest and most minimal support for democracy exists in post-communist Eastern European states (Norris & Inglehart 2004, pp. 147, 154). These findings militate strongly against the "clash of civilizations" argument proffered by Samuel Huntington (Huntington 1996; cf. Norris & Inglehart 2004, pp. 135–38), and they are supported by other studies such as that conducted by Steven Fish (2002). If Muslims are not against democracy in predominantly Islamic states, one can hardly expect them to be naturally or doctrinally disposed to adopt antidemocratic values in America or in other Western democracies.

But there is more to the story than this. For I expect that Muslims hold special prospects for enlivening and revivifying liberal democracy, and, in particular, for reaching the increasing numbers of citizens of liberal democracies who display dissatisfaction with traditional institutions and sources of religious authority.[28] The disaffected are legion in European Union member states, where one finds decreasing numbers of church-going citizens in every country except Italy (Norris & Inglehart 2004, p. 73). Traditional religious beliefs have "steadily declined" in Western Europe, since the 1960s, with the percentage of citizens with no religious affiliation increasing over time (Norris & Inglehart 2004, pp. 86, 87; cf. pp. 88–89, 104–06). What is more, the number of people reporting belief in God has fallen, since 1947, in all advanced democracies save the United States and Brazil.[29] America remains interestingly anomalous, retaining quite high levels of religious belief and observance,[30] with a good explanation for this still wanting, although there is some reason to think that secularizing trends may be present in the United States as well (Norris & Inglehart 2004, pp. 84–88, 91–93, 240).

Citizens of postindustrial societies show "increasing interest" in the meaning and purpose of life: they seem to be thinking more about such questions now than they did in previous decades (Norris & Inglehart 2004, pp. 74–75). Norris and Inglehart infer from this finding that "spiritual concerns" have increased across publics (Norris & Inglehart 2004, p. 75), but that conclusion remains tenuous: the fact that more people report thinking about life's meaning could simply mean that they are puzzled or confused about their life's direction, instead of indicating that they are actually affirming anything spiritual at all.[31]

It appears that these broad swaths of people seek something to believe in: one surmises that they are those who have lost their faith—or who never acquired any—and are adrift. The disaffected are surely not newly-autonomous individuals, directing their lives from the inside in self-critical, reflective ways. One finds no evidence that citizens of democratic polities have become more autonomous in any significant sense. Indeed, it would be quite a magical feat for personal autonomy to take root in those who seem simply have lost or forsaken traditional sources of normative or spiritual authority. I expect that many of these citizens are well-suited for heteronomy: their natural dispositions, interests, and inclinations dispose them to a fine and fruitful life according to a *nomos* that does not vaunt the critically-independent attitudes and dispositions emblematic of personal autonomy (Swaine 2010). After all, personal autonomy is difficult to achieve, and it is not as if an autonomous life has no risks attached. Those who seek high levels of autonomy can suffer from bad decisions resultant from a lack of *nomos*, difficulty in belonging with communities, and anomie. It seems quite reasonable that a heteronomous life is a more realistic aspiration for many democratic citizens, and that such ways of life could be fulfilling, worthwhile, and constructive. Those well-suited for heteronomy could also embrace cardinal principles of liberty of conscience: the unaffiliated might affirm, as part of their specific conceptions of the good, the need politically to keep conscience free to accept the good, to reject the bad, and to distinguish between the two (Swaine 2006). Principles of liberty of conscience are suitable and auspicious for Western Europe's democracies, and for America, too, which has a historical, long-standing commitment to that value.

Engagement and Renewal: The Promise of Muslim Minorities

Healthy political deliberation is vital for the advancement of principles of conscience in liberal democracies, apart from having its own, independent values and ends, and it is crucial for the basic legitimacy of a liberal order. I believe that Muslims can and indeed must be part of the important effort to promulgate principles of conscience and to renew the promise of democratic polities, and here I will outline three ways in which Muslims can do so.

In the first place, more liberal-minded Muslims are auspiciously placed to address fellow Muslims who have not yet adopted principles of liberty of conscience or views favorable to liberal democracy. Indeed, some Muslims seem largely to have rejected democratic societies outright, and others seem only to see prospects for a fallen life in *jahili* or "ignorant" liberal democracy.[32] There are three general things that Muslims can do to assist, here. First, they can promulgate principles of liberty of conscience to fellow Muslims, working to convince and persuade them of the central importance of liberty of conscience in Islam. A number of scholars and activists are already pursuing work in this area (see, e.g., An-Na'im 1990, 2008). Muslims can, for example, demonstrate that the adoption of principles of conscience is fully consistent with the pillars of Islamic belief, and point out that such principles are readily identifiable in the Koran and *hadith*. To take these principles to Muslims, direct engagement in social networks will be crucial and efficacious (Swaine 2006, pp. 121–56). Such direct interaction might not count as deliberation in a properly political sense, but it would be no less important: non-Muslims often do not have access to these religious and social networks. In the course of generating such interactions, Muslims can aim to give their fellow Islamic believers reasons they should accept, for the cases they promote; some of those reasons will be drawn from Islamic doctrine, and also grounded in universal principles of liberty of conscience. Such engagement can help others to understand the role and importance of deliberation: it emphasizes the need to give reasons back and forth, and to be respectful of others, and the interactions can prepare minority groups for ameliorated political deliberation. These practices also help others to understand and appreciate why citizens deserve reasons they should accept for the political and legal impositions of their countries, and how the process of offering and discussing those reasons lends legitimacy to the outcomes that are ultimately produced (cf. Asad 2003, pp. 6–7).

Second, more liberal Muslims can engage with other Muslims on specific and persisting issues that need to be addressed. Sexual liberalization and women's equality loom large, here, as matters on which there is notable dissonance between Muslim minorities and other members of liberal democracies. On a more global level, Norris and Inglehart found that predominantly Muslim countries differ from their Western counterparts on gender roles and sexual liberalization, showing real divisions in that regard (Norris & Inglehart 2004, pp. 150–52, 154). Western countries are becoming increasingly permissive with regard to sexual mores, displaying greater women's equality, too. In Islamic societies, however, publics remain deeply traditional with respect to their views on women, divorce, abortion, and homosexuality. Norris and Inglehart encapsulate their findings as follows, "[t]he central values separating Islam and the West revolve far more centrally around Eros rather than Demos" (Norris & Inglehart 2004, p. 134).[33]

This discrepancy between predominantly Islamic societies and liberal democracies is important and worth careful consideration: many Muslims in Western democracies are recent immigrants from Islamic societies, and traditionalism on gender roles and sexual norms is presumably influenced by patterns of human migration. However, inculcation and advancement of cardinal liberal principles could deftly be used to modify Muslims' views on women and sexuality, not just in liberal democracies but in other countries as well. And this is something that should be done: it seems simply true that men and women are moral equals, for instance, and that any case to the contrary is very hard to defend, especially given what people have learned regarding women's capacities since they began enjoying greater recognition, equality of opportunity, and esteem. Women's liberty of conscience demands respect, and it is sensible to work to promulgate this view to others. On more specific issues, more liberal-minded Muslims could assist in efforts to impress upon traditionalists the fact that women are fundamentally equal to men and deserving of equal educational opportunities and protections. Principles of conscience also provide structure to what can and cannot be allowed by way of marriage, domestic life, and divorce. Muslims unfavorably disposed to liberal-democratic norms could be offered reasons they should accept, grounded in principles of conscience, with regard to why liberal government shall not allow excessively young marriages, permit multiple marriages, or tolerate physical abuse in a domestic environment (cf. Abdo 2006, pp. 11–36, 41; Monsma & Soper 2009, p. 220). Here, too, Muslims can look to the Koran and *hadith*, and also to what one hopes will be helpful argumentation and ideas from political theory and philosophy, for assistance and grounding. To be clear, I am not saying that everyone should be persuaded to think that no differences exist between men and women, that people are equal in virtue or natural capacities, or anything of the sort. Principles of conscience permit latitude in social and domestic life, provided that women meaningfully opt into those arrangements, remain there without undue duress or coercion, and have freedom of exit.

With regard to the sexual permissiveness of liberal democracies, I suspect that there are few hard and fast rules on what kinds of behavior to permit, where such behavior may take place, or how much of it to allow. The lines that societies draw change over time, and in many cases the new limits do not seem to be set in unreasonable places. What are thought of as reasonable standards on abortion or homosexuality, for instance, wax and wane, and there appears to be a range of legitimate, acceptable outcomes for qualifications and restrictions on both forms of behavior. Nevertheless, I expect that citizens need to be more sensitive to changing standards of reasonableness on matters of sexual permissiveness. Indeed, the case of Muslim minorities in liberal democracies is an instructive example of how standards of reasonableness not only can change, but should be altered. For Muslims have been mischaracterized and maligned as unreasonable people, with critics contending that they cannot or will not propose fair terms of cooperation; that they are people bereft of moral sense; that Muslims are excessively irascible and uncivilized; or that they are irredeemably patriarchal and awful to women.

Muslims who are not especially receptive to the sexual mores of liberal democracies could be approached anew with the notion that there are numerous ways of life that governments ought to permit, even though one may not countenance or wish to pursue the paths oneself. The requirements of liberty of conscience support such a position: as a matter of basic tolerance, there is reason to affirm the view that government shall permit citizens to live in their own way, broadly speaking, distasteful though many of the practices may be to oneself, just as government must permit people to live lives of modesty and chastity. There will and should be a good deal of room for contestation on just what practices and ways of life ought to be permissible, but principles of conscience help to structure the range of possibilities.[34] And a similar approach could be used to modify views regarding the extent to which apostasy should be punishable, or in cases where people feel compelled to challenge, modify, or abandon faith. Society must allow people to depart from their faith because of the more primary principle that conscience must be free, and because even if one has found the true faith, political power must not be used to try to keep one affixed to it.

I do not expect that existing traditionalist views on gender or sexuality bespeak anything about Islam itself. This is because many Muslims take no issue with women's equality, or with laws protecting sexual permissiveness or homosexuality. Neither would it be correct to presume that Islamic polities' attitudes on gender and sexuality testify to some intrinsic or irreparable flaw in their societies. After all, even in more permissive liberal democracies, one need only to look back a matter of decades to find a time when women were shut out of high office and prevented from holding important positions in employment; and women still lag behind men in the workplace. What is more, it was only recently that American states and other liberal democracies ridded themselves of more restrictive laws regarding sexuality and decency. Indeed, contemporary American women, dressed for a day at the beach, were they transported to a summer beachfront in England or Ireland of the 1950s, would promptly be arrested. My point is not that Western democracies are too lax in their regulations of sexual decency; it is that liberal societies are oddly glib and self-satisfied about their state of advancement, whereas they were considerably repressive in the recent past and continue to face various social issues on this front.

As for the receptivity of Muslims to such engagement and argumentation, there are encouraging prospects. Abdo reports that young Muslims with whom she interacted "don't want to practice faith blindly"; instead, they seek "rational explanations" for their faith (Abdo 2006, p. 19; cf. pp. 22, 86).[35] The case I present supports a measure of *ijtihad*, without recommending or requiring Muslims to aspire to the critical independence emblematic of personal autonomy.[36] One appreciates that there exists a series of intricate, subtle issues with respect to *ijtihad*. Nevertheless, to the extent that it is an endeavor of personal reasoning that yields reward (even if one proceeds conscientiously but ultimately errs in judgment), *ijtihad* is a practice that could certainly be employed by those who do not possess personal autonomy. *Ijtihad* also

appears to be fully consistent with liberty of conscience, and it resonates with the three principles I have identified. Naturally, I am not
suggesting that there is some need for Muslims fully to democratize
the notion or practice of *ijtihad*, or that pains should be taken to try
to "vest every Muslim...with the competence to be a jurist" (Abou
El Fadl 2004, p. 124). My point is simply that the history and importance of *ijtihad* in Islam could lend itself to a variety of contemporary
applications—for example, whether Koranic verses proscribe youthful
musical expression—and could be applicable to issues of gender and
sexuality (see Abdo 2006, p. 113).

The third special prospect for Muslim minorities in liberal democracies concerns the promotion of principles of liberty of conscience
and related democratic values in the citizenry at large. In this regard,
Muslims can assist in demanding better treatment and appreciation of
liberty of conscience, both for themselves and others. Liberty of conscience is a value on which the religious and nonreligious can converge,
and it appears to be unique in that regard. But there are also other values that democratic citizens could reconsider and better embrace, and
there are three notable ways in which Muslims can assist to promote
that end.

First of all, Muslims can demonstrate their equanimity and fair-
mindedness by supporting liberty of conscience and religious liberty for
all. They can do this partly via respectful argumentation and reasoning
in public fora, and also through the examples that they set in public and
private life, in their interactions with others.[37] Second, Muslims can
continue to be exemplary citizens in what they affirm and how they
affirm it. Muslim minorities in liberal democracies have shown distinctive virtues in their affirmation of racial equality, their efforts to overcome poverty, and their work to secure housing for those in need.[38]
These features of Muslim life harmonize well with the values of liberal
democracies, and, as Kamali notes, cooperation in good and beneficial works is itself an important part of Islam (Kamali 1997, p. 79). In
addition, Muslims shall continue to resist drugs and alcohol, and can
fend off "Westoxication" more generally.[39] Many Muslims refuse to be
beholden to the materialism and banality of quotidian life in America
or elsewhere (Abdo 2006, p. 28). There is good reason to endorse such
attitudes, grounded in values of self-reliance, independence, and simple
moral rectitude. Muslims can also be patient and unflappable in their
dealings with suspicious and unreasonable others, too, as appropriate.[40] These features might successfully be joined to "rising activism"
in human rights, globalization, environmental concerns, and women's

issues (Norris & Inglehart 2004, p. 183), although such engagement would remain a matter of prerogative for Muslims individually.

Third, Muslims in liberal democracies can look to liberal non-Muslims for allies. These will be people wishing to demonstrate respect for Islam, who are committed to the promise of pluralistic, democratic life, and who share a dedication to fighting the spread of corruption on earth.[41] There will be a need to call upon and correct liberals when they go wrong, however, and also to admonish liberals when their voices go silent or they lose their spine. For while not all liberals will abandon Muslim minorities in times of need, many will, even though the lily-livered will have condemned the maltreatment of Muslims and expressed reproach for socially apathetic and politically detached indivduals. Muslims and non-Muslims can work together to ameliorate or overturn such policies as *laïcité* or the Patriot Act, along with other policies that are insufficiently accommodating or respectful of religion.

Conclusion

I have in this chapter identified central values of political liberalism and democratic citizenship, and considered their compatibility with respect to commitments of Muslim minorities in liberal polities. Reciprocity, mutual respect, equitableness, rational inquiry, and inclusiveness stand among the positive values of citizenship; those values are harmonious with the Islamic faith, and there is good reason to believe that Muslims can affirm them in their interactions with others, participating and deliberating as excellent citizens in liberal democratic life.

I note finally that the ideas and strategies I present could be pursued concurrent with renewed efforts to resolve various international issues and conflicts. Muslims and non-Muslims might deliberate and interact together, to try to work toward more healthy and normalized relations between Western democracies and predominantly Muslim societies. These prospects have been short-circuited by current wars and conflicts in the Middle East; but those wars will eventually come to some sort of resolution, and one can at least hope that they will not have set matters back too far, when they conclude. The point is that Western democracies could be better encouraged to deal fairly and squarely with countries in the Middle East, and entreated to do so on the principled, identifiable, and defensible grounds that a liberalism of conscience supports.

Liberal democracies must not fold in front of the darker, misguided theocratic aspirations that some segments of the Islamic world continue to hold, and more radical and recalcitrant parties from various groups and traditions might not be able to be reached by the strategies and arguments I present. But the efforts I have outlined could be employed in efforts to speak anew to foreign publics and peoples, and to address those citizens of liberal democracies who view Muslims with undue suspicion and distrust. In the end, concerned and right-minded citizens of liberal democracies should take note of the need to better engage and include the Muslims in their midst. For demographic facts, legitimacy, and the very future of liberalism require it; and a liberalism of conscience can assist by bringing greater comity, respect, and peace to the world, delivering on the great promise that political liberalism and Islam jointly affirm.

Notes

1. See also Schmidt (2004), Chapter 6, *passim*; Klausen (2005), pp. 81–104, 122–31. Cf. Pipes (1983); Kedourie (1992); Miller (1996); Bawer (2006); Bowen (2007, 2009).
2. Cf. generally Verba, Schlozman, & Brady (1995), pp. 37–48, esp. pp. 42–43, *passim*. See also Klausen (2005), pp. 47–48, 76–78, *passim*.
3. See also Young (2000), pp. 19–21; Daniels, (1999), p. 200.
4. Gutmann & Thompson (2004), pp. 27–29, 79, 90; the authors appear to limit prospects for consensus to groups that are not intractably large.
5. Young (2000), pp. 17, 175–77; see also Bohman (1996), p. 14; Habermas (1996), Chapter 7; Mansbridge (1999), pp. 224–25; Knight & Johnson (1994).
6. Gutmann & Thompson (2004), pp. 13, 23, 58, 98, 126, 133. See also Swaine (2006), Chapters 1, 4.
7. Cf. Raz (1998); Holmes (1995), Chapter 8.
8. See Rawls (2005), pp. 211–54. See also Kant (1983).
9. See also Schauer (1999), Shapiro (1999).
10. Cf. Sanders (1997), pp. 348, 370.
11. See Bohman (1996), pp. 7, 17. See also Fearon (1998), pp. 44–68.
12. Gutmann & Thompson (2004), pp. 133–35 ff. To say that mutual respect is part of the meaning of reciprocity is not necessarily to suggest that the former is the normative ground of the latter; cf. p. 134.
13. I treat the matter of whether mutually-acceptable reasons are requirements of public reason in Swaine, "Deliberate and Free: Heteronomy in the Public Sphere," *Philosophy & Social Criticism*, Vol. 35, Nos. 1–2 (2006): 183–213 (hereinafter Swaine, 2009a).
14. Cf. Gutmann & Thompson (1996), defining reciprocity as "seeking fair terms of cooperation for their own sake" (p. 2).
15. Cf. generally Hampshire (2000).
16. Bohman (1996), p. 26; see also Bohman's nontyranny, equality, and publicity conditions (pp. 35–37).
17. Mansbridge (1999), p. 213; but cf. her subsequent suggestion that it applies only "fairly unproblematically" (p. 222).

18. See Young (2000), esp. Chapters 1–3; Habermas (1996), pp. 76–79, 315–16, 373–87.

19. Cf. Hampshire's proceduralist view, in Hampshire (2000).

20. Young (2000), p. 23; cf. p. 52. This is a sophisticated restatement of a comment made by King Edward I, in his summons of the Model Parliament in 1295: "What touches all, should be approved of all." See also Manin (1987), at pp. 352, 359.

21. See Dahl (1989) for an extended list of conditions required for ideal deliberation.

22. Bohman (1996), p. 5; Bohman also suggests that cooperation is an important element of deliberative democracy.

23. Young (2000), pp. 7, 43–44; cf. generally Elshtain (1995). See also Sanders (1997), pp. 359–62; Bohman (1996), pp. 16, 34.

24. Gutmann & Thompson (2004), p. 20; cf. p. 126. Bohman (1996) expresses a similar view, describing what he calls "precommitment" and "proceduralism" in deliberation (pp. 47–53), and advocating a "dynamic" view of public reason (p. 75 ff.).

25. Kamali (1997), pp. 49–51, 52–60 ff. See also March (2006, pp. 402–03 ff).

26. Ali (1999), pp. 325–36 (Surah 6, Verse 108).

27. It would not be a great leap to ask Muslims to aim to offer reasons that others should accept, in the process of deliberation on matters of public concern, which is a standard for public reason that citizens of liberal democracies ought to affirm. See Swaine (2006), Chapter 2; Swaine (2009a). Cf. Asad (2003), pp. 14–15.

28. Norris & Inglehart (2004), pp. 104–05. See also Norris (1999); Pharr & Putnam (2000).

29. Norris & Inglehart (2004), p. 89. The authors find that the younger generation in post-communist Europe "has not experienced a significant revival of religious values, belief, or behavior" (p. 131). Cf. Monsma & Soper (2009), p. 171.

30. Norris & Inglehart (2004), pp. 224–25; see generally pp. 83–110. See also Jelen & Wilcox (2002); Monsma & Soper (2009), p. 17.

31. Cf. Norris & Inglehart's discussion of the bricolage of personal beliefs common to adherents of New Age religions (2004, p. 88).

32. Cf. generally Qutb (n.d.); Moussalli (1992); Cook (2005), pp. 102–06, 107–10, 128–61, *passim*.

33. See also Soper (2009), p. 67. Cf. March (2006), p. 374; Bower (2007), Chapter 8; Klausen (2005), Chapter 6.

34. I suspect that such discussions could benefit from a reworked and more plausible version of the distinction between internal and external preferences, although I cannot address the matter here.

35. Cf. Mahmoud (2005), pp. 54–57, 79, 80–82, 97, 132–37; Bower (2007), pp. 70–72.

36. See Saeed & Saeed (2004), p. 97. See also Kamali (1997), p. 45; Abdo (2006), p. 21. Cf. Swaine (2009; 2010).

37. One's example to others would not itself be deliberative *per se*, but it can still be noble, influential, and consistent with the values and ideas for which I have argued here.

38. Cf. Norris & Inglehart (2004), p. 189.

39. See Saeed & Saeed (2004), p. 111; see also Soroush (2000); Safi (2003). Cf. Maududi (1979, 1980, 1990).

40. Cf. Saeed & Saeed (2004), p. 82.

41. See Surah 5, Verse 33 (Yusuf Ali [1999], pp. 257–58).

C H A P T E R   4

Multiculturalism in the West and Muslim Identity

Tariq Modood

Blaming Multiculturalism, Blaming Muslims

The critique of multiculturalism in Europe that focuses on Muslims and is so prevalent today predates the terrorist attacks of 9/11 and their aftermath, though in Britain at least 2001 is a pivotal year. During the late spring and early summer of that year there were urban disturbances in a number of northern English towns and cities where young, mainly Pakistani Muslim men played a central role. The official response was that the riots were due to a one-sided multiculturalism having facilitated, even encouraged, segregated communities that shunned each other. All subsequent events seem to point in the same direction. In 2004 a swathe of British civil society fora and institutions of the center-left or the liberal-left held seminars or produced special publications with titles such as *Is Multiculturalism Dead?, Is Multiculturalism Over?, Beyond Multiculturalism,* etc.[1] This critical, sometimes savage discourse reached a new peak with the London bombings of July 7, 2005 and the abortive bombings of July 21. The fact that most of the individuals involved were born and/or raised in Britain, a country that had afforded them or their parents refuge from persecution and poverty and sometimes a newfound freedom of worship, led many to conclude that multiculturalism had failed—or worse, was to blame for the bombings. The multinational commentary in the British media included William

Pfaff who stated that "these British bombers are a consequence of a misguided and catastrophic pursuit of multiculturalism" (Pfaff 2005), with Gilles Kepel observing that the bombers "were the children of Britain's own multicultural society" and that the bombings have "smashed" the implicit social consensus that produced multicultural- ism "to smithereens" (Kepel 2005), and Martin Wolf concluding that multiculturalism's departure from the core political values that must underpin Britain's community "is dangerous because it destroys politi- cal community...(and) demeaning because it devalues citizenship. In this sense, at least, multiculturalism must be discarded as nonsense" (Wolf 2005). Francis Fukyama offered a more balanced analysis but concluded that "countries like Holland and Britain need to reverse the counterproductive multiculturalist policies that sheltered radicalism, and crack down on extremists" (Fukuyama 2005).[2]

Not only is there disillusionment with and anxiety about multicul- turalism among the center-left, but Muslims[3] and multiculturalism have become mutually implicated politically, especially in Europe, not least in becoming unpopular both in themselves and as part of the unpopu- larity of the other (Modood 2007). In what follows I respond to this situation by restating a conception of multiculturalism, which clearly distinguishes it from certain narrow forms of liberalism, but which places it squarely within an understanding of democratic citizenship and nation-building, though this is far from a simple reaffirmation of either. My argument consists of sketching a conception of citizenship with which multiculturalism fits better than the narrow conception of liberalism that I will discuss. To put it another way, I offer a "multicul- turalised" version of democratic citizenship and national identity.

Multicultural Citizenship

Just as social democrats have a notion of positive equality around socio- economic equality, what one might call social citizenship, I would like to make a parallel case for positive equality in connection with the symbolic dimensions of public culture. Citizenship describes not only a legal status and set of rights but is amplified by a certain kind of politics. I have nothing specific to say about the former, the basic foundational levels of citizenship except that they are necessary—in the way a skeleton is to a living body—to a wider meaning of citizenship. T. H. Marshall (1973) famously conceptualized a wider citizenship as a series of historical-logical developments, each necessary to later stages, by which legal rights such as habeas corpus were gradually extended to include rights of political participation and then later to social rights such as the right of citizens to receive healthcare funded by the state. These developments were the result of a long deliberative process, involved a history of political struggles, not least in extending the body of citizenry, the rights-holders, from an aristocratic male elite to all adults. With some plausibility it has been argued that through egalitarian movements such as the politics of difference, the second half of the twentieth century has seen the emergence of a fourth stage in the form of a demand for cultural rights (Roche 1992; Turner, 1993), while also seeing an erosion of some social rights. Social citizenship has certainly not been accultural; rather it has been informed by an assumption of cultural homogeneity, such as its support of a male breadwinner model of the nuclear family (Lister 2003). The homogeneity has been particularly vulnerable to social change and change in attitudes and critiqued by feminists whose work—as with the public-private distinction—others have built upon. I would like to outline an understanding of this historically developing citizenship, which has not been a simple linear process, in terms of three over-arching characteristics—non-transcendent pluralism, multilogical, and dispersed—rather than by types of rights, though like Marshall I believe the citizenship I speak of is particularly informed by British history, though it can be seen at work in many other places too.

The British or pluralist conception citizenship is necessarily non-transcendent. Citizens are individuals and have individual rights but they are not uniform and their citizenship contours itself around them. Citizenship is not a monistic identity that is completely apart from or transcends other identities important to citizens; in the way that the theory—though not always the practice—of French republicanism demands. The creation of the United Kingdom created new political subjects (for my purpose citizens, though strictly speaking, for most of the history of the United Kingdom, subjects of the Crown) but did not eliminate the constituent nations of the United Kingdom. So a common British citizenship did not mean that one could not be Scottish, English, Irish, or Welsh, and so allowed for the idea that there were different ways of being British—an idea that is not confined to constituent nations but also included other group identities. The plurality, then, is ever present and each part of the plurality has a right to be a part of the whole and to speak up for itself and for its vision of the whole.

Moreover, the conception of citizenship I am drawing on is multi-logical. The plurality speaks to each other and it does not necessarily agree about what it means to be a citizen. There can be a series of agreements and disagreements, with some who agree on X and disagree on Y; some who disagree on X may agree and others disagree on Y and so on. But there is enough agreement and above all enough interest in the discussion for dialogues to be sustained. As the parties to these dialogues are many, not just two, the process is more aptly described as multilogical. The multilogues allow for views to qualify each other, overlap, synthesize, modify one's own view in the light of having to co-exist with that of others', hybridize, allow new adjustments to be made, new conversations to take place. Such modulations and contestations are part of the internal, evolutionary, work-in-progress dynamic of citizenship.

The third feature of this conception, related to citizenship not being monolithic, is that action and power are not monopolistically concentrated and so the state is not the exclusive site for citizenship. We perform our citizenship and relate to each other as fellow citizens, and so get to know what our citizenship is, what it is composed of, not just in relation to law and politics but also civic debate and action initiated through our voluntary associations, community organizations, trades unions, newspapers and media, churches, temples, mosques etc. Change and reform do not all have to be brought about by state action, laws, regulation, prohibitions, etc. but also through public debate, discursive contestations, pressure group mobilizations, and the varied and (semi-) autonomous institutions of civil society.

Difference and Equality

Multiculturalism gives political importance to a respect for identities that are important to people, as identified in minority assertiveness, arguing that they should not be disregarded in the name of integration or citizenship (Young 1990, Parekh 1991, Taylor 1994). Sociologically we have to begin with the fact of negative "difference": with alienness, inferiorization, stigmatization, stereotyping, exclusion, discrimination, racism etc; but also the senses of identity that groups so perceived have of themselves. The two together are the key datum for multiculturalism. The differences at issue are those perceived both by outsiders or group members—from the outside in and from the inside out—to constitute not just some form of distinctness but a form of alienness or inferiority that diminishes or makes difficult equal membership in the wider society or polity. There is a sense of groupness in play, a mode of being, but also subordination or marginality, a mode of oppression, and the two interact in creating an unequal "us-them" relationship.[4] The differences in question are in the field of race, ethnicity, cultural heritage or religious community; typically, differences that overlap between these categories, not least because these categories do not have singular, fixed meanings.

These groups—or given the variety and looseness of the forms they can take, "groupness" may be better—have a political character and give rise to the processes and outcomes of political struggles and negotiations around the fact of difference. To those struggles and outcomes in which certain kinds of "differences" are asserted and certain claims are made, recognition or accommodation is sought and not considered illegitimate. Multiculturalism, as I am using it, refers to the struggle, the political mobilization but also the policy and institutional outcomes, to the forms of accommodation in which "differences" are not eliminated, or not washed away but to some extent "recognized". Through group assertiveness and mobilization, and through institutional and policy reforms to address the claims of the newly settled, marginalized groups, the character of "difference" is addressed; ideally, a negative difference is turned into a positive difference, though in most contemporary situations something of each is likely to be simultaneously present.

To speak of "difference" rather than "culture" as the sociological starting point is to recognize that the difference in question is not just constituted from the "inside," from the side of a minority culture, but also from the outside, from the representations and treatment of the minorities in question. Moreover, as I have said, it is also to recognize that the nature of the minorities, and their relationship to the rest of society, is not such that "culture" is a stand-alone alternative to race, ethnicity, religion and so on.

Multiculturalism is not, therefore, about cultural rights instead of political equality or economic opportunities; it is a politics that recognizes that post-immigration groups exist in Western societies in ways that both they and others, formally and informally, negatively and positively are aware that these group differentiating dimensions are central to their social constitution. So, rather than derive a concept of multicultural politics from a concept of culture, it is better to construct it with the specific claims, implicit and explicit, of the post-war extra-European/non-white immigration and settlement, and their struggles and the policy responses around them to achieve some form of acceptance and equal membership.[5]

Though some liberal thinkers may take issue with my conception of group equality, I believe, then, that the concept of equality has to be applied to groups and not just individuals (e.g., Parekh 2000)[6]. Different theorists have offered different formulations on this question. Charles Taylor (1994), for example, argues that when we talk about equality in the context of race and ethnicity, we are appealing to two different albeit related concepts—*equal dignity*, and *equal respect*. Equal dignity appeals to people's humanity or to some specific membership like citizenship and applies to all members in a relatively uniform way. A good example is Martin Luther King, Jr.'s demand for civil rights. He said black Americans want to make a claim upon the American dream; they wanted American citizenship in the way that the constitution theoretically is supposed to give to everybody but in practice failed to do so. This universalist idea is evident in antidiscrimination policies where we appeal to the principle that everybody should be treated the same. But Taylor, and other theorists in differing ways, also posit the idea of *equal respect*. If equal dignity focuses on what people have in common and so in principle is gender-blind, color-blind and so on, equal respect is based on an understanding that difference is also important in conceptualizing and institutionalizing equal relations between individuals.

This is because individuals have group identities and these may be the ground of existing and long-standing inequalities such as racism, for example, and the ways that some people have conceived and treated others as inferior, less rational and culturally backward. While those conceptions persist they will affect the dignity of non-white people, above all where they share imaginative and social life with white people. The negative conceptions are likely to precipitate direct and indirect acts of discrimination—they thus will eat away at the possibilities of equal dignity. They will affect the self-understanding of those who seek to be equal participants in a culture where ideas of their inferiority, or even just of their absence, their invisibility, is pervasive. They will stand in need of self-respect and the respect of others, of the dominant group; the latter will be crucial for it is the source of their damaged self-respect and it is where the power for change lies (Du Bois 1903).

A denigration of a group identity, or its distortion, or denial—the pretence (often unconscious because it is part of a culture rather than a personal thought) that a group does not exist—the withholding of recognition or misrecognition is a form of oppression (Taylor 1994). It is a form of inequality in its own right but also threatens the other form of equality, equal dignity, the fulfillment of which can be made impossible by stereotypes or a failure to recognize the self-definitional strivings of marginal groups.

The interaction and mutuality between the two kinds of equality runs the other way too. Equal respect presupposes the framework of commonality and rights embodied in equal dignity. Hence it is quite wrong to think of the latter in terms of universalism and the former as a denial of universality. For not only does the concept of equal respect grow out of a concern with equal dignity but it only makes sense because it rests on universalist foundations. It is only because there is a fundamental equality between human beings or between citizens that the claim for respect can be formulated. As Taylor says, there is a demand for an acknowledgement of specificity but it is powered by the universal that an advantage that some currently enjoy should not be a privilege but available to all (Taylor 1994: 38–39). Hence we must not lose sight of the fact that *both* equal dignity and equal respect are essential to multiculturalism; while the latter marks out multiculturalism from classical liberalism it does not make multiculturalism normatively particularistic or relativist.

Multiculturalism, then, seeks the goal of positive difference and the means to achieve it, which crucially involve the appreciation of the fact of multiplicity and groupness, the building of group pride among those marked by negative difference, and political engagement with the sources of negativity and racism. While the focus is not on anything so narrow as normally understood by "culture," and multicultural equality cannot be achieved without other forms of equality, such as those relating to socioeconomic opportunities, its distinctive feature is about the inclusion into and the making of a shared public space in terms of equality of respect as well as equal dignity.

Some qualifications are appropriate at this point. I do not mean that simply claiming to be a group or an oppressed group is enough to ensure recognition. If a racist organization like the British National Party (BNP) claimed to be speaking for a group (white working class) and demanded political representation such claims would have to be demonstrated in a public dialogue. While I think a case can be made for the marginalization and even the disrespecting of white working class people in relation to some policies that portray them as unequivocal racists, it is not the case that the BNP represents such a group or that the policies of the BNP are what is needed to extend respect to white working class people. Moreover, even when there is a case for recognizing a group it does not follow that everything that some members of that group identify as practices that need support should be supported. Some communities might say that "honor killings" are a custom that ought to be preserved but I would not wish to be interpreted as saying that such practices do not constitute murder. In talking about supplementing equal dignity with equal respect I am assuming a strong background framework of individual rights. My point is that individual rights do not exhaust the basis of multicultural equality. While the latter must be constrained by the former this leaves considerable space for equal respect, some of the boundaries of which cannot be determined in advance but need to be identified through multicultural dialogues. In such dialogues we should be able to criticize the practice of any group but we must take care to avoid being influenced by prevalent stereotypes that identify certain groups with some unacceptable practices of some of their members. Respect for groups is not a blank check; nor must we blank out groups in the name of individual rights.

It should now be evident that a deep resonance exists between citizenship and multicultural recognition. Not only do both presuppose complementary notions of unity and plurality, and of equality and difference, but the idea of respect for the group self-identities that citizens value is central to citizenship. Moreover, seeing citizenship as a work in progress and as partly constituted, and certainly extended, by contestatory multilogues and novel demands for due recognition, as circumstances shift, means that citizenship can be understood as conversations and renegotiations, not just about who is to be recognized but about what is recognition, about the terms of citizenship itself. At one point, it is the injuries of class that demand civic attention; at another there is a plea for dropping a self-deluding "color-blindness" and of addressing racialized statuses through citizenship. The one thing that civic inclusion does not consist of is an uncritical acceptance of an existing conception of citizenship, of "the rules of the game" and a one-sided "fitting-in" of new entrants or the new equals (the ex-subordinates). To be a citizen, no less than to have just become a citizen, is to have a right to not just be recognized but to debate the terms of recognition, whether from within one's own group or without (Benhabib, 1992 and Fraser, 1992).

3+1 Implications for Liberal Citizenship

Multiculturalism arises within contemporary liberal egalitarianism but it is at the same time in tension with, and a critique of some classical liberal ideas. Specifically, it has four major implications for liberal citizenship. Firstly, it is clearly a collective project and concerns collectivities and not just individuals. Secondly, it is not color/gender/sexual orientation "blind" and so breaches the liberal public-private identity distinction that prohibits the recognition of particular group identities in order that no citizens are treated in a more or less privileged way or divided from each other. These two implications are obvious from the discussion so far but the next two implications are less obvious and more controversial. The first of these is that multiculturalism takes race, sex and sexuality beyond being merely ascriptive sources of identity, merely categories. Traditional conceptions of liberal citizenship are not interested in group identities and have shunned identitarian politics; its interest in "race" is confined to anti-discrimination and simply as an aspect of the legal equality of citizens.[7] Strictly speaking, race is of interest to liberal citizenship only because no one can choose their race: while some features (such as skin color or hair texture) visibly distinguish persons from one another, race is more commonly a way of being categorized by the society around them by reference to some real or perceived biological features, and so one should not be discriminated against on something over which one has no control. But if, as I have argued, equality is also about celebrating previously demeaned identities (e.g., taking pride in one's blackness rather than accepting it as a merely "private" matter), then what is being addressed in antidiscrimination, or promoted as a public identity, is a chosen response to one's ascription, namely pride, identity renewal, the challenging of hegemonic norms and asserting of marginalized identities and so on. Of course this is not peculiar to race/ethnicity. Exactly, the same applies to sex and sexuality. We may not choose our sex or sexual orientation but we choose how to politically live with it. Do we keep it private or do we make it the basis of a social movement and seek public resources and representation for it? In many countries the initial liberal—and social democratic and socialist—response that the assertions of race, political femininity, gay pride politics and so on were divisive and deviations from the only political identity that mattered (citizenship; and/or class, in the case of socialists) soon gave way to an understanding that these positions were a genuine and significant part of a plural, center-left egalitarian movement.

Marginalized and other religious groups, most notably Muslims, are now utilizing the same kind of argument and making a claim that religious identity, just like gay identity, and just like certain forms of racial identity, should not just be privatized or tolerated, but should be part of the public space. In their case, however, they come into conflict with an additional fourth implication of liberal citizenship. This additional conflict with liberal citizenship is best understood as a "3+1" rather than merely a fourth difficulty because while it is not clear that it actually raises a new difficulty, for many on the center-left this one, unlike the previous three is seen as a demand that should not be conceded.[8] One would think that if a new group was pressing a claim that had already been granted to others then what would be at issue would be a practical adjustment and not a fundamental principle. But as a matter of fact, the demand by Muslims for not just toleration and religious freedom but for public recognition is indeed taken to be philosophically very different to the same demand made by black people, women and gays. It is seen as an attack on the principle of secularism, the view that religion is a feature, perhaps uniquely, of private and not public identity.

Hence it is commonly found in the op-ed pages of the broadsheets, that Muslims (and other religious groups) are simply not on a par with the groups with which I have aligned them. It is argued that woman, black and gay are ascribed, involuntary identities while being a Muslim is about chosen beliefs, and that Muslims therefore need or ought to have less legal protection than the other kinds of identities. Some analytical political theorists have elaborated the distinction on which this argument rests by categorizing diminutions in opportunities that result from the belief of individuals as "expensive tastes" that are of no normative interest to egalitarians and should not be compensated for through state intervention. For instance, disputing cases such as the exemption from wearing motorcycle safety helmets given in United Kingdom law for turban wearing Sikhs on the grounds of their religious duties, Barry argues: "The position of somebody who is unable to drive a car as a result of some physical disability is totally different from that of somebody who is unable to drive a car because doing so would be contrary to the tenets of his or her religion" (Barry, 2001: 37). Whatever the merits of his specific argument (for a critique, see Owen and Tully, 2007), to argue thus is not so much as to draw a line between say religion and race or gender, but to undermine the politics of recognition as a whole. For the case of religious groups like Muslims is much closer sociologically to the standard cases of equal opportunities for other disadvantaged groups . For example, there are relevant senses in which being a Muslim is not about choice, and certainly not simply about religious beliefs, any more than being a Jew is or being a Catholic in N. Ireland. Indeed, being a Muslim is no less sociologically defined than gender is (or indeed disability is in many contemporary analyses of disability (see Chapireau and Colvez, 1998). To think otherwise is sociologically naïve (and a political con). The position of Muslims today in countries like Britain is similar to the other identities of "difference" as Muslims catch up with and engage with the contemporary concept of equality. No one chooses to be or not to be born into a Muslim family. Similarly, no one chooses to be born into a society where to look like a Muslim or to be a Muslim creates suspicion, hostility, or failure to get the job you applied for. Of course how Muslims respond to these circumstances will vary. Some will organize resistance, while others will try to stop looking like Muslims (the equivalent of "passing" for white); some will build an ideology out of their subordination, others will not, just as a woman can choose to be a feminist or not. Again, some Muslims may define their Islam in terms of piety rather than politics; just as some women may see no politics in their gender, while for others their gender will be at the center of their politics.

I reject, therefore, the contention that equality as recognition (uniquely) does not apply to oppressed religious communities. Of course many people's objections may be based on what they (sometimes correctly) understand as conservative, even intolerant and inegalitarian views held by some Muslims in relation to issues of personal sexual freedom. My concern is with the argument that a commitment to a reasonable secularism rules out extending multicultural equality to Muslims and other religious groups.

I proceed on the basis of two assumptions, firstly that a religious group's view on matters of gender and sexuality, which of course will not be uniform, are open to debate and change; and secondly, that conservative views are not necessarily a bar to multicultural recognition.[9] Those who see the current Muslim assertiveness as an unwanted and illegitimate child of multiculturalism have only two choices if they wish to be consistent. They can repudiate the idea of equality as identity recognition and return to the 1950s liberal idea of equality as color/sex/religion etc blindness (Barry 2001). Or they must appreciate that a program of racial and multicultural equality is not possible today without a discussion of the merits and limits of secularism. For we have reached a moment, at least in Western Europe, where the most assertive claims to public recognition are being made by Muslims. To say to them that their claims *qua Muslims* cannot be recognized, as a matter of principle, because religion is a private matter, while simultaneously extending symbolic and policy recognition to people defined by gender, race, culture, nationality, sexual orientation and so on is not viable

(Modood 2007, chp. 4; Modood 2010). It is to be open to the charge of double standards and will inevitably provoke resentment.

Muslims and Identity

Identity, for some is a matter of background, while for others it is fore grounded in a politics of difference. So it is with Muslims. Even with those for whom a Muslim identity is in many contexts not just a background, it does not follow that it is the religious dimension that is most salient: it can be a sense of family and community; or collective political advancement; or righting the wrongs done to Muslims. Indeed, we cannot assume that being "Muslim" means the same thing to everyone. For some Muslims—like most Jews in Britain today—being Muslim is a matter of community membership and heritage; for others it is a few simple precepts about self, compassion, justice and the afterlife; for some others it is a worldwide movement armed with a counter-ideology of modernity; and so on.

British Muslim identity politics was stimulated, if not virtually created, by the *Satanic Verses* Affair of the late 1980s and beyond (Modood 1992). Muslims began to make demands for recognition and civic inclusion into a polity that had up to that point misrecognised them (as black or Asian) or had kept them invisible and voiceless; a polity that was struggling to recognize gender, race and ethnicity within the terms of citizenship but was not even aware that any form of civic recognition was due to marginalized religious groups. The crisis led many to think of themselves for the first time as Muslims in a public way, to think that it was important in their relation to other Muslims and to the rest of British and related societies. This is for example movingly described by the author, Rana Kabbani, whose *Letter to Christendom* begins with a description of herself as "a woman who had been a sort of underground Muslim before she was forced into the open by the Salman Rushdie affair" (Kabbani 1989: ix). Such shocks to Muslim identity are hardly a thing of the past. The present situation of some Muslims in Britain is nicely captured by Farmida Bi, a New Labour Parliamentary candidate in Mole Valley in 2005, who had not particularly made anything of her Muslim background before 7/7 but was moved by the London bombings to claim a Muslim identity and found the organization, Progressive British Muslims. Speaking of herself and others as "integrated, liberal British Muslims" who were forced to ask "am I a Muslim at all?" she writes: "7/7 made most of us embrace our

Muslim identity and become determined to prove that it's possible to live happily as a Muslim in the West" (Bi 2006).

This conviction that one must speak up as a Muslim is of course nothing necessarily to do with religiosity. Like all forms of difference it comes into being as a result of pressures from "outside" a group as well as from the "inside." In this particular case, both the "inside" and the "outside" have a powerful geo-political dimension. The emergence of British Muslim identity and activism has been propelled by a strong concern for the plight of Muslims elsewhere in the world, especially (but not only) where this plight is seen in terms of anti-imperialist emancipation and where the United Kingdom government is perceived to be part of the problem—tolerant of, if not complicit in or actively engaged in the destruction of Muslim hopes and lives, often civilian. Political activity, charitable fund raising, the delivering of humanitarian relief, and sometimes the taking up of arms has taken place in connection with Palestine, Kashmir, Bosnia, Chechnya, Kosovo, Afghanistan, and Iraq, just to mention the most prominent cases. As a consequence, Muslims have been perceived by some other Britons as disloyal and have experienced recurring and deepening tensions connected with dual loyalties and alienation from New Labour, initially seen as a champion of British Muslims (Werbner 2004). It is not that unusual, even for successful, integrated and respected minorities, to be strongly identified with an international or a "homeland" cause; British and American Jews in relation to Israel and Cuban-Americans in relation to Cuba are notable examples. Yet, as these latter cases demonstrate, these causes are usually those where one's government is either neutral or on your side. That British, American, and Australian (perhaps to some extent most Western) Muslims are having to develop a sense of national citizenship, to integrate into a polity, which has a confrontational posture against many Muslim countries and is at war or occupying some of them in what is perceived by all sides to be a long term project, is an extremely daunting task and I suppose one has to say that success cannot be taken for granted. Moreover, domestic terrorism, as well as political opposition, has become part of the context. The danger of "blowback" from overseas military activity is, as the London bombings of July 2005 and various other incidents have already shown, considerable and capable of destroying the movement towards multicultural citizenship.

There is, then, a crisis of multiculturalism, that I have been arguing must not be responded to in panic but with a cool reappraisal of what multiculturalism is and what is needed for it succeed. One of the reasons why I do not think we should simply give up and pursue a less attractive political goal is that I am impressed by how many British Muslims have and are responding to the crisis, namely, with a concern to stand up for their community through civic engagement and a refusal to give up on their Muslim identity or being part of democratic citizenship. Despite this dependency on overseas circumstances outside their control and so where one might anticipate passivity and a self-pitying introspection, what is clear from many Muslims is their dynamism, energy, and confidence that they must rise to the challenge of dual loyalties and not give up on either set of commitments. Ideological and violent extremism is indeed undermining the conditions and hopes for multiculturalism, but, contrary to the multiculturalism blamers I began with, this extremism has nothing to do with the promotion of multiculturalism but is coming into the domestic arena from the international.

National Identity and Being British

Multiculturalism has been broadly right and does not deserve the desertion of support from the center-left let alone the blame for the present crisis. It offers a better basis for integration than its two current rivals, namely, "social cohesion" and "multiculture" (Meer and Modood, 2009). For while the latter is appreciative of a diversity of interacting lifestyles and the emergence of new, hybridic cultures in an atmosphere of "conviviality," it is at a loss as to how to sympathetically deal with the claims of newly settled ethno-religious groups, especially Muslims, who are too readily stereotyped as "fundamentalists" (Modood, 1998). Some advocacy of multiculturalism has, however, perhaps overlooked or at least underemphasized the other side of the coin, which is not just equally necessary but is integral to multiculturalism. For one can't just talk about difference. Difference has to be related to things we have in common. The commonality that I have been emphasizing, in common with most multiculturalists and others, is citizenship. I have emphasized that this citizenship has to be seen in a plural, dispersed, and dialogical way and not reduced to legal rights, passports and the franchise (important though these are). I would now like to go further in suggesting that a good basis for, or accompaniment to, a multicultural citizenship is a national identity.[10]

Many multiculturalists and others for whom equality and difference are politically important do not agree with me but national identity seems to be relevant here. This is partly because conceiving of citizenship in the very broad way that I have outlined already begins to overlap with much of what we mean when we speak of the "national," as in, for example, the national news, national history, national dynamism, national malaise, and national agenda, etc. Indeed, modern democratic citizenship has nearly always—if not in theory, then in fact—been accompanied by a national identity. Of course, these have not usually been welcoming of difference and sometimes have actively suppressed it, so I am not simply recommending unreformed historical models of national identity.

We in Europe have overlooked the fact that where multiculturalism has been attempted, with more or less success, as a state project or as a national project—Canada, Australia, and Malaysia for example—it has not just been coincidental with but integral to a nation-building project, to creating Canadians, Aussies, and Malaysians etc. Even in the United States, where the federal state has had a much smaller role in the multicultural project, the incorporation of ethno-religious diversity and hyphenated Americans has been about country-making, civic inclusion, and making a claim upon the national identity. This is important because some multiculturalists, or at least advocates of pluralism and multiculture (the vocabulary of multiculturalism is not always used[11])—even where they have other fundamental disagreements with each other—argue as if the logic of the national and the multicultural are incompatible (Gilroy 1987 and 2004,[12] Anthias and Yuval-Davis 1992, Sayyid 2000 and 2007, Joppke 2004,[13] Cannon 2006, Preston 2007, O'Donnell 2007). Partly as a result many Europeans think of multiculturalism as antithetical to rather than as a reformer of national identity.

No one can deny that national identity, even where it has been connected to a national citizenship, has simultaneously or at other times been involved in ideological forms of nationalism that have led to exclusion, racism, military aggression, empires, and much more. But looking at recent and contemporary history, especially in Western Europe and countries like Canada, it appears that it is possible to disconnect national identities from strong forms of nationalism. Perhaps it is also possible to disconnect citizenship from national identities, and so from the national altogether, perhaps to invest our civic loyalties and sense of belonging into some principles of a human rights based political order, what Habermas (1992) calls "constitutional patriotism." I would concede that recent trends in the countries mentioned above, where for many, especially younger people, citizenship can be prized but nationality is looked at with suspicion or indifference, are just as supportive of the idea of a non-nationalism national identity of the kind I am arguing for as they are of the fading of national identity.[14] Nevertheless, my judgment is that attitudes such as constitutional patriotism or cosmopolitanism are not affective enough for most people, especially the relatively non-political, at times of crisis. They are unlikely to hold people together and to give them the confidence and optimism to see through the present crisis of multiculturalism. Indeed, what we see happening is that it is all too easy in these times of fear and panic for ordinary, decent people to be very anxious and—where multicultural national identities are weak or at least are not inclusive of Muslims—to wrap themselves in strong nationalisms, militarisms, and other dichotomizing, confrontational ideologies.

Moreover, it does not make sense to encourage strong multicultural or minority identities and weak common or national identities; strong multicultural identities are a good thing—they are not intrinsically divisive, reactionary or fifth columns—but they need a framework of vibrant, dynamic, national narratives and the ceremonies and rituals that give expression to a national identity. It is clear that minority identities are capable of having an emotional pull for the individuals for whom they are important. Multicultural citizenship requires, therefore, if it is to be equally attractive to the same individuals, a comparable counter-balancing emotional pull. Many Britons, for example, say they are worried about disaffection among some Muslim young men and more generally a lack of identification with Britain among many Muslims in Britain. As a matter of fact, surveys over many years have shown Muslims have been reaching out for identification with Britain. For example, in a Channel 4 NOP survey done in spring 2006, 82 percent of a well constructed national sample of Muslims said they very strongly (45 percent) or fairly strongly (37 percent) felt they belonged to Britain.[15] Yet the survey also found that many Muslims did not feel comfortable in Britain. For example, 58 percent thought that extreme religious persecution of Muslims was very likely (23 percent) or fairly likely (35 percent); and 22 percent strongly agreed (11 percent) or fairly strongly agreed (11 percent) that the 7/7 London bombings were justified because of British support for the United States war on terror—in each case the figures were higher among the young.[16] The last set of views are connected to foreign policy and so in some cases cannot be changed without a change in policy but nevertheless to not build on the clear support there is for a sense of national belonging is to fail to offer an obvious counterweight to the ideological calls for a violent jihad against fellow Britons.

A sense of belonging to one's country is necessary to make a success of a multicultural society. Not assimilation into an undifferentiated national identity; that is unrealistic and oppressive as a policy. An inclusive national identity is respectful of and builds upon the identities that people value and does not trample upon them. Simultaneously respecting difference and inculcating Britishness is not a naïve hope but something that is happening and leads everyone to redefine themselves. Perhaps one of the lessons of the current crisis is that in some countries, certainly Britain, multiculturalists, and the left in general, have been too hesitant about embracing our national identity and allying it with progressive politics. The reaffirming of a plural, changing, inclusive British identity, which can be as emotionally and politically meaningful to British Muslims as the appeal of jihadi sentiments, is critical to isolating and defeating extremism. The lack of a sense of belonging to Britain that can stand up to the emotional appeal of transnational solidarities is due to several causes, including causes that belong to the majority society and not the minorities. One of these is exclusivist and racist notions of Britishness that hold that non-white people are not really British and that Muslims are an alien wedge. Another, and this time from the Left, is the view that there is something deeply wrong about rallying round the idea of Britain, about defining ourselves in terms of a normative concept of Britishness—that it is too racist, imperialist, militaristic, elitist, and so on—and that the goal of seeking to be British in the present and the future is silly and dangerous, and indeed, demeaning to the newly settled groups in the population (Preston 2007). But if the goal of wanting to become British, to be accepted as British and to belong to Britain is not a worthwhile goal for Commonwealth migrants and their progeny, what then are they supposed to integrate into? And if there is nothing strong, purposive, and inspiring to integrate into, why bother with integration? And if inspiring and meaning-conferring identities can be found elsewhere—in some internationalist movement—that's just fine and if that's at the expense of your country and its citizens, well they don't really matter all that much in the ultimate scheme of significance? We cannot both ask new Britons to integrate and go around saying that being British (or English) is a hollowed-out, meaningless project whose time has come to an end. This will rightly produce confusion and will detract from the sociological and psychological processes of integration, and offer no defense against the calls of other loyalties and missions. Today's national identities certainly need to be re-imagined in a multicultural way but if this is thought impossible or unnecessary then multiculturalism is left not triumphant but with fewer emotive resources.

So integration—like multiculturalism as a whole—is not simply or even primarily a minority problem. If too many white people do not feel the power of Britishness, it will only be a legal concept and other identities will prevail, including ones that will be damaging to multicultural citizenship. Earlier in the paper, I recognized that the development of a British Muslim identity was dependent on overseas events and international politics. I am now pointing out that whether and what kind of integrative citizenship takes place is inevitably dependent upon majority attitudes and interests. I believe that in many circumstances, as in Britain, the best support for multicultural citizenship is a national identity but I am unsure if there is enough interest among white Britons in a British national identity. It is therefore to be welcomed when politicians of the left show an interest in British national identity. A leading example of this is Gordon Brown, the recent United Kingdom Prime Minister. He has argued for the need to revive and revalue British national identity in a number of speeches, most notably at the Fabian 2006 Annual Conference, entitled "Who Do We Want to Be? The Future of Britishness" (Brown, 2006). Brown wants to derive a set of core values (liberty, fairness, enterprise, and so on) from a historical narrative yet such values, even if they could singly or in combination be given a distinctive British cast, are too complex and their interpretation and priority too contested to be amenable to be set into a series of meaningful definitions. Every public culture must operate through shared values, which are both embodied in and used to criticize its institutions and practices, but they are not simple and uniform and their meaning is discursively grasped as old interpretations are dropped and new circumstances unsettle one consensus and another is built up. Simply saying that freedom or equality is a core British value is unlikely to settle any controversy or tell us, for example, what is hate speech and how it should be handled. Definitions of core values will either be too bland or too divisive and the idea that there has to be a schedule of value statements to which every citizen is expected to sign up to is not in the spirit of a multilogical citizenship (Brown 2005). The national identity should be woven in debate and discussion, not reduced to a list.

Let me conclude with the Commission on Multi-Ethnic Britain (CMEB) report (aka The Parekh Report). It suggested that if people are to have a sense of belonging to society as a whole, to have a sense of sharing a common fate with fellow citizens and nationals they must be able to feel "that their own flourishing as individuals and as communities is intimately linked with the flourishing of public institutions and public services" (CMEB 2000: 49). The report insisted that this sense of belonging required two important conditions: the idea that one's polity should be recognized as a community of communities as well as a community of individuals; and the challenging of all racisms and related structural inequalities (CMEB 2000: 56).[17] It is clear in the CMEB report, and I hope from this paper that the concepts of recognition and belonging are about much more than culture and cultural rights. They are interpretations of the idea of equality as applied to groups who are constituted by differentia that have identarian dimensions that elude socioeconomic concepts. The realization of multicultural equality is not possible in a society in which the distribution of opportunities is restricted by "difference" but it cannot be confined to socioeconomic opportunities. For central to it is a citizenship and the right to make a claim on the national identity in which negative difference is challenged and supplanted by positive difference (Modood 1992).[18] We cannot afford to leave out these aspects of multicultural citizenship from an intellectual or political vision of social reform and justice in the twenty-first century. Rather, the turning of negative difference into positive difference should be one of the tests of social justice in this century.

This paper and the book on which it is based is a response to the crisis of multiculturalism that has been brewing as a result of Muslim political assertiveness in the West, the support among some western Muslims for anti-imperialist Muslim causes in Muslim countries, and above all to the terrorist activity by a few Muslims, including against fellow citizens. I have restated a conception of multicultural citizenship that makes a case for multiculturalism, arguing that the accommodation of Muslims is reasonable and just, should not be rejected as antithetical to progressive politics and can be achieved through dialogue and negotiation within a multicultural citizenship and an inclusive nationality (Modood 2007). In most Anglophone countries and in parts of Western Europe we have begun moving in this direction. We need to reconnect with that movement. That is the best way to overcome the present state of fear, polarization, and ultimately the suicide-bombings in our cities. The "best way," but I am conscious that multiculturalism offers only part of the answer, for it itself cannot flourish in a context of fear, terrorism, and the neo-conservative United States–United Kingdom international project of controlling Muslims. So, I cannot conclude on a clear note of optimism. But we do need some optimism and belief in ourselves if we are to limit the damage that is currently being done to our multicultural politics and prospects for the future. The twenty-first century is going to be one of unprecedented ethnic and religious mix in the West. In the past, multicultural societies tended to flourish only under imperial rule. If we are to keep alive the prospect of a dynamic, internally differentiated multiculturalism within the context of democratic citizenship, then we must at least see that multiculturalism is not the cause of the present crisis but part of the solution.

Notes

This chapter is based on Chapters 3, 4, and 6 of Tariq Modood's *Multiculturalism: A Civic Idea* published by Polity Press.

1. For example, Prospect, The Observer, The Guardian, the Commission for Racial Equality, open Democracy, Channel 4, and the British Council. In the light of this flood of open discussion and criticism it is extraordinary that comments by some academics were presented anonymously in the national professional paper, *The Higher,* 17 March 2006.

2. Not all of these commentators are of the center-left and so highlight the new convergence against multiculturalism.

3. By "Muslim" I mean someone who thinks they are a Muslim—for religious, familial, communitarian, political, or other reasons—and is accepted as such by other Muslims (cf., Modood and Ahmad 2007 and Meer 2008).

4. In Modood 2007 I clarify that I do not mean terms such as "groupness," "mode of being," "subordination," "identity," and so on to denote univocal, internally undifferentiated concepts (see my discussion of Wittgenstein's concept of "family resemblance" in Chapter 5).

5. I therefore dissent from the approach, especially found in the United States, to use "multiculturalism" to capture a politics aimed at addressing the needs of all disadvantaged groups (e. g., women, people with disabilities etc. This approach finds theoretical expression in Iris Young's "politics of difference" (Young, 1990), in which it has been quipped the minorities amount to about eighty percent of the population for all are represented except for able-bodied, white, middle-class males.

6. This is my principal difference with Anne Phillips's "multiculturalism without culture" (Phillips 2007; Modood 2008).

7. In this respect Will Kymlicka and other liberal multiculturalists represent a radical break with traditional liberalism.

8. A recent example is the Euston Manifesto http://eustonmanifesto.org/joomla/index. php?option=com_content&task=view&id=12&Itemid=41

9. It is clear that "moderate" Muslim public figures in Britain are divided on homosexuality (Modood and Ahmad 2007) in just the way that all religions seem to be divided today.

10. For a very helpful elaboration of nationality, though which in places takes a too circumscribed a view of multiculturalism, see Miller 1995.

11. For a discussion of the differences and tensions between communitarian multiculturalism and "multiculture," see Modood, 1998 and Meer and Modood 2010.

12. Gilroy 2004 presents most contemporary stirrings of English/British national identity as a form of melancholia, a depression introduced by a loss of Empire.

13. I do not share the view that the "national-identity dimension of multiculturalism has nothing in common with the minority-focussed politics of recognition" (Joppke 2004: 244). Much of what Joppke describes as accommodation in fact is what I have argued is recognition and not, as Joppke thinks, toleration.

14. Of course for some, especially, younger people, even citizenship is not prized and certainly not compared to entertainment and shopping. So, if all we wanted to do was to follow trends, even constitutional patriotism would look out of date.

15. Full survey at http://www.channel4.com/news/microsites/D/dispatches2006/muslim_survey/index.html

16. "Justified" here does not necessarily mean approval of the bombings (for other questions about political violence elicited much less support) but more a sense that one thing causes another—the cause of the bombings lies in Anglo-American foreign policy. A Populous *The Times* Poll of British Muslims, 6 February, 2006 found that 7 percent agreed with "There are circumstances in which I would condone suicide bombings on UK soil."

17. For an example of a discussion on how to challenge persistent employment inequalities, see the review of positive action in employment and concluding recommendations in Dhami, Squires and Modood 2006.

18. As I stated earlier this does not mean that every feature of a minority group, no less than of a majority group, can be made "positive." It is enabling groups, rather than every practice, to be made positive that is being argued for here.

CHAPTER 5

Is Being Muslim a Fact or a Challenge?
A Perspective on Muslim Identity, Citizenship, and Islamic Education

YEDULLAH KAZMI AND ROSNANI HASHIM

Like most religious communities Muslims do not constitute a mono-lithic, undifferentiated community but display a rich variety of differences. This fact is not appreciated by Muslims and non-Muslims alike. Needless to say, this fact is hardly ever acknowledged in the discourse of Muslim education. This essay explores ways that this absence can be filled. Hence the challenge for Muslim educators is twofold: to design a learning and teaching situation that not only tolerates, but celebrates difference without surrendering commonality, and to imbue Muslims with sufficiently robust historical consciousness to be effective historical actors. If educators meet this challenge successfully then the issue of citizenship can also easily be resolved.

The discussion that follows is presented as *a* perspective on education and deliberately eschews any attempt to engage in constructing a grand theory or a meta-narrative of education. Grand theories or meta-narratives not only have a tendency to still the movement of history but also incline toward negating differences. Insensitivity to history and blindness to difference has been the bane of much of the thinking on Islamic education. This has accrued for the most part by focusing primarily on *what* to teach rather on *who* is being taught. These negative tendencies have been compounded when the question "what to teach?" is answered with reference to life here after with only a cursory glance, if at all, at the concrete world here and now. When, however, we focus on the agent in his/her concreteness then history and differences are necessarily highlighted. Hence the grounding assumption of the perspective being sketched out here is that history and difference are constitutive of human experience. The task for a Muslim interested in offering guidelines, at best heuristic, for designing Islamic education is to hammer out a perspective that acknowledges the constitutive role of history and difference while remaining true to the spirit of the Qur'an; a perspective that views difference as part of a larger common fabric. It is to elaborate and make clear this issue that is fundamental to the perspective presented here that a distinction between "who is a Muslim" and "what is it to be a Muslim" is invoked. This distinction turns on the assumption that a Muslim should not view his/her identity as a Muslim as given but rather see it as something to be created in a given socio-historical context and hence regard it as a challenge. The discussion begins with a general introduction to the issue, which is followed by the sketching of the formal structure of self-identity[1] and the cultural, social, and political tendencies that thwart that formation, and culminates in the discussion of how the use of the formal structure of self-identity can include the conceptual tools with which to answer the question posed in the topic.

A General Introduction

Each one of us as a concrete being is always already located in some history, tradition, and culture. To think of concrete human beings, therefore, is to think of them in an historical, cultural context. We are not our biology but our history, tradition, and culture. Although we are our history and culture we are nevertheless each unique. To say that we are constituted by history and culture is not to deny the uniqueness of each individual but rather to point to the task or the challenge we each take up in designing our uniqueness in the context of our history and culture. To put it a little differently, that we are born in a culture that bears a tradition that has a history is a given fact of our being human; what we make of this fact, however, is not a given. The uniqueness of my identity, therefore, is not a given but lies ahead in the future as a project that I alone can undertake; no one can undertake it for me and no one can be responsible for it but me. Hence, how I use the cultural resources available to me is a task for which I am responsible. What I become within the horizon of my historical moment is my choice. This chapter is an attempt to answer the question, should a Muslim regard his/her Muslim identity as a fact or as a challenge? In order to draw out the full social, historical, and ethical import of the question posed a further related distinction between "who is a Muslim?" and "what is it to be a Muslim?" is made and expressed as a set of questions. However, before tackling the central issue the formal question, "how to structure one's identity?" has to be addressed.

The formal structure of self-identity

The problem described above can also be stated as society having two dialectically related poles: the social and the existential. This relationship, like all dialectical relationships, is always in conflict. The social is the objective social reality that confronts the individual as a social fact existing independent of him or her, and the existential is my relationship to myself mediated by society. The relationship I have with myself is of the same general nature as my relationship to my body; I experience myself as not being identical with my body. To be aware of this issue is to be cognizant of the existential fact that identity is something that is not given on a silver platter but for which each one of us is responsible for creating and shaping. To view it as a challenge is to consider what this entity that is *me* is as one's life project.

To take up a project is not like choosing a profession, although it could be part of it, but rather to make sense of who or what one is, i.e., to engage in self-interpretation. Self-interpretation, like the interpretation of a text, is hermeneutical in nature where the meaning of the parts is determined by the anticipated meaning of the whole, while the meaning of the whole is concurrently shaped by the meaning of the parts. For example in reading a sentence we make sense of the words with reference to the anticipated meaning of the whole sentence and the meaning of the sentence is dependent on the meaning of each word. In a life-project as self interpretation a similar strategy is in operation where the meaning of individual events in one's life are interpreted in light of the overall project one is engaged in and the project undergoes revisions in light of the meaning of the individual events. Hence the life-project has a narrative structure where events of life are made sense of by stringing them together as in a story where they make sense. The upshot of this is to regard one's life as a narrative where the author is oneself. I create myself as I write my self; I am what I become; there is no *me* prior to or independent of the narrative.

It should not be assumed that one can or is able to write his/her narrative without the help or influence of others in society. Human endeavor cannot create something out of nothing; every time we create, be it a poem, a novel, a piece of music, or even a philosophical treatise we rely on what is already there to learn *how* to create and also *what* to create. To be creative is not to create something so totally and entirely new that it has no antecedent, for, even if it were possible, no one will be able to understand it. To be creative is to use the old words in a new way, to arrange them differently, to say something that has not been said before; to be creative is to discover the *possibilities* of saying new things in the old vocabulary, and possibly sometimes to create a new vocabulary. Each creative act does not change the vocabulary in any fundamental way but rather makes it more flexible, more expansive by enriching the pool of meaning the words in the vocabulary articulate. Creative human beings enrich their culture by contributing to the store of meaning that people participating in that culture find helpful in making sense of their lives and help them to be more creative.

There is a great deal that we humans have in common, however remote in time and space we may be from each other, that allows us to understand each other. Hence our reach in trying to write our narrative should not only be vertical in time i.e., limited to our own contemporary culture, but rather it also must be horizontal and reach back into history. Because we cannot jump out of our times and culture, other times and other cultures will have to be mediated by our contemporary culture.

In writing the narrative that is *me,* the fact of my death is not a casual event that just happens to end my narrative, but rather a fact that is of paramount importance to the entire project. The awareness of the fact of my death constitutes my existence as human. Human beings, of all other creatures, know that they are finite; they are born to die. It is against the backdrop of the final end of my life that the choices I make are crucial and critical to whom and what I become; I get only one shot at living my life. Death gives the need to create my narrative an urgency that otherwise it would not have.

Due to my situatedness in a world, when I take a stand with respect to myself I simultaneously also take a stand with respect to that world. The world and I are not two independent entities confronting each other but implicated in each other; I am constituted by the way I am situated in the world. When I take a stand with respect to my self I also take a stand with respect to the world that shapes me. This brings to the fore the question: to what extent am I aware of being shaped by the world, the failure of which is evasion of the responsibility to be free, i.e., to be? The grave consequence of evading the responsibility of designing my own narrative, in the ways and for reasons discussed above, is that I willingly or unwittingly surrender this responsibility to anonymous others. Then I am no longer the author of my narrative and I have jeopardized my uniqueness.

When I take a resolute stand with respect to myself by projecting into the future what I am to become, I become ethical. No shaping or designing is possible without a call for some ethical judgment. Ethics is an essential part of a life-project that guides the choices regarding which possibilities are to be appropriated from those that are offered. To be ethical, in the sense used here, means to take responsibility of one's life, to be the author of the narrative one is creating. To be ethical, therefore, is contrasted with being moral. To be moral is to know and follow the rules of the game, while being ethical is to creatively use the rules in making novel moves that define you. However, there is often tension between the two in real life situations. What precipitates the tension is the imposition of one way of playing the game or one way of being a Muslim.

This raises the questions: under what circumstances and for what reasons do I shrink away from this responsibility? Our everyday social existence does not for the most part give us any hint or clue of this issue. Going about our everyday life "we are impressed with such issues as how to get good marks if we are students, as adults we want to be more successful, to make more money, to have more prestige, to buy a better car, to go places, and so on" (Fromm 1991, p. 217). In the hurly burly of daily life the question of identity is viewed as entirely meaningless, diverting attention from more important issues and hence avoided as irksome for not having any true significance for getting on with one's life. The busier and more competitive life becomes, the more this question recedes into irrelevancy.

Generally, we shirk the responsibility when and if made aware of it, because we find ourselves having neither the skills nor the discipline to cope with it. This fills us with anxiety. We just do not know what to do. To escape from anxiety we try to busy ourselves even more with tasks with identifiable rewards hoping that the frenzied activity will prove a reliable bulwark against the impending anxiety attack. Or else we casually buy into the view that identity is synonymous with social status, and hence becoming a function of prestige and power thereby transforming the existential issue of identity into a social issue of prestige, status, and power.

Closely associated with this notion of identity is one acquired by virtue of the socially assigned roles one plays. On this view one's role as a teacher, doctor, or engineer defines one's identity; I am or become what I am trained to do; my profession is my identity. Or my identity is defined by such roles as that of a father, mother, son, daughter, or student. However, what happens to my identity when I lose my job, my wealth? When the social conditions change or are no longer extant my identity has to undergo a makeover or perhaps even withers away rendering the individual invisible. In other words, I have no control over who I am; I am a creature of situations and circumstances, they make or unmake me. One moment I have an identity and the next moment I am a cipher. Such identities are called "manufactured" precisely because they are structured and designed by somebody else, and are external to me. Manufactured identity levels off my uniqueness. When I back away from my responsibility of creating myself and society steps in, the tension between the two poles of social existence slackens.

Being a Muslim as a narrative structure

As a Muslim one faces a choice, one can either exist at the level of a social fact, which is defined in most cases by virtue of one's birth, or instead build on this fact by giving a unique expression to being a Muslim. It should be made abundantly clear that the difference between the existential and the social is not presented as an either/or situation as if to say that when one takes the existential choice one automatically opts out of society or becomes asocial, but rather refers to the distinction, discussed above, between taking the responsibility of designing oneself or letting anonymous others define and characterize you. The distinction between "social fact" and "challenge" is not between existing in society or outside it, but rather between two modes of social existence: between being reconciled to, content with the givenness of the identity of being a Muslim or viewing being a Muslim as a becoming. It is a challenge because it entails facing up to and accepting the existential task of designing oneself in the ever-changing historical context of one's existence. The existential enterprise is very much a social enterprise.

This point can further be made clear with the help of responses to two related but different questions and judging which is more significant, "who is a Muslim"? and "what is it to be Muslim"? The response to the first question is obvious: in a nutshell, a Muslim is one who believes in one God and the Qur'an as the divine book and recognizes Prophet Mohammed (peace be upon him) as the last prophet of Allah. Although true, belief in Allah and the Qur'an in and by itself defines one as a Muslim at the level of a fact, albeit a spiritual fact. In short it is purely a spiritual definition. It does not take account of the fact that we are thrown into history and responsible for giving unique expression to being a Muslim. The proper response to the second question builds on the spiritual fact in the context of concrete historical and cultural reality. The second question is more significant because it assumes the purely spiritual definition and places it in historical context and exhorts Muslims to define themselves in the context in which they find themselves. In other words, it confronts me with the challenge to realize my Muslimhood as the project of my life that characterizes me in my uniqueness that expresses what it is to be a Muslim in a specific and determinate historical context. This is only possible if I do not reduce my Muslimhood to a mere given fact for which I am not entirely responsible but take it as my responsibility to design myself as a Muslim. This in turn is possible only if I make my identity as a Muslim an issue that requires that I take a resolute stand with respect to being a Muslim. It does not in any sense mean that I take liberties with the universal spiritual definition of what it is to be a Muslim.

This point can be best illustrated with the help of the analogy of playing a game, say, of soccer. The game of soccer, like any other game, is only possible because of certain ground rules to which everyone adheres. A good player, however, is one who although playing by the rules brings something unique to the game; he/she plays it a little differently thereby contributing to the game by making the game exciting to watch. Such a player is creative in making moves that rules allow but no one has yet made and if made makes them better or makes them in the most unlikely situations. No one before Pele, the brilliant Brazilian soccer player, had ever tried the scissor kick, yet once he demonstrated it is possible it becomes part of the repertoire of the accepted soccer moves, thereby enriching the game on the field both for the players and the spectators. It is important to recognize that uniqueness is only realizable in and through the game governed by rules.

Although governed by the same rules, each game is historically unique. Although necessary, my knowledge of the rules is not sufficient to put me in the class of good or great players. My mastery of the game and hence my dexterity on the field cannot be reduced to my knowledge of the rules but rather depends on my ability to make the moves that the rules permit in response to my awareness of the ever changing dynamic situation on the field in each instance of the play. The issue is not whether the players know the rules but how to play by the rules. The crucial distinction is between knowing *that*, i.e., the rules, and knowing *how* to play. Knowing the rules is part of the overall competency of a good player, yet one may know the rules and still be an indifferent player. In other words, the ability to play well far transcends the knowledge of just the rules; the ability to play well cannot be reduced to the knowledge of rules. To be a great artist or a great player one needs that special something that whatever its called can never be reduced to following the rules. According to Gadamer (1975), "The players are not the subject of play: instead play merely reaches presentation through the players" (p. 2). What makes the continuity of the game possible are the rules that do not change from one game to the next. However, what keeps the interest of both the players and the spectators are the novel and interesting ways the challenges of each game are met and how new moves are invented and old ones refined within what is permitted by the rules.

With the help of the analogy of the game we can now perhaps make sense of the distinction between "who is a Muslim?" and "what is it to be a Muslim?" and begin to understand what it means that I recognize that as a Muslim I exist in a specific historical context and that my being a Muslim or my Muslimhood is to be realized in large part in my response to the specific contingencies I face in that historical context. Yet my being a Muslim is not given to me in history but only finds expression in history. However, what finds expression through history is given in the book called the Qur'an that forever transcends history. To recognize the full import of the distinction invoked above is to acknowledge that a Muslim is a being on whom it is incumbent to exist in two spaces simultaneously: the spiritual and the historical. While the Qur'an locates human beings in the spiritual space, the life of the Prophet (peace be upon him) shows how human beings are to give expression to, to make sense of being so located through the medium of history (Kazmi 2000).

In response to the question "what is it to be a Muslim?" the correct answer would be, one who knows the basic rules of the game called Islam; one, being situated in a particular historical situation, whose ability *to be* unfolds in time; one whose being is becoming. In other words, to take history seriously does not imply we take the Qur'an any less seriously but rather to feel the need to ground it in history, which is not to render the Qur'an subject to the contingencies of history but rather to subject the contingencies of history to the Qur'an. For if the

Qur'an is to guide us it has to guide us through the squalor of history generated contingencies. The question "what is it to be a Muslim?" refers to, following the example of the Prophet (peace be upon him), giving spiritual expression to our historical existence. The inability to play or not to learn to play is contrary to the rules of the game of Islam. The Qur'an demanded and the prophet acted to change the course of history. Furthermore, the Qur'anic injunction is clear; Allah does not change the circumstances of human beings unless they first act in and on the world (Al-Qur'an, v. 13:11).

The correct answer to the question "what is it to be a Muslim?" should exhort us to build and create our identity out of the materials history makes available to us by shaping them to our purpose. In short, it entails that each Muslim take up the ethical responsibility of being the author of his/her narrative. Humans are doomed, in a manner of speaking, to be free, however limited that may be, to choose to become. What elevates us above angels is our freedom to be, but this path of freedom is paved with difficulties and snares that trouble an unwary traveler at every step. With this freedom comes the awesome responsibility of choice, a challenge of no mean proportion. However, a Muslim is given the Qur'an, or the *Furqan* (distinguisher of good and bad) to guide him/her in his/her historical journey. Yet the fact of possessing the Qur'an, does not by itself make the challenge of trying to define his/her unique identity as a Muslim just disappear, although no doubt it makes it less forbidding. A Muslim still has to apply the Qur'an and the issue is how to relate to it. In the subsequent sections we will examine the challenges of citizenship in a diverse society, in light of our definition of the Muslim identity.

Muslim society and the challenges of diversity

In the past, we tended to live within our own circle of people having a common language, culture, and tradition. We rarely needed to negotiate with others who did not share our commonalities. Yet in the last hundred or so years two major events have occurred, one technological and other social, which have changed the world in dramatic ways. Thanks to technological innovations we find ourselves living today in what Marshall McLuhan calls the global village. And in recent years there has been a great movement of populations from one part of the world to another. The reasons for the diaspora are various and controversial and there is no reason to rehearse them here. Both have contributed to the disruption and dislocation in the taken for granted cultural and social horizons of the people. For the purpose of this discussion the latter event is of greater importance.

People of diverse ethnic, cultural, and religious backgrounds find themselves living today as each other's neighbors. While no country ever had a homogeneous population, today the heterogeneity is more marked and cuts deeper into the taken for granted cultural horizon of a society. Thus the issue is: should the old cultural horizons be preserved or changed? If they remain unchanged the new arrivals will be marginalized, causing them to be disaffected and contributing to social unrest. And if they are to change then both the new and the old have to play a cooperative and collective role. It is in this context that the issue of Muslim identity as a fact or challenge is seen as having relevance for a concrete social world that Muslims find themselves living in.

Muslims in their newly adopted homelands face a variety of challenges, regardless of the country they migrated to—whether it is in North America, Western Europe, Australia, or New Zealand. Most of these challenges are similar to those faced by other minority communities within these countries such as relocation, preservation of traditions and language, and acculturation to the dominant society. However, Muslims also encounter challenges and opportunities that are related to the nature of their faith, Islam. "The Islamic faith and its practice involve special obligation and responsibilities that shape the way Muslims as individuals and groups respond to the conditions of these societies" (Voll 1991, p. 205). Several issues related to Islam are involved. Some of these issues involve problems while others involve challenges. According to Haddad and Lummis (1987), the classic issue for Muslim minorities everywhere concerns "how to live an Islamic life in a non–Muslim country" (p. 155). Haider (1985) puts it in another way, "Perhaps the most frequently and hotly debated issue among these Muslims (migrants of Western Europe and North America) is the 'Islamic survival of the next generation'" (p. 54). Sachedina (n.d), recalling the struggle of Ali Shariati and Iqbal for the Muslim youth, rephrased the issue as a question, "Having found ourselves here and now what shall we do to remain Muslim (in the literal rather than the cultural sense of the word meaning "one who submits to the will of God)" (para. 8)?

Implicitly they are all asking, "what is it to be a Muslim?" This has become a pressing problem only now when they find themselves living in a new country and amidst a foreign culture. However they fail to realize that the issue is endemic to Muslim identity and not just an issue of those Muslims living in the West if we recognize the importance of the historical dimension of human existence. The issue first has to be problematized philosophically to lead to successful social resolution of it and hence the critical importance of understanding identity issues as a challenge to Muslims in different and varying situations.

Turning now to countries where the identity of Muslims is an issue. France and the United States represent paradigm cases of the different responses to the issue. In France the issue is dramatically put on the public stage by the French government's knee-jerk reaction to Muslim women wearing *hijab* and the recent declaration making covering of face in public places illegal, subjecting Muslim women who persist to legal persecution. This reaction hardly encourages Muslims in France to forge their unique Muslim identity as French Muslims. A more fruitful approach would have been to try to understand why Muslim women chose to dress that way instead of trotting off banal generalities that the veil represents subjugation of females by Muslim males.

Given that there is no consensus among Muslim scholars regarding whether the wearing of *hijab* or covering of face is the most appropriate dress for Muslim women, and when a vast majority of Muslim women in Southeast Asia do not cover their faces, the practice of it by some women in Europe has to be understood with due regard to social conditions rather than viewed in ideological terms. In short, the issue is why some chose to do so. One plausible explanation could run something like the following: Muslims coming to live in Europe find themselves living among not too friendly aliens and surrounded by a culture that at key points was at odds with theirs giving rise to an identity crisis. Coming, as most of them did, from lower middle class and working class backgrounds and predisposed to be conservative, their experience in France did nothing to encourage them to change their customs and practices but in fact reinforced them. Suffering from identity insecurity they took refuge in tried and tested modes of behavior and practices in order to hold on to their threatened identity. Rather than to step out of their comfort zone and make their Muslim identity an issue on the way to forging a new identity as European Muslims they hunkered down with the one they were most familiar with and justified their decision with the help of the most narrowly defined literal reading of the rules of Islam. From this perspective it is the French government in particular and Europeans in general who are being narrow minded and conservative and not Muslims.

Some, however, have tried to explain the French government's stringent reaction to Muslim women's insistence on wearing *hijab* or veil with reference to France's unique notion of a secular state; a notion, dating back to revolutionary France that holds all religions as anathema and hence forbids display of religious symbols in public institutions. This view of a secular state is in stark contrast to the one that is accepted in countries like the United Kingdom, the United States, and India, among others, which grants all religions equal weight and is indifferent to none. Whether the official French explanation is justification or explanation is debatable.

In other words, the French government is not prepared to concede that their taken for granted cultural horizon has to be modified, to be made more flexible to create space within it where Muslims in France could undertake the challenge of being French Muslims without fear of jeopardizing their Muslim identity. The French obduracy will succeed only in driving a wedge between the private and public space of a Muslim; he/she will be a Muslim at home and French in public and never the twain shall meet. This is a recipe for split personalities and not for a healthy citizenry. A Muslim in France is being forced to live at the level of moral existence and denied the possibility to exist ethically.

In the United States the situation is very different. If in France the relationship between the government and the Muslims is one fraught with tension and latent hostility the one across the Atlantic can be best characterized as one of benign neglect; the government has no views about it one way or the other. The Muslims in the United States cannot look to government agencies like the public school system to help them in this regard. But the atmosphere of benign neglect is most conducive for the Muslims in the United States to struggle with the issue of their identity without any substantial help or hindrance from the government. The issue of identity is their individual and collective ethical responsibility. The issue turns on their deciding whether to be Muslims who happen to be Americans or Americans who happen to be Muslims. In this regard their situation is very similar to that of the Jews who started to come to the United States in large numbers in the early part of the last century. They started off wanting to be Jews who happen to be Americans but over the years increasingly become Americans who happen to be Jews. It has to be recognized, however, that the tide of anti-Semitism that was on the rise then was no small or trivial consideration in their slide toward the latter. Now why should this distinction make a difference?

If the notion of citizenship has to do just with one's loyalty to the country and state then it is a very one dimensional notion though a necessary aspect. An equally important aspect, for a country like the United States, is what you as a citizen contribute to the repertoire of meaning available in the culture. A Muslim who happens to be American is nourished and sustained by sources and resources from beyond national boundaries. It is, furthermore, part of his/her identity to cultivate those intellectual, cultural and spiritual activities, and mental habits that are necessary for the preservation of that identity's uniqueness. The issue is not if there is a fundamental contradiction between being a Muslim and being an American but rather what type of Muslim an American Muslim is going to be. The type of Muslim one turns out to be depends on what one gives ontological priority to. If as a Muslim you give ontological priority to being a Muslim over being an American then you work to preserve your Muslim identity over time and contribute to the general repertoire of the American meaning system something unique drawn from sources that lie far beyond and in turn enrich both the ways of being a Muslim and the American culture. If on the other hand you give priority to being an American then your cultural and intellectual horizons are limited to one country because your identity does not require resources from outside the national boundaries to sustain and maintain itself. And as a result both your understanding of Islam and the cultural depth of the available meaning of the host country suffer. Hence the distinction is crucial. And this distinction is predicated on the distinction between who is a Muslim and what it is to be a Muslim.

For Muslims in the West to pull it off they have to feel secure enough to venture beyond their habitually secure cultural zones to draw their narrative story lines from the majority culture and thereby forge an identity that is French/British/American and Muslim simultaneously. Only then the dichotomy between being French/British/American and being Muslim would appear as a false one. Muslims in France, Britain, and the United States bring with them a heritage of a rich and sophisticated culture that the host cultures should draw upon to make their own culture richer. The more diverse the culture the richer it is, allowing its members to draw upon a rich repertoire of story lines in forging their respective identities. For Muslims to feel secure the Western countries have to show more than benign neglect, particularly in the face of rising Islamophobia in the West. As Charles Taylor (1991) has noted, "Equal recognition is not just the appropriate mode for a healthy democratic society. Its refusal can inflict damage on those who are denied it, according to a widespread modern view. The projecting of an inferior or demeaning image on another can actually distort and oppress, to the extent it is interiorized" (p. 49).

What are the issues for a Muslim living in an almost total Muslim nation such as Pakistan and Saudi Arabia, or a majority yet plural Muslim nation such as Malaysia or Syria? For Muslims living in a majority Muslim nation the challenge would be how to exhort Muslims to go beyond the fact of being Muslim, that is, how to make the shift from "who is a Muslim?" to "what is it to be a Muslim?" This is to move from seeing their identity as a fact to their identity as a challenge. This is badly needed because the tendency is for Islamic education to be taught in a manner of prescribing the rules of the game, rather than to be creative, and to construct new moves within the parameters allowed by the Qur'an. Without much challenge internally, it is natural for the Muslims in these countries to inherit an ossified identity or to take the Qur'an literally, ignoring the historical context of being a Muslim.

And here is where identity and citizenship are closely linked. The issue of citizenship in these countries does not revolve around being a minority but rather around being Muslims of different racial and cultural origins. Despite being from the same *ummah Islamiyya,* Muslims who do not belong to the dominant race are discriminated against in terms of education, social welfare, and economic and political freedom. There are clear policies in regard to this in Saudi Arabia and in the United Arab Emirates such that non-Arab students who have spent all their lives in these countries and are yet denied public higher education and thus either have to pay considerable sums of money to study in private institutions or go study abroad, in Malaysia, for example, where it is affordable. It is easy in these countries to justify education that does not go beyond teaching the rules of the game or to discourage students from a creative use of the Qur'an on religious grounds in order to preserve the status quo. That would require teaching students to go beyond learning grammar and be critical and creative and to interpret the Qur'an in a more contextual manner. The environment seems to choke those who desire to translate the Qur'an in a manner appropriate for their times, which at times conflicts with the official translation accepted by the powers that be. The attempt to change is resisted and curbed. As a consequence of this, many Muslim intellectuals have left their homeland for the West, which is seen as democratic and allows for intellectual and religious freedom. This has been the case with many Muslim scholars such as Fazlur Rahman, Abdulkarim Soroush and Ismail al-Faruqi to name only a few.

Then there is the issue of non-Muslim minorities living in countries with Muslim majorities. In his work, *On Identity,* Amin Maalouf (2000), a famous Lebanese Christian author, editor, and director of a Beirut daily living in France noted that "from the outset, and ever since, the history of Islam has reflected a remarkable ability to coexist with others" (p. 48). Thus, in many, though by no means all, cases it was relatively easy in the past for non-Muslim citizens to live in Muslim countries and be treated fairly. This was especially true in how the Muslims treated the Jews in Andalusia, Egypt, and in many other countries. In such countries, the relationships of Muslims with non-Muslim minorities were harmonious and supported by mutual respect.

Maalouf (2000) asks "Why has the Christian West, which has a long tradition of intolerance and has always found it difficult to coexist with "the Other," produced societies that respect freedom of expression, whereas the Muslim world, which has long practiced coexistence, now looks like a stronghold of fanaticism?" (p. 50). Given the testimony of history, a simple answer is that to the extent Muslims have shown and practiced intolerance toward people of different faiths they have deviated from the spirit of Islam. But to venture a little less simple answer would be to see the rise in intolerance as partly the result of a Muslim identity crisis.

Muslims find themselves today living in a world in which their self-understanding as a Muslim i.e., their identity is increasingly out of sync with the rest of world. When Muslims look at the world from the perspective of their self-understanding as Muslims the world appears fairly incomprehensible and at times threatening and hostile. Finding the world threatening and/or hostile they, like the Muslim women in Europe, retreat to the comfort of just blindly and uncritically following the rules of the game, where the slightest relaxation of the rules is experienced as a threat to identity and to Islam. This gives some the moral justification to destroy and kill whoever is perceived as a threat to their identity and to Islam. Tolerance is a weakness they believe they cannot afford as they fight for the survival of Islam, all the while blissfully unaware that Islam is not under threat but rather their historically obsolete identity. Now of course this sense of being out of sync with the world is not articulated anywhere but presented here just as a hypothesis that may help explain why many Muslims by and large act the way they do. No doubt this hypothesis is fairly broad and general and treats Muslims as a monolithic block, yet despite the shortcomings it may have some heuristic value.

And this has been the result of intellectual stagnation of Muslims *qua* Muslims. It is due to this intellectual stagnation that the distinction between who and what it is to be a Muslim is supposed to both highlight and show a way to remedy it through education by empowering Muslims to be able to write their own narratives and shape their own identities. Quite often it is reflected in their inability to reconcile what they believe in and what they know that renders them *qua* Muslims intellectually inert. The issue of their identity can be best summed up by saying that they see themselves and behave as an engineer, sociologist, etc. who happens to be a Muslim rather than defining themselves as a Muslim who happens to be an engineer, sociologist, or whatever. The identity their profession has conferred upon them has priority over their identity as Muslims. To put it more starkly they exercise their intellect when they are not acting as Muslims and when acting as Muslims they see no reason to exercise their intellect. In other words, learning and knowing the rules of Islam and hardly ever venturing to learn how to become a player in the historical arena with the help of those rules is what circumscribes the life of a Muslim today for the most part.

Such Muslims fail to recognize that the Qur'an's proscriptions and prescriptions, its do's and don'ts can be viewed as describing a circle where Muslims are to create their respective narratives, that is, to be creative in the ways sanctioned by the Qur'an resulting in an identity that is spiritually specific yet historically current. And it follows that any transgression of the circle would make a narrative as a Muslim incoherent.

Conclusion

The issue is that Muslims have to face up to the radical ethical choice regarding their identity that has serious consequences for the way they relate to the world. The choice is between viewing identity as wholly a fact of being a Muslim by the accident of birth or to accept the responsibility of designing oneself as a Muslim in light of the Qur'an. The choice is between two different stances one can take regarding ones identity as a Muslim: between one that does not recognize that history is constitutive of our identity and one that squarely faces up to the contingencies of history and accepts the individual responsibility of shaping, creating one's identity out of what history makes available to one. The choice is not between being a good or bad Muslim in some absolute ethical sense but what would contribute most to Islam as a historical project that unfolds in time. The issue ultimately turns on recognizing that only when we adopt the historical stance can we succeed in coming up with solutions and answers to the problems and questions that history throws across the path of Muslims.

And one among several challenges facing Muslims living in the West today is how to preserve their spiritual integrity and yet be effective members of societies that in their dominant practices are not Islamic. Historically speaking this is not entirely a new phenomenon. Islam, through the course of its history took root in different cultures and acquired local color without however compromising, for the most part, its essential integrity, thus creating a diverse array of Muslim cultures across a wide swath of the world. This was a slow process that took place behind the backs of the Muslims, so to speak. This was never, however, recognized as a challenge. The failure to recognize this as a challenge has resulted in the view that there is just *one* way of being a Muslim.

One consequence of this is the unnecessary dissonance created in the lives and psyche of Muslims migrating to live in countries where Muslims have not lived before compounding the problem of integration and citizenship. Muslims in the West can and should be as creative in defining themselves as Muslims as they are in their chosen field of expertise. This will result not only in a much more nuanced understanding of the Qur'an but equally in an Islamic identity more closely calibrated with the local culture and history. This is not however a plea to conform to whatever culture one finds oneself in but an exhortation to Muslims to be creative in defining themselves and thus contributing to the local cultural scene; for Muslims to be different but not alien.

Note

1. Anyone at all familiar with Martin Heidegger's first major book *Being and Time* will not fail to notice his influence running right through the discussion. Because his influence is so pervasive, constant citing from this book is dispensed with for fear of the discussion being considered too pedantic and replaced with an acknowledgment for the sake of intellectual honesty. See Martin Heidegger. *Being and Time.* trans. John Macquarrie & Edward Robinson. New York: Harper & Row Publishers, 1968.

CHAPTER 6

Dealing with Difference: Religious Education and the Challenge of Democracy in Pakistan

Matthew J. Nelson

For most of the last thirty years, since Prime Minister Zulfiqar Ali Bhutto was removed from power in a military coup led by General Zia-ul-Haq in 1977, the education sector in Pakistan has become increasingly privatized. This push in the direction of the private sector has generated a growing interest in the nature of local consumer demands, including demands in favor of a modern "religious" education.[1]

Within this demand-driven landscape, basic statistics designed to show "how much" religious education local children receive have tended to attract far more attention than specific details regarding the "content" of that education. What follows is an attempt to address this imbalance in light of nearly 800 qualitative interviews conducted in Pakistan, drawing special attention to (a) new data regarding the shape of existing enrollment patterns (who studies "where") and (b) new data regarding the content of local "religious" demands (who studies "what").

This second set of concerns, regarding the content of local religious demands, is closely related to an expanding body of literature concerning the relationship between religion, religious education, and democracy.[2] Here the question boils down to an enduring interest in the extent to which it might be possible for those with an attachment to ongoing market-oriented reforms to work *within* the context of local consumer demands (that is, within the context of local demands in favor of religion) while, at the same time, working to advance the cause of democracy. When do the terms of a modern religious education and those of a democratic education overlap?

I argue that religious responses to religious and sectarian *difference*—that is, religious responses to the issue of religious and sectarian *pluralism*—lie at the heart of this issue. Many of those I met in the context of my interviews insisted that the terms of democracy and, more specifically, democratic "equality," are enhanced if, in the context of a modern religious education, students are instructed to move *beyond* the terms of diversity in a bid to illuminate the terms of homogeneity, conformity, or consensus. Democratic "equality," in other words, requires an effort to "overcome" the specific terms of diversity: *e pluribus unum* (out of many, *one*). There were, however, some who rejected this view. This group—accounting for roughly 8 percent of my total interview sample (N = 794)—argued that the terms of "equality" did *not* require any effort to promote the terms of religious or sectarian homogeneity. Instead, they argued that the terms of democratic equality were comfortable with persistent forms of religious, sectarian, and doctrinal diversity: *in uno plures* (in one, there are *many*).[3]

Drawing special attention to the nature of local consumer demands in Pakistan, this chapter does not focus on "the extent to which local children are engaged in some form of religious education." Instead it stresses "the ways in which those engaged some form of religious education articulate their relationship with religious difference, sectarian diversity, and debate." Part One draws attention to the link between local consumer demands and persistent demands "in favor of religion." Part Two takes up the competing views of diversity mentioned above (*e pluribus unum* v. *in uno plures*) in an effort to tease out the implications of each view for those with an interest in the relationship between Islam, Islamic education, and democracy.

Local Educational Demands
(Religious vs. Non-Religious): Who Studies Where?

During the summer of 2003, and then again in 2004–2005, I worked with two research assistants from Lahore to interview the parents of roughly 3,500 school-aged children throughout Pakistan. In 2003, these interviews were used to document the nature of local educational demands in and around the district of Rawalpindi. In 2004–2005, this effort was expanded to include sixteen districts nationwide.[4]

In each district we interviewed 40–50 respondents, including a mix of men and women, rich and poor, educated and illiterate, Muslim, non-Muslim, Sunni, Shi'a, and so on, along with several different sectarian sub-groups (Deobandi, Barelwi, etc.). As compared to the population as a whole, our sample of 794—each representing an average of 4–5 children—was biased in favor of urban respondents, male respondents, and those with slightly higher levels of education. This bias was not intentional, but, in the analysis of our data it was important. In fact when it came to specific questions regarding the meaning of "a good education," male respondents (as a group) tended to be slightly more conservative than those living in urban areas and those with higher levels of education. Indeed, competing biases *within* our sample (for example, conservative *male* respondents versus change-oriented *urban* respondents) made for robust aggregate data that, nevertheless, require careful scrutiny.

Regarding the nature of local consumer demands, we asked our respondents to identify their top two educational priorities from a list of five options including (a) basic education (that is, basic literacy), (b) religious education, (c) vocational education, (d) liberal education (that is, education focused on the cultivation of critical thinking skills), and

Table 6.1 Educational Preferences: Religious vs. Non-Religious

	Basic	**Religious**	Liberal	Vocational	Civic	---	TOTAL
Gender: First + Second Choice (combined)							
GENDER							
Male	14.4	**37.7**	8.1	20.6	18.4	0.8	100
Female	12.9	**35.3**	8.8	18.2	24.7	0.0	100
TOTAL	14.2	**37.4**	8.2	20.3	19.3	0.7	100
Education: First + Second Choice (combined)							
EDUCATION							
No school	21.6	**45.1**	1.0	22.6	9.8	0.0	100
Primary	13.0	**41.7**	7.6	20.3	16.0	1.5	100
Matriculation/FA	13.8	**37.7**	8.4	19.9	19.9	0.4	100
University	13.9	**33.1**	9.7	20.3	22.3	0.8	100
TOTAL	14.2	**37.4**	8.2	20.3	19.3	0.7	100

(e) civic education.[5] In response we found that "religious" education was selected nearly twice as often as anything else, particularly among local men and those with lower levels of education (see Table 6.1, above). In fact, overall, we found that *more than 62 percent identified religious education as their "top" educational priority.*[6]

Even if most parents were inclined to stress the merits of a sound religious education, however, we noticed that *the overwhelming majority did not approach their educational options (for example, religious v. non-religious options) as a zero-sum game.* Instead, most sought to construct a careful balance, including both types of education at the same time. Existing attachments to religious education notwithstanding, in other words, most parents did not seek to educate their children exclusively in a local *maktab* (mosque-based school) or *madrasa*. On the contrary, most simply expected their children to attend more than one school at the same time, usually traveling to their local *maktab* or *madrasa* before (or after) their "regular" school day.[7]

The importance of this attachment to "hybrid" enrollments is difficult to overstate. In fact "part-time" enrollments were extraordinarily important for those with an interest in religious education broadly defined.[8] While it may be true, in other words, that the number of students enrolled on a "full-time" residential basis in the context of their local *madrasa* remains rather *small*—according to the World Bank, less than 1.5 percent of the total student population—the number who receive a *maktab* or a *madrasa*-based education on a "part-time" basis is in fact extremely *large*.[9] Local attachments to religious education, in other words, do not express themselves in terms of aggregate full-time enrollment data. Instead they emerge in the form of part-time data— data that, I would argue, remain woefully under-represented in the literature.

This is an important point to keep in mind because, more often than not, scholars turn to quantitative data regarding "full-time" enrollments—for example, in the context of private *madrasas* or English-medium schools—to establish or explain larger political trends, trends that push in the direction of (secular) democracy or (religious) extremism. The underlying conclusion is of course familiar: "more" religious education is believed to be associated with "more" extremism, less religious education is believed to be associated with less extremism, and so on—not only at the level of individuals, but also in aggregate terms, for instance, in the Northwest Frontier Province (NWFP), where "more *madrasas*" are said to produce "more extremism," and, in due course, more instability and violence. Indeed, this approach has become almost *de rigueur* in the policy-oriented literature regarding religious education and, especially, Islamic education in South Asia.[10]

Tariq Rahman draws considerable attention to this view in his book *Denizens of Alien Worlds: A Study of Education, Inequality, and Polarization in Pakistan* (2004).[11] In particular he notes that "where you study" (on a full-time basis) has a tendency to shape "how you think" about the terms of religion, religious diversity, and democracy. Those enrolled full-time in the context of their local *madrasa*, for instance, are said to be less enthusiastic about the notion of "equal rights" for religious and sectarian "others" (defined as Hindu others, Christian others, or Ahmedis) than their "less religious" peers. In fact they are said to be considerably less tolerant—and, as such, more susceptible to various forms of extremism—than those who receive their training in other types of schools.

Even as Rahman notes that full-time *madrasa* students express higher levels of anxiety regarding the possibility of "equal rights" for religious and sectarian "others," however, a thorough understanding of the link between local *madrasas*, their students, and the question of extremism tends to remain somewhat elusive. Indeed, even if full-time *madrasa* students express higher levels of anxiety regarding the "equal rights" of "others," it is impossible to ignore the fact that, as per the World Bank, "full-time" *madrasa* students represent a very small portion of the total student population. Full-time *madrasa* students, in other words, may hold particular views—views that, even apart from the question of extremism, appear to challenge particular features of democracy—but, even so, the *number* of these students, defined as a percentage of "all students" or even "students of religion," remains rather *small*.

A deeper understanding of the relationship between Islam, Islamic education, and democracy *nationwide* is in fact impossible to extract from any account of Pakistan's "full-time" (exclusively religious) *minority*. For this, a deeper understanding of Pakistan's "part-time" (mixed education) *majority* is essential.

This is particularly true because, so far, our understanding of this part-time mixed-education majority remains deeply divided. On the one hand, Tariq Rahman maintains that this majority is relatively "tolerant," at least when compared to the "intolerant" minority enrolled (full-time) in the context of local *madrasas*. And yet, at the same time, Peter Bergen and Swati Pandey (2006) have pointed out that seventy of the world's seventy-nine leading Muslim terrorists (that is, 89 percent) were drawn from precisely this group—that is, this modern (mixed-education) majority.[12] In fact for those with an interest in developing a

more sophisticated understanding of the link between religious education and extremism (or democracy), the challenge does *not* lie in any
understanding of what I would describe as the demographic extremes
(defined in terms of "full-time" enrollments). Instead, the challenge
lies in grappling with the divergent trajectories that exist within what
I have chosen to describe as Pakistan's modern, mixed-education
majority.[13]

What is the nature of the religious "content" that this majority
encounters in the context of its religious education? And, perhaps more
importantly, how does this content address the question of "tolerance"
vis-à-vis religious and sectarian "others"? Is this mixed-education
majority pushed in the direction of moderation, as Rahman suggests,
or militancy, as Bergen and Pandey contend? This is, briefly stated,
the question that I will take up and address in the remainder of this
chapter.

Religious Education and the Challenge of Diversity in Pakistan: Who Studies What?

As noted above, the nature of local educational demands in Pakistan is
fairly clear. Parents are attracted to the possibility of a "mixed" education that combines religious as well as non-religious elements.

With particular reference to the issue of religion, however, the question arises: *what exactly is the nature of the religious community that most
parents would like their children to join?* In fact, turning to the issue of religious and sectarian diversity, the question becomes: *how exactly should
this issue—this issue of diversity—be examined or explained?* Do local parents believe that some of the different groups *within* Islam (for instance,
Sunnis and Shi'as) should be acknowledged (or not) in the context of
their children's schools?

In the course of my interviews (2003–2005), the responses I received
to such questions were not related to a pattern in which local parents
sought to *acknowledge* specific expressions of difference. On the contrary most sought to *avoid* any expression of difference altogether. In
fact, throughout Pakistan, I found that sectarian differences of opinion
had come to resemble something like the proverbial "elephant in the
living room." Everyone could see these differences. Everyone could
feel the mounting pressure associated with their expanding influence and importance. Everyone knew about the sectarian massacres in
Sialkot (October 2004), Multan (October 2004), and Islamabad (May

2005)—just to name a few. But, even so, and in a remarkable challenge to most of the existing literature concerning the question of sectarian diversity in Pakistan, these differences were surprisingly difficult to discuss.[14] As one of my respondents noted, "*ikhtilafaat ke bare men baat kar-ke, ladai shuru hoti hai; hamen chup rahna chahiye!*" Or, "people fight if they talk about differences; we should just keep quiet!"

For several years, scholars like A. H. Nayyar and Ahmed Salim in Islamabad (2004) and Rubina Saigol in Lahore (1994, 2000) have attempted to break this silence, looking for ways to revisit—and revitalize—the study of religious diversity in the context of *both* religious *and* non-religious schools.[15] In particular, Nayyar, Salim, and Saigol, along with scholars like K. K. Aziz (2004), have gone out of their way to discuss the treatment of "Muslim" versus "non-Muslim" differences in an effort to show how several different types of schools have persistently sought to eliminate any positive regard for such differences, first by constructing a simple *awareness* of "non-Muslim" others and, then, by encouraging an explicit effort to *exclude* them "for the sake of the nation."[16]

My own interviews led me to many of the same concerns. But, as my work unfolded, I found myself returning to the question of religious and sectarian difference in a slightly different way, moving away from any special interest in "Muslim" versus "non-Muslim" differences (that is, religious differences) in favor of a special focus on the differences *among* local Muslims (that is, sectarian differences) instead. In fact, following up on some of the work completed by Mohammad Qasim Zaman (1998, 2002), Syed Vali Reza Nasr (2000), and Yoginder Sikand (2004), my own research drew me to the fact that many of the most conspicuous expressions of religious identity—particularly in the context of local *madrasas*—did *not* emerge from any effort to exploit the terms of "religious" difference. On the contrary, I found, these expressions were rooted in a rather specific set of concerns regarding sectarian difference (and the threat of sectarian fragmentation) instead.[17]

The most consistent message in the context of a modern religious education, in other words, was not, "They're different!" (referring, quite specifically, to the substantive differences associated with any number of religious "others"). No, the most conspicuous message was almost exactly the opposite. The most conspicuous message was, "We are, as Muslims, exactly and permanently *the same!*"[18] Deobandi Sunnis, Barelwi Sunnis, Twelver Shi'as, Ismaili Shi'as, and so on, all one and the same: *e pluribus unum.*[19]

In fact I quickly realized that it was not any specific expression of religious or sectarian difference, but rather *the terms of difference itself* that left my respondents feeling uneasy. Difference itself was the thing that most had come to regard as un-desirable, unacceptable, and, at some level, even "un-Islamic."[20]

Of course Nayyar, Salim, and Saigol were not entirely incorrect in their attempt to highlight the importance of ongoing educational efforts to eradicate specific notions of "otherness." They simply highlighted the rhetoric of eradication as *expulsion* over and above the far more common rhetoric of eradication as religious and sectarian *assimilation*. The former, if you will, pushes "others" away. The latter pulls them in. And, as my research unfolded, I discovered that, among those I interviewed, the latter was far more common.

To be sure, some insist that specific efforts to downplay or deemphasize difference—even to the point of denying its existence—must be regarded as an indication of "moderation," particularly insofar as local Muslims attempt to deny local expressions of difference in an effort to avoid any possibility of disagreement, inequality, or conflict. But in my view, these efforts to deny the existence of difference are, themselves, an important source of friction. Indeed, for those with an interest in fortifying the relationship between Islam, Islamic education, and *democracy*, the question becomes: what does it mean to privilege an approach that seeks to deny the existence of "difference" and, more specifically, "differences of religious opinion?" What does it mean to believe that the terms of religion require a persistent effort, not to *acknowledge* these differences, but rather simply to *ignore* them—indeed, to *eradicate* them through some form of sectarian *assimilation*? What does it mean to speak of both "religion" and "democracy" without any appreciation for "difference?"

Dealing with Diversity: Sectarianism the Elephant . . . in the Living Room

The religious landscape in Pakistan is of course deeply fragmented. But in every part of this landscape I encountered a rather similar trend—in many ways, a deeply *assimilationist* trend. Muslims in sectarian group A sought to assimilate those in sectarian groups B and C; Muslims in sectarian group B sought to assimilate those in A and C; and so on. In fact, this language of assimilation (as a bid for "equality") remained more or less *exactly the same* as I travelled from one part of the sectarian landscape to the next. Those in sectarian group A expressed their assimilationist aspirations in almost exactly the same language as those in groups B and C (and so on and so forth). The denial of difference was astonishingly consistent, with each group using almost exactly the same expressions to insist that, ultimately, "there is only one Islam."[21]

For those with an interest in promoting the terms of peace and social harmony, the implications of this religiously aspirational language—this language of inclusion-as-assimilation bound up with the notion that *there can be only one Islam*—are really quite profound.[22] In fact the remainder of this chapter will assess these implications in the context of two very different approaches to the question of difference in general.

The first approach, drawn from the work of scholars like Nayyar, Salim, and Saigol, maintains that, throughout Pakistan, local schools have paid "too much" attention to the issue of religious and sectarian difference. Here, the terms of peace and social harmony—in effect, the antidote to this persistent preoccupation with difference—are said to lie in a deliberate effort to ensure that "existing attachments to difference" are *diminished*: *e pluribus unum* (out of many, *one*).

The second approach, however, is exactly the opposite. This approach maintains that the problem does not involve "too much" difference, but rather "too little." In fact, from this perspective, the terms of peace and social harmony are believed to expand if the terms of difference are not diminished but rather continually and carefully *discussed*: *in uno plures* (in one, there are *many*).

In order to explain exactly how I came to stress the special value of this second approach, defining "the problem" as one of *avoiding* rather than *exaggerating* the issue of difference, it is necessary to turn, more specifically, to some of the challenges I faced in the context of my field research—challenges that emerged whenever I tried to ask about the notion of sectarianism, or sectarian "differences of opinion," in the context of local schools.

When I arrived in Pakistan, I assumed that I could simply step off the bus and ask local parents to discuss the nature of local sectarian boundaries. I simply assumed, for instance, based on my reading of specific disputes articulated by local religious scholars (*ulema*), that I would be able to ask local parents to tell me how (or if) they wanted their children to hear about sectarian differences of opinion regarding, say, the status of the first four caliphs—Abu Bakr, Omar, Uthman, and Ali—or different "styles" of prayer (Sunni, Shi'a, and so on).

But in fact I assumed too much. Confronted with a series of "pretest" questions regarding issues as common as the status of the first four caliphs—that is, the *khalifa-e-rashidun* or "rightly guided caliphs" (and the notion, typically associated with Shi'as, that the fourth caliph, Ali, was particularly important)—for instance, many simply looked at my research team with a clear sense of concern, as if they were being confronted with a pop quiz that would decide the fate of their souls. "*Men to aap ki baat bilkul nahin samajhta hun,*" they complained. "*Mere khyaal men, aap ko kisi maulvi se baat karna chahiye,*" or "I don't really know what you're talking about. You'll have to ask a *maulvi* about that."

I must have gone through forty test questions, each round more refined than the one before it, trying to determine where local parents would place the (sectarian) boundary surrounding their children's religious education:

"Do you think that, in the context of Islamiat [Islamic Studies]," I asked, "local schools should employ different teachers for different sects, or one teacher for everyone?" *Most Common Answer:* One teacher for everyone. "Okay. If you're a Sunni [in the case of Sunni respondents], would you be upset if your child's teacher were a Shi'a?' *Answer:* Yes, absolutely. "Okay. Why should Sunni teachers prevail?" *Answer:* Because Sunnis are in the majority. "Right. If the population of both groups were exactly the same, do you think they should receive exactly the same amount of attention in the curriculum?" *Answer:* Yes—yes of course.

Initially, I was confused, but eventually I came to understand that my respondents were less concerned about the finer points of religious doctrine, ritual practice, or religious and sectarian *boundaries* than they were about essentialized religious-cum-political *majorities*—a formulation in which, I discovered, everyone sought to favor, or promote, a local "majority" that included them. In fact the terms of majoritarianism were generally seen as a proxy for *ijma*, "consensus," and "truth." Muslim majoritarianism here; Sunni majoritarianism there; Sunni "Deobandi" here; "Madani" Deobandi there—each one religiously "superior" for no reason other than its role in constructing and sustaining some notion of "majoritarianism," "conformity," and "power."

In fact, apart from the shifting terms of doctrinal conformity (read: majoritarianism set apart from any interest in the question of minority rights), the finer points of Muslim discourse were generally regarded as elite matters, better left to those with knowledge and understanding—that is, quite literally, the *ulema*. At the very least, most people were inclined to leave enduring matters of religious "discussion" or sectarian "debate" to those who had read the Qur'an in a language they could actually understand—an experience that, owing to highly regarded pedagogical traditions associated with the transmission of the Holy Qur'an in Arabic, most of my respondents had never actually had.

As I was running out of test questions, however, it dawned on me that, even as I was trying to sketch a specific set of sectarian "boundaries," most of my respondents were simply on a different page. In fact, for most of my respondents, the question of sectarian difference boiled down to an extremely simple question regarding the value of religious "conformity" versus *kufr* (infidelity), solidarity versus "sin," and so on.[23] Indeed, even as the "elephant" began to rear its head in violence—the sectarian massacres in Sialkot (October 2004), Multan (October 2004), and Islamabad (May 2005) were no secret—the elephant itself (that is, the problem of difference) remained extremely difficult to discuss. As Khaled Ahmed pointed out in his roundup of the Urdu press for *The Daily Times* in Lahore (May 2006), "sectarian conflict is routinely denied...as if an admission of it would destroy Islam." "All mullahs do it," he added, "but so do most citizens."[24]

Dealing with Diversity: Sectarianism the Elephant... Goes to School

Again and again, my research team was informed that "a good education" is a "mixed" education—one that, apart from providing a thorough grounding in non-religious subjects like English, Urdu, mathematics, and the natural sciences, must teach children to follow "the example of the Prophet." This made a great deal of sense, but the more we asked about "the example of the Prophet," the more we found that most people were simply unprepared to provide much in the way of any programmatic details. In fact, every individual in every sectarian community was inclined to articulate the same relatively undifferentiated desideratum: every individual was expected to become a perfect reflection of the Prophet himself. One prophet, one faith, one practice, *one way: e pluribus <u>unum</u>*.

Again, this is not to say that religious or sectarian differences were completely eliminated. They simply weren't discussed. When our respondents pointed out that "a good education teaches children to follow the example of the Prophet," for instance, the overwhelming majority were *not* saying that "good Muslims follow the example of the Prophet, but they do so in many different ways." On the contrary, most were inclined to ignore the elephant altogether, insisting that "all good Muslims" interpret the example of the Prophet "just exactly as I do."[25]

As one respondent said, summing up the specific substance of this view with reference to the issue of "equality": "*Jab sab bilkul ek jaise hain, to sab baraabar hote hain. Jhagda ka matlab jaahil hai.*" "When everyone is *exactly the same*," he argued, "equality is enhanced." "Difference implies disagreement [*jhagda*], and disagreement implies a deep lack of religious understanding [*jahiliyya*]." In fact, he noted, the language of local Muslims was a language that people around the world had come to regard as familiar. This language was, first and foremost, a language of equality—a language of "equality-as-homogeneity" and "harmony," a language of "conformity" and "consensus."

Eventually, as our interviews came to an end, we asked our respondents to address five rather critical questions designed to find out exactly how local parents—rich, poor, Sunni, Shi'a, and so on—understood the *content* of their children's religious education vis-à-vis the question of sectarian difference. Did local parents feel that the notion of equality required students to move "beyond" diversity (*e pluribus unum*) or not (*in uno plures*)?

First, we asked our respondents whether the curriculum for Islamic Studies should "mention" (*zikr karna*) some of the different groups within Islam—for example, Sunnis, Shi'as, Deobandi Sunnis, Barelwi Sunnis, and so on. Fully two-thirds revealed an attachment to the notion of equality-as-homogeneity, arguing that "these differences should be ignored" before adding something like "it's not necessary to mention them," because "there is only one Islam."

We then proceeded to ask a slightly more specific question to solicit the same type of information. "Everyone knows that different Muslims say their *namaz* (prayers) in different ways," we noted. "Sunnis have one style; Shi'as another." Then, having established that this was in fact the case, we asked our respondents whether the syllabus for Islamic Studies should attempt to *explain* these differences or *ignore* them. Again, about 62 percent said these differences should be ignored, noting that all students should be expected (even required) to say their prayers in exactly the same way.

In the next question, we concentrated more explicitly on the views of those who said that religious education should "ignore" sectarian differences in the performance of *namaz*. If sectarian differences were ignored, we asked, how should the parameters of *namaz* be explained in their children's schools? "If everyone thinks that *their* style is the *correct* style," we'd say, "how should *disagreements* be resolved?"

At this point, most of our respondents appeared profoundly vexed. Eventually, however, they came up with one of two types of answers.

Seventy percent continued to insist that there should be one style of *namaz* for all students and, within this group, more than half said something like, "I don't know how to achieve this, but there should be one method according to the Qur'an and the *hadiths* [that is, the sayings of the Prophet]." (In other words, all children should be taught to follow "the [singular] example of the Prophet.") The remaining 30 percent said, "there should be one method, and that method should be decided by (a) the Sunni majority, (b) the *ulema*, or (c) the government."

Finally, cutting straight to the point, we posed an open-ended question, asking our respondents to tell us why Sunnis and Shi'as occasionally come to blows in Pakistan. This time, nearly 75 percent were inclined to ignore the elephant of sectarian difference altogether: "What are you talking about?" they'd say. "There hasn't been any sectarian conflict in my area." Or, "there's really no tension [read: "no difference"] between them; they simply fight at the behest of local *maulvis*, local politicians, and [especially] foreign interlopers." Indeed, after noting that "sectarian conflict is routinely denied by all concerned," Khaled Ahmed went on to point out, in the same article for *The Friday Times* (May 2006), that, in this climate of persistent denial, "a kind of collective sickness makes us blame sectarian violence on [outside agents associated with] the United States and India." Or, as Imtiaz Ahmed explained, drawing attention to a similar trend in *The News* (April 2006), "leading clerics would have us believe that [there] is always an alien hand...at work" when it comes to "sectarian killings."[26]

At the end of our interviews, however, we posed one last question, and this question almost invariably turned the conversation upside down. "If there are Sunnis and Shi'as today, and there will continue to be Sunnis and Shi'as in the future," we asked, "how should we teach our children to avoid fighting? Should we teach them to pretend that differences don't exist—to imagine that everyone is exactly the same? Or should we teach them to acknowledge and appreciate the differences that *do* exist?"

At this point, roughly 80 percent said that sectarian differences should be recognized (See Table 6.2). In other words, when confronted with the *fact* of difference, even conflict, and the need to address it themselves, rather than historically dubious claims regarding the *possibility* of unity (at some point in the future), as articulated by the *ulema*, more than half of the 62 percent who originally sought to "ignore differences" stepped forward to *reverse* their position and cast a vote for "diversity."

Table 6.2   Creating Peace: Ignore Differences or Acknowledge/Appreciate Differences

	Ignore	**Acknowledge**	...	*TOTAL*
AGE				
18–39	4.3	**82.5**	13.2	100
40–69	6.8	**78.2**	15.0	100
TOTAL	5.4	**80.6**	14.0	100
GENDER				
Male	6.2	**80.7**	13.1	100
Female	1.2	**78.6**	20.2	100
TOTAL	5.6	**80.4**	14.0	100
EDUCATION				
No school	7.8	**88.2**	3.9	100
Primary	4.4	**77.9**	17.7	100
Matriculation/FA	6.3	**83.5**	10.2	100
University	5.0	**77.1**	17.9	100
TOTAL	5.6	**80.4**	14.0	100
INCOME				
Rs. 1,000–2,500	6.4	**82.5**	11.1	100
Rs. 2,500–5,000	4.8	**85.0**	10.2	100
Rs. 5,001–10,000	6.6	**80.1**	13.3	100
Rs. 10,001–20,000	6.7	**78.3**	15.0	100
Rs. 20,001–50,000	2.7	**71.2**	26.0	100
Rs. 50,001+	0.0	**100.0**	0.0	100
TOTAL	5.7	**80.5**	11.5	100

Moving Forward:
From "E Pluribus Unum" to "In Uno Plures"

Slowly but surely, as my research came to a close, I began to see that Pakistan's educational marketplace was shaped by two (closely related) trends. In the first instance, existing markets were shaped by local demands for a modern multifaceted education, one in which *religious* education continued to play an important and persistent part. In the second instance, however, I noticed that existing education sector markets were shaped by a push in the direction of religious or sectarian *homogeneity*. In fact, homogeneity was often believed to be the most appropriate expression of a modern Muslim identity, such that standard market regulations designed to protect and preserve the terms of market "diversity" were seen (by many) as "an affront to Islam itself."

Insofar as this was the case, however, the basic parameters of the education sector landscape become fairly easy to discern: on the one hand, market structure, and, on the other, local values. The first aspect was described in Part I. The second, focusing on the value of conformity and "the singular example of the Prophet," was discussed in Part II. In the end, however, the underlying thrust of my work came to rest on an account of *the combined effect* of these two elements.

Part I: Market structure (e.g. private sector religious education)

                 +

Part II: Value content (e.g. unity/equality)

                 ↓

Conclusion: Market-based demands for unity/equality/stability
              "*E Pluribus Unum*"

Briefly stated, the education sector landscape in Pakistan combines an appreciation for two closely related processes—on the one hand, the emergence of market-oriented forces that compel each educational "firm" (for example, each *madrasa*) to expand its market share (up to, and including, the pursuit of a monopoly); and, on the other, an appreciation for "the unity, the equality, and indeed the stability" that this emerging monopoly could be said to represent.

As my research unfolded, I began to see how the quest for monopoly control that emerges in the context of a contemporary private sector religious education is, ultimately, a quest that derives its core support, not merely from the fact that leading *madrasas* are committed to the creation of religious, sectarian, or doctrinal "monopolies," but rather from the widely held notion that "monopoly control in the context of religious education" amounts to *a good thing*. Indeed I quickly discovered that this push for monopoly control—this push for a *monolithic* conception of Islam—was generally regarded as a push for unity, harmony, stability, and a particular conception of "equality" (*e pluribus unum*) as opposed to religious "fragmentation" or *fitna* (chaos).[27] And, of course, precisely insofar as this was the case, efforts to push in the direction of monopoly tended to enjoy widespread (and growing) support—even in the context of several *different* and, indeed, otherwise *competing* sectarian domains. Each group simply expected to establish its *own* "true" monopoly.

Conclusion

Economists with an interest in market forces typically argue that the terms of social harmony are less dependent on the creation of a homogenizing *monopoly* than the persistence of variety and *diversity*. In fact, they note, antitrust regulations are generally regarded as desirable insofar as they attempt to limit the strength of some market actors for the sake of the market as a whole. Unfortunately, this logic appears to become less attractive whenever we shift our attention away from local "markets" toward "the nation"; indeed, when it comes to "the nation" and, for that matter, the *ummah* as a whole, this appeal to market-oriented diversity seems to run into all kinds of resistance, with many remaining firmly convinced that diversity-enhancing regulations are designed to enhance the destructive terms of "competition" at the expense of some larger community "whole."

Significantly, the terms of "monopoly control" in Pakistan have come to be regarded as the most appropriate expression of core religious values by a sizable Muslim majority. In fact, for many different sections of this majority, religious and sectarian "diversity" (*ikhtilaaf*) have come to be regarded as, for all intents and purposes, "religiously anathema." Precisely insofar as this is the case, however, the terms of pluralism, as a common feature of democracy, tend to face a number of rather serious constraints. Indeed the question arises: *how might those with an interest in bridging the gap between Islam, Islamic education, and democracy begin to address (or counter) this attachment to the language of monopoly even within the context of a modern Muslim education?*[28] Is it possible to engage local demands for "religious" education while, at the same time, finding ways to appreciate the terms of religious difference, sectarian diversity, and ongoing political debate?

In a recent White Paper regarding education (December 2006), the government of Pakistan noted that, in the context of future educational reforms, public sector syllabi should seek to avoid what the government described as religious or doctrinal "details" if these details "are known to be divisive." In particular, the government noted that Pakistani "textbooks must never foster, or lead to, sectarianism." "All divisive material," the paper explained, "[must] be weeded out of the national curriculum and [each provincial] textbook."[29]

This was, of course, a familiar refrain. In fact for all intents and purposes the government merely succeeded in reinforcing the language of the private sector and, within this, the language of local educational demands—in effect, the demands of those (namely, the majority) who sought to *ignore* the terms of religious and sectarian difference in favor of a persistent appeal for unity, conformity, and consensus: *e pluribus unum* (out of many, *one*).

Moving beyond the homogenizing aspirations of this demand-driven majority, however, I found that, on the margins, *the language of monopoly did not persist entirely unopposed*. On the contrary, as my data clearly reveal, "exceptional" cases remained. To be sure, the views expressed in these exceptional cases were, themselves, quite mixed; in fact most of those who said that sectarian differences should be "acknowledged" went on to say that these differences should be acknowledged *only in an effort to expose local children to "that which must be avoided."* In other words, even apart from the majority 62 percent who felt that sectarian differences should be ignored altogether, an additional 29 percent felt these differences should be mentioned *only in an attempt to insure that local children would be able to recognize (and, in due course, avoid) specific expressions of difference.*

There was, however, one set of exceptional cases that seemed to depart from this trend. This category of cases, representing just 8 percent of my total sample, appeared to articulate a different language—one that, I believe, points to the possibility of what Martin Marty (2005) described as an expression of *religiously informed civic pluralism.*[30] "There is, of course, only one Islam," explained one member of this group—adding that, after all, "there is no god but God." But even so, he declared, coming straight to his main point, "there may be many different ways to find God." In fact, drawing attention to the terms of a commonly cited (but deeply contested) *hadith*, he explained that "the differences *within* Islam are themselves an important blessing." "*Iktilafaat hamaare, vo bhi Allah ki rehmat hoti.*" "These differences [within Islam]," he said, "these are also a sign of God's grace."[31]

In Pakistan, private-sector educational demands reflect a persistent set of demands "in favor of religion." But, more often than not, these demands appear to reflect a language of religious "uniformity" and unbending "monopoly" control. The challenge does not involve any effort to move away from these demands "in favor of religion." Instead it lies in an effort to maintain a certain appreciation for these demands while, at the same time, addressing their reaction to—indeed their *denial* of—the terms of "difference" within.

Throughout Pakistan, many insist that the terms of democratic "equality" cannot be reconciled with those of religious and sectarian "diversity." In fact most of those I met appeared to favor the construction of a "democracy without difference." But, as my work progressed,

I began to realize that those who disagreed (a small minority) should not be underestimated. On the contrary, those who succeed in apprehending and embracing what I have chosen to call "the [sectarian] elephant in the living room" represent an important religious and political alternative—an alternative that, I believe, may help to address the fact of sectarian difference while, at the same time, working to avoid its most fearsome and destructive effects.

Notes

1. See Matthew Nelson, 2006, "Muslims, Markets, and the Meaning of "A Good Education" in Pakistan," *Asian Survey*, 46:5.

2. See, for example, Amy Gutmann, 1995, "Civic Education and Social Diversity," *Ethics*, 105:3, pp. 557–579; Stephen Macedo, 1995, "Liberal Civic Education and Religious Fundamentalism: The Case of God v. John Rawls," *Ethics*, 105:3, pp. 468–496; 1995, "Multiculturalism for the Religious Right? Defending Liberal Civic Education," *Journal of the Philosophy of Education*, 29, pp. 223–238; Veit Bader, 1999, "Religious Pluralism: Secularism or Priority for Democracy?" *Political Theory*, 27:5, pp. 597–633; and Lucas Swaine, 2001, "How Ought Liberal Democracies to Treat Theocratic Communities?" *Ethics*, 111:2, pp. 302–343.

3. See also Isaiah Berlin, *The Hedgehog and the Fox* (NY: Simon and Schuster, 1953).

4. For an account of the research undertaken in 2003, see Nelson 2006. Selected districts included Lahore, Faisalabad, Multan, Sialkot, Bahawalpur, Okara, Jhang, Muzaffarabad, Karachi I, Karachi II, Hyderabad, Larkana, Quetta, Sibi, Peshawar, and Dera Ismail Khan.

5. In the context of the interviews, the five definitions of "a good education" were articulated as follows: (a) *basic education*: "Some people say that a good school teaches students how to read and write. In other words, good schools provide students with basic reading skills and basic math skills"; (b) *religious education*: "Some people say that a good schools create good Muslims; in other words, a good school is a school that provides students with strong values and strong religious beliefs"; (c) *liberal*: "Some people say that good schools teach students how to solve problems and think for themselves"; (d) *vocational*: "Some people say that good schools prepare students to find good jobs"; and (e) *civic*: "Some people say that good schools teach students to become good citizens, showing respect for the laws of their country."

6. See John Damis, 1974, "The Free-School Phenomenon: The Cases of Tunisia and Algeria," *International Journal of Middle East Studies*, 5:4, pp. 434–449; Dale F. Eickelman, 1992, "Mass Higher Education and the Religious Imagination in Contemporary Arab Societies," *American Ethnologist*, 19:4, pp. 643–655; Patricia Horvatich, 1994, "Ways of Knowing Islam," *American Ethnologist*, 21:4, pp. 811–826.

7. Middle-class families with parents who call the mullah from a local *madrasa* to teach their children at home, like those who visit their local *madrasa* on a part-time basis, rarely identify their ties to local *madrasas* on survey instruments that fail to inquire about "part-time enrollment" or "religious education in the home." In fact the religious education of these students tends to remain unreported in the literature.

8. See also Nelson, 2008, "Religious Education in Non-Religious Schools: A Comparative Study of Pakistan and Bangladesh," *Journal of Commonwealth and Comparative Politics*, 46:3, pp. 337–361.

9. See Nelson 2008. Andrabi et al. agree that most families are inclined to include both religious and non-religious education in the context of their educational "portfolio," but they limit this observation to the level of the household, suggesting that, within a given household, it is not uncommon to find one child attending a *madrasa* and the others enrolled in public or private schools. In many cases, however, this balance extends to the level of individual students; in other words, many students attend *both* religious *and* non-religious schools *at the same time*. Even Andrabi et al. point out that, "although the household data can tell us whether a child is enrolled full-time in a *madrasa*, it cannot tell us if a child goes for an hour on any given day to study the Qur'an." See Tahir Andrabi, March 2005, "Religious School Enrollment in Pakistan: A Look at the Data," Harvard University Kennedy School of Government Working Paper No. RWP05-024; World Bank Policy Research Working Paper No. 3521, p. 4.

10. For a detailed discussion of this policy-oriented literature, see C. Christine Fair, *The Madrassah Challenge: Militancy and Religious Education in Pakistan* (Washington, DC: U.S. Institute of Peace, 2008), pp. 1–13. For examples, see Jessica Stern, "Pakistan's Jihad Culture," *Foreign Affairs* (2000), 79:6, pp. 115–126; Peter Singer, "Pakistan's Madrassahs: Ensuring a System of Education not Jihad," Analysis Paper 41 (Washington, DC: Brookings, 2001); International Crisis Group, "Pakistan: Madrassahs, Extremism, and the Military," ICG Asia Report 36 (Islamabad, 2002).

11. See Tariq Rahman, *Denizens of Alien Worlds: A Study of Education, Inequality, and Polarization in Pakistan* (Karachi: Oxford, 2004).

12. See Peter Bergen and Swati Pandey, 2006, "The Madrasa Scapegoat," *The Washington Quarterly*, 29:2, pp. 117–125.

13. Among those with children enrolled exclusively in a *madrasa*, 80 percent identified religious education as their top priority. Among those with children enrolled exclusively in a private school, this figure dropped to just 58 percent. The majority, however, lay in between this 60–80 percent band. Seventy-three percent of those with children in a local government school *and a madrasa* identified religious education as their top educational priority; 62 percent with children in a private school *and a madrasa* selected religious education as their top priority. The only outlier involved affluent families with children who studied in a local government or private school and, then, in the afternoon, with a local *maulvi* at home. Only 51 percent of this group identified religious education as their top educational priority. Still, each group included more than 50 percent who felt that religious education should be regarded as a "top priority."

14. For an alternative perspective, see S.V.R. Nasr, 2000, "The Rise of Sunni Militancy in Pakistan: The Changing Role of Islamism and the Ulama in Society and Politics," *Modern Asian Studies*, 34:1, pp. 139–180; also 2000, "International Politics, Domestic Imperatives, and the Rise of the Politics of Identity: Sectarianism in Pakistan, 1979–1997," *Comparative Politics*, 32:2, pp. 179–190.

15. A.H. Nayyar and Ahmed Salim, *The Subtle Subversion: The State of Curricula and Textbooks in Pakistan* (Islamabad: Sustainable Development Policy Institute, 2004); Rubina Saigol, "Boundaries of Consciousness: The Interface between the Curriculum, Gender, and Nationalism," in N.S. Khan, R.S. Saigol, and A.S Zia, eds., *Locating the Self: Reflections on Women and Multiple Identities* (Lahore: ASR, 1994); Rubina Saigol, *Symbolic Violence: Curriculum, Pedagogy, and Society* (Lahore: SAHE, 2000).

16. See Nelson 2008. See also K.K. Aziz, *The Murder of History: A Critique of History Textbooks Used in Pakistan* (Lahore: Vanguard, 2004).

17. See Jamal Malik, "Dynamics Among Traditional Religious Scholars and Their Institutions in Contemporary Pakistan," in Nicole Grandin and Marc Gaborieau, eds., *Madrasa: La Transmission du Savoir dans le Monde Musulman* (Paris: Editions Argument, 1997), pp. 168–82; Mohammad Qasim Zaman, *The Ulema in Contemporary Islam: Custodians of*

Change (Princeton: Princeton, 2002); Syed Vali Reza Nasr, 2000, "The Rise of Sunni Militancy"; Yoginder Sikand, March–April 2004, "Ecumenism and Islam's Enemy Within," *Himal South Asia*, <http://www.himalmag.com/2004/march_ april/opinion_3.htm>

18. "In some countries," notes Robert Hefner, "the resulting fragmentation of authority ... has pluralized social power and been a force for democratization." But in others, "the struggle has often abetted the ascent of a "neofundamentalism" hostile to pluralism." In fact, he notes, "religious politics in Muslim countries today often lead to heightened demands for a unitary profession of the faith." "Multiple Modernities: Christianity, Islam, and Hinduism in a Globalizing Age," *Annual Review of Anthropology*, 27 (1998), pp. 91–92. For Hefner, these demands for a unitary profession of the faith tend to proceed "from above," provoking calls for pluralism "from below." My research indicates that these demands for a unitary profession of the faith emerge "from below" as well.

19. As Tariq Rahman points out, "there was much more acrimonious theological debate among the Shi'as and Sunnis and among the Sunnis themselves during British rule than is common nowadays.... The followers of the main debaters sometimes exchanged invectives and even came to blows," he writes, "but [they] never turned to terrorism as witnessed in Pakistan's recent history." *Denizens*, p. 85. Today it seems that discussion and debate are actively discouraged, leading to "politics by other means" (violence). In fact a persistent failure to "acknowledge the elephant in the living room" appears to be closely related to the scourge of sectarian violence.

20. For a more detailed account of *ikhtalaaf*, or difference, in Islam and the problems associated with it, see Taha Jabir al "Alwani, The Ethics of Disagreement in Islam" (Herndon, VA: The International Institute of Islamic Thought) <http://www.usc.edu/dept /MSA/ humanrelations/alalwani_disagreement/>

21. See also Michael G. Peletz, "Islam and the Cultural Politics of Legitimacy: Malaysia in the Aftermath of September 11" in *Remaking Muslim Politics: Pluralism, Contestation, Democratization*, Robert W. Hefner, ed. (Princeton: Princeton University Press, 2005), pp. 240–272. According to Peletz, "there is a strong current throughout the entire Muslim community in Malaysia that questioning any aspect of Islam could well lead to divisions within the *ummah*, and that exposing or widening divisions of the latter sort amounts to "letting down the side" and thus an erosion of Muslim ... sovereignty, which is necessarily tantamount to treason." In other words, he notes, "there is an overdetermined reluctance to debate the ontological status of apostasy and many other issues linked to religion," p. 261.

22. See also Aziz al-Azmeh, "Populism Contra Democracy: Recent Democratist Discourse in the Arab World," in Ghassan Salame ed., *Democracy without Democrats? The Renewal of Politics in the Muslim World* (London: I.B. Taurus, 1994), pp. 112–129.

23. See also Peletz, pp. 264–265.

24. See Khaled Ahmed, "Deoband-Barelvi War Amid Clerical Lying," *The Daily Times* (Lahore), 23 May 2006; see also "Sorry, Your Extremism Is Showing," *The Daily Times*, 12 May 2006; "How We Deny Sectarianism and Then Pay for It," *The Daily Times*, 4 September 2006.

25. See Peletz, p. 263.

26. Khaled Ahmed, "Deoband-Barelvi War"; Imtiaz Ahmed, "Sectarian Menace and Perpetual Denial," *The News* (Islamabad), 18 April 2006, p. 1.

27. The term *fitna* is widely used, often with reference to the emergence of bitter sectarian rivalries following the death of the Prophet Mohammad in 632CE; the assassination of the second caliph Uthman in 656CE; and, finally, the martyrdom of Hussein, the son of the fourth caliph Ali, in 680CE. See Gilles Kepel, *The War for Muslim Minds: Islam and the West* (Cambridge, MA: Belknap Press, 2004).

28. For a more detailed discussion of these issues, see Kevin McDonough, 1998, "Can the Liberal State Support Cultural Identity Schools?" *American Journal of Education*, 106:4,

pp. 463–499. For an attempt to spell out the terms of religious *regulation* in keeping with the terms of religious *pluralism*, see Donald M. Sacken, 1988, "Regulating Nonpublic Education: A Search for Just Law and Policy," *American Journal of Education*, 96:3, pp. 394–420. For concerns about the effect of "too much" pluralism, see J. Harvie Wilkinson III, 1995, "The Law of Civil Rights and the Dangers of Separatism in Multicultural America," *Stanford Law Review*, 47:5, pp. 993–1026; David Blacker, 2000, "Proceduralism and the Orthodox Backlash against Students' Rights," *American Journal of Education*, 108:4, pp. 318–355.

29. See Government of Pakistan, December 2006, "Education in Pakistan: A White Paper," pp. 53–54.

30. See Martin Marty, *When Faiths Collide* (Oxford: Blackwell, 2005), p. 70, 76–81.

31. This reconceptualisation of the relationship between Islam and civic pluralism has been articulated by different scholars in different ways. See, for example, Mohammad Allama Iqbal, 1934, *The Reconstruction of Religious Thought in Islam* (Oxford); Fazlur Rahman, 1982, *Islam and Modernity: Transformation of an Intellectual Tradition* (Chicago: University of Chicago Press); 2000, *Revival and Reform in Islam: A Study of Islamic Fundamentalism*, Ebrahim Moosa, ed. (Oxford: Oneworld); Abdolkarim Soroush, 2000, *Reason, Freedom, and Democracy in Islam* (Oxford); and so on.

CHAPTER 7

Muslim Schools, Social Movements, and Democracy in Indonesia

ROBERT W. HEFNER

Events in the early 2000s cast a momentary pall over Indonesia's 47,000 Islamic schools. A few years earlier, in the late 1980s, the state Islamic university system initiated curricular reforms that transformed it into one of the most forward-looking in the entire Muslim world. In the 1990s, students and faculty from the same system played a proud role in Indonesia's democracy movement, one of the largest the Muslim world has ever seen (see Kraince 2003). Following the collapse of President Soeharto's "New Order" regime (1966 to May 1998), however, radical Islamist militias with ties to conservative Islamist schools sprang up in cities and towns across the country. In a few places, the militants got into street fights with democracy activists and the police. Several dozen Islamic boarding schools also initiated campaigns to dispatch *mujahidin* fighters from Java and Sumatra to the eastern provinces of Maluku and north Maluku, where, from 1999–2003, almost 10,000 people died in fierce Christian-Muslim violence (see Feillard and Madinier 2006, 95–151; van Bruinessen 2002; Hefner 2005, 273–301).

Concerns about the political disposition of the country's Islamic schools were further heightened with the 2002 bombings of a beach-front pub in south Bali, where more than 200 people perished, most of them Western tourists. The men eventually convicted of the attack were members of the terrorist Jemaah Islamiyah, and were discovered to have ties to an Islamic boarding school in Lamongan, East Java. Some Western observers saw these incidents as proof that at least some among Indonesia's Islamic schools had become training camps for al-Qa'ida militants intent on opening a "second front" against Western interests (Abuza 2003).

Notwithstanding these developments, and notwithstanding a few radical schools, the state of Islamic education in Indonesia is healthy and of enormous comparative interest. Indonesia's Muslim schools are among the most intellectually dynamic in the entire Muslim world. Some 5.7 million or 13 percent of Indonesia's 44 million primary and secondary students are today enrolled in madrasas, which in Indonesia are Islamic schools which combine religious and general education. An additional three million students attend full-time Islamic boarding schools (*pondok pesantren*), most after first attending a middle or high school of a general studies nature. The curriculum controversies that have raged in recent years in some Muslim-majority countries over the place of "secular" subjects in Islamic schools have in Indonesia long been resolved. On their own initiative, Muslim educators began to introduce general education into their curricula in the 1910s and 1920s, and the trend was general by the 1960s. Indonesian Muslim schools were also pioneers of girls and women's education. Today, girls make up slightly more than half of the student body in the madrasa wing of Islamic education, and about 47 percent of the students in boarding schools (Azra, Afrianty, and Hefner 2007).

In this chapter, I step back from the general history of Islamic education in Indonesia and examine several smaller trends which are, despite their scale, of comparative interest. I focus on a new breed of Islamic schools of a "social movement" nature. By social movement schools, I refer to educational institutions that aim, not merely to impart knowledge and values to children, but to use the networks and perceptual frames that religious education provides to critique and reform state and society. With its appeal for a deeper Islamization of self and society, Islamic education in Indonesia has long displayed many of the characteristics political sociologists identify with social movements. However, it was only in the 1980s and 1990s that a significant number of schools began to interpret this mission in an activist and nationally organized way. A minority among a minority, a tiny proportion of the movement schools have in turn interpreted their activist mission in a politically *radical* manner. However, rather than being harbingers of educational radicalization, the very success of social movement schools generally has drawn the overwhelming majority squarely back to the political and cultural center.

That educational center has itself been buffeted by a development of great comparative interest. It is that the overwhelming majority of Muslim educators have concluded that constitutional democracy is compatible with Islam, and is the best form of government for Indonesia. This is indeed a great transformation of Islamic educational culture. But the change has proved challenging. Even as they say they subscribe to democratic values, most educators also insist that divine law (*shari`a*) should in some sense serve as the basis of the state. The primary question with which mainstream Muslim educators will grapple in years to come is not radicalization, but how to balance the ideals of democracy with the ethical imperatives of God's law.

Schooling as Social Movement

The history of Islamic education in Indonesia demonstrates that the country's schools have shown a remarkable aptitude for competing in a rapidly changing educational marketplace. Although market forces explain some of the Islamic sector's dynamism, it is clear that the religious–educational marketplace is embedded in a larger world subject to forces more varied than price signals among autonomous individuals (McPherson 1983). Indeed, to invoke a notion from economic philosophy, one of the more striking features of religious education is that, rather than just satisfying preexisting "consumer preferences," religious schools help to produce the very demand to which they respond. In this and other regards, the goals of Islamic education are not merely individual. Among the pious, education is seen as part of a collective duty to Islamize society, turning believers away from things un-Islamic and toward those commanded by God.

Viewed from this perspective, Indonesia's Islamic schools bear a partial resemblance to the social movements to which political theorists have turned their attention in recent years. In Sidney Tarrow's oft-cited phrase, social movements are "collective challenges, based on common purposes and social solidarities, in sustained interaction with elites, opponents, and authorities," and seeking a fundamental change in existing institutions and hierarchies (Tarrow 1998, 4; Wiktorowicz 2004). Much social movement literature implies that the state is the primary target of movement leveraged change. However, not all social movements are state-centric in orientation. As with movements in other religious traditions, Islamic social movements tend to be as much concerned with changing citizens and society as they are with challenging the state.[1]

The parallel between social movements and Islamic schooling is even more striking when one looks at the way in which religious schools create social organizations and cultural frames for assessing and reforming the social order. Here a brief theoretical aside is in order. Social movement theory arose in reaction to "strain" and "grievance" explanations of protest movements in political sociology; these were regarded as flawed in two ways. First, strain theories assumed that the mere presence of injustices or tensions in society was sufficient to generate protest movements (Wiktorowicz, 2004, 8; Wickham 2002, 6–8). Second, in emphasizing a unitary social psychology, strain theorists implied that actors who join social movements are more stressed out than rational, seeking compensatory release rather than an effective instrument for mobilization and change.

Social movement theorists responded to strain theory's presuppositions by pointing out that injustice and grievances abound in all societies, but they do not always result in organized social protest. The emergence of the latter depends on social processes far less automatic than strain theories implied. In particular, theorists argued, the emergence of social movements depends on three conditions: the existence of social networks where actors can communicate and mobilize; opportunity structures in political society that provide openings through which the mobilization can move without incurring repression; and, last but not least, leaders capable of formulating "cultural frames" that resonate with popular grievances, inspiring people to join the movement.

Of course, the analogy between social movements and Islamic schools begins to wear thin once one recalls that historically most schools were founded for reasons that had little to do with creating a unified movement. In Indonesia as in many other parts of the Muslim world, traditionalist educators are notorious for the way they jealously guard their institutional autonomy. This is not an attitude that lends itself to the cohesive leadership highlighted in social movement theory. By comparison with social movements, too, the ends to which Islamic education are put are highly varied. To state the point in more theoretical terms, education's impact on the habits and ideals of its charges is typically diffuse in its forms rather than efficiently instrumentalized toward the achievement of a single valued end.

Notwithstanding these differences, it is indisputable that Islamic schooling creates network resources ("social capital") with the potential to draw social actors into organizations and projects that extend well beyond the school yard. It is well known, for example, that boarding school (*pesantren*) education in Indonesia creates a bond between student and teacher infused with a deep sense of gratitude and obedience. The bond in turn gives rise to enduring social solidarities that can be deployed for ends other than those of education or piety. Whether in the ulama-led peasant rebellion in late nineteenth century West Java or the phoenix-like resilience of the Nahdlatul Ulama in the twentieth century, modern Indonesian history abounds with examples of Muslim educational networks being put to broader social uses. Indeed, more generally, the twentieth century political competition associated with what are known in Indonesian studies as *aliran politik* ("political streams") was in part the result of what one might describe as the "social movementization" of preexisting educational networks, both Muslim and secular nationalist (Geertz 1965, 127–8).

The most striking parallel between Islamic schooling and social movements, however, has to do with the "framing processes" in which both engage (Snow et al., 1986). To create an effective movement, social movement theorists emphasize, the cultural frames created by leaders must 1) diagnose some chronic problem in society in a manner that resonates with the needs of people; 2) recommend a strategy for the problem's remedy; and 3) provide a rationale that motivates actors to support the proposed course of remedial action. If any among these conditions is not met, the movement will not gain traction.

The most critical element in the framing process is the frame's ability to resonate with the perceptions and aspirations of broad masses of people in society. As Quintan Wiktorowicz has noted, "Such reverberation...depends upon not only its consistency with cultural narratives, but also the reputation of the individual or group responsible for articulating the frame, the personal salience of the frame for potential participants, the consistency of the frame, and the frame's empirical credibility in real life " (Wiktorowicz 2004, 16; cf. Benford and Snow 2000).

Some proponents of Islamic schooling in Indonesia have long acted in ways that bear an uncanny resemblance to the framing processes highlighted in social movement theory. For example, in Muslim educational circles in twentieth century Indonesia, an oft-heard line was that the main cause of the country's problems was the failure of ordinary Muslims to fulfill their religious obligations. The key to improving state and society, then, lay in Muslims learning to observe their religious duties more faithfully.

On the question of the nation-state, the message Muslim educators in Indonesia have conveyed has, to say the least, varied. With the partial exception of the tumultuous period from 1955–1965, when the country was torn by a bitter rivalry among communist, nationalist, and Islamic parties, the majority of educators has downplayed the need to transform the state or engage in any other radical social project. Inasmuch as they have been concerned with political issues, Indonesia's Muslim educators have tended to be nationalist and system reforming rather than radical or system upending. Most align themselves with the Islamic-but-pluralist nationalism of mainstream groups like the Muhammadiyah and Nahdlatul Ulama.

Since the early-1990s, however, a few school movements have arisen and offered frames demanding a more far-reaching transformation of politics and society. Even among these schools, only a tiny number advocate what amounts to a revolutionary restructuring of state and society (see below). Islamist revolution is not the preferred end of most of the new generation of social movement schools. The majority subscribes to the notion that what is most needed is a gradualist and peaceful Islamization of state and society.

The most notable example of moderate social movement schools of this latter sort are those associated with what has come to be known in recent years as the "integrated Islam school" (*sekolah Islam terpadu*) movement. Integrated schools are part of a multistranded educational movement that, to the surprise of many, became one of the fastest growing trends in Islamic education in the post-Soeharto era.

The Integrated School Movement

The first principle of integrated Islamic education is that, rather than confining religious instruction to one or two subjects, it should be interwoven into subjects across the school day. Although not all proponents of integrated Islamic schools are familiar with the broader history, the more intellectually sophisticated understand that the movement is related to efforts by the U.S.-based (now deceased) Palestinian academic, Isma'il Raji al-Faruqi. In the 1970s and 1980s, al-Faruqi and his colleagues formulated a blistering critique of Western science and education, accusing both of materialist and secularist biases. Al-Faruqi insisted that if Muslims are to use these disciplines at all, their content must be "Islamized" through their reconstruction around the ideal of the essential unity of God (*tawhid*).[2]

In today's Indonesia, the curricular implementation of the integrated education ideal usually proves to be somewhat less ambitious than one might expect based on the model's genealogy. The majority of integrated Islam schools cater to the Muslim middle class and lower-middle class, and they base their curriculum on modules prepared by the state Ministries of Education and Religion. They do so, not because of government pressures, but because many of their students hope to go on to college, and college admission requires demonstrated mastery of the national core curriculum. The integration of religious themes into the general curriculum nonetheless does make a difference in both the style of teaching and the school atmosphere. As one educator at an integrated-Islam school in Tangerang, West Java observed, "Even when we teach a course like mathematics, we try to refer to examples from the life of the Prophet Muhammad, who was a trader, and his trading activities can be used to illustrate mathematical concepts."[3]

Since the fall of the Soeharto regime, hundreds of integrated Islam schools have sprung up, most of them in urban and suburban areas. The fastest-growing networks are those associated with two groups of a moderate Islamist persuasion, the Prosperous Justice Party (PKS) and the Hidayatullah movement.

The Prosperous Justice Party and Integrated Education

The PKS is a center-right party similar in organization and ambition to Turkey's Welfare Party and its successor, the AK (Justice) party. Founded three months after Soeharto's resignation in May 1998, the PKS won 1.3 percent of the vote in the 1999 elections and an impressive 7.3 percent five years later. Most of the PKS leadership had a background in the Islamist student movement of the 1980s and 1990s, and was at first influenced by a moderately conservative wing of Egypt's Muslim Brotherhood. In the 1980s, Indonesian students returning from Egypt brought back Brotherhood ideas on movement tactics and organization. One of the main ideas they borrowed was that character formation and religious education (*tarbiyah*) are the best ways to build a movement for social change. The students also learned that the most effective way to carry out this character shaping is through the formation of intimate learning circles (*halaqah*) and support groups (*usrah,* literally "family") where cadres try to implement God's law in all aspects of their lives. The members' behavior is supposed to be so ethically exemplary that it gradually brings about the transformation of society and—through nonviolent means and at some unspecified future date—the state.

The first *tarbiyah* cells sprouted on Indonesian campuses in the early 1980s. By the mid-1980s, *tarbiyah* Islamists had begun to win control of state-sanctioned religious training programs (Lembaga Dakwah Kampus) on those same campuses. By the early 1990s, *tarbiyah* activists had captured student senates at most state universities. In March 1998, at the height of student protests against President Soeharto, *tarbiyah* representatives from sixty colleges came together to form the Indonesian Muslim Student Action Committee or KAMMI (Komite Aksi Mahasiswa Muslim Indonesia; see Machmudi 2006). Although a latecomer to the anti-Soeharto campaign, KAMMI went on to play a central role in the final push to drive Soeharto from power (see Madrid 1999). Three months after Soeharto's resignation in May 1998, the KAMMI leadership came together with several like-minded groups to establish a new party, which they named the Justice Party (*Partai Keadilan*). Like the student group from which most of its leadership had originated, the party's central aim was to promote Indonesia's continuing but peaceful Islamization (see Aspinall 2005, 128–31, 148–54).

The party had less than a year to prepare for the first national legislative elections in 1999, and it won just 1.3 percent of the vote. In the aftermath of that first election, party officials chose to relax their heretofore strict cadre training requirements for membership. Between 1999 and 2004, party membership quadrupled, allowing the party (now renamed the Prosperous Justice Party or PKS) to establish new branches and more than quadruple its share of the vote in the 2004 elections. During campaigning that year, the party downplayed the question of implementing *shari`a*, and instead emphasized its commitment to clean government and efficient public services. In my interviews in Yogyakarta and Jakarta during these years, party officials took pains to point out that their soft-peddling of *shari`a* was not just a strategic ploy. Rather, the tactic reflected party leaders' conviction that the implementation of Islamic law was a long-term goal that could only be realized when the Muslim public had a deeper understanding of the law.[4] In all these regards, the PKS approach differed from the top-down and immediatist tack favored by militant Islamists in the Crescent Moon and Star Party (PBB) and the Indonesian Council of Mujahidin (MMI).[5]

It is this moderate Islamist organization, then, from which the largest current in the integrated school movement emerged in the early 2000s. Each of the schools in this network is locally financed and formally independent from the national PKS leadership. However, directors at most schools are happy to acknowledge that they are informally tied to the PKS. Schools vary, however, in the degree to which they encourage or require staff to affiliate with the PKS. The directors of the six schools that I visited in 2005 and 2006 did not advertise their ties to the PKS, but parents and older students were well aware of the high regard in which faculty held the party.

Although the first principle of integrated Islamic education has to do with curriculum, most proponents of integrated schools see the "mixing" to which they are dedicated as implying commitment to a second and more ambitious principle, touching on the relationship of Muslim schools to society. In particular, schools are supposed to serve, not only as places for training young students, but as motors for the Islamization of society. A second grade teacher at an integrated Islam school in Tangerang, West Java, described the mission in the following terms:

> "Our understanding of *terpadu* [integrated] is seen in the way we encourage parents to become active in the school and teachers to become active in the community. You know in most public schools in Indonesia parental involvement in education stops at the entrance to the school. We don't agree with that. Many of our teachers are parents, and part of our mission is to allow them to become active in the community, particularly with regard to religious affairs.... Our goal is not just education in the narrow sense but *da'wa* [religious "appeal" or predication]. And the main purpose of *da'wa* is to make the entire society more Islamic."

Not all PKS-linked schools interpret their mission in the same activist terms. At another school in West Java, the teachers with whom I spoke remarked that they felt it imprudent to mix politics and education too directly. The school director explained that most students at the school came from families with backgrounds in the traditionalist Nahdlatul Ulama. "Talking about politics with these parents might only cause bad feelings." Other teachers and administrators interviewed in 2005 and 2006, however, made clear that they had no such qualms about using schools to engage the broader community. As one teacher in Yogyakarta explained to me in December 2006, "The PKS is a party of *da'wa*, and the purpose of *da'wa* is not just to make Muslims more individually pious, but to build a better society and, at some point, a better state. Our religion commands us to do this."

Hidayatullah's Populist Integralism

Headquartered in Jakarta and Gunung Tembak, a small village south of Balikpapan, East Kalimantan, the Hidayatullah school network was also founded on the principle that while teaching children Islamic schools should also catalyze the transformation of society. As of 2007, the movement operated 133 schools in cities and towns across Indonesia. Demonstrating that the parallels between Islamic school networks and social movements are not an artifact of analysts' imaginations, in 2000 the Hidayatullah organization officially transformed itself from an educational foundation into a political movement. Today it has some 200 chapters. The movement's central premise is that "the backwardness of the Muslim world has been caused by a tendency to understand the holism of Islamic teaching in an only partial manner."[6]

The Hidayatullah began in 1973 with the establishment of a small pesantren in what was at the time a forested corner of East Kalimantan. The pesantren's five founders included individuals from traditionalist and modernist backgrounds. However, from the beginning the movement was largely modernist in spirit, with a strong emphasis on the Qur'an and Sunna, and notably less on the study of classical religious commentaries. In his youth, Abdullah Said, chief among the school's founders, had been active in the Association of Indonesian Muslim Students (PII), a modernist student organization; he had also attended well-known modernist boarding schools in Gontor and Bangil (Hasan 2000, 87). Said is said to have been inspired in part by the life and ideals of Kahar Muzakkar, leader of an Islamist rebel movement that had operated in South Sulawesi in the 1950s and early 1960s.[7]

But Said was no political radical. In the 1960s, he had also been active in the Indonesian Student Action Union, known by the acronym KAMI (not to be confused with the above KAMMI), which had assisted General Soeharto in his campaign to topple President Soekarno and undermine the Communist Party. After moving to East Kalimantan, Said and his colleagues took care *not* to be seen as Islamist opponents of the New Order government. They maintained cordial relations with local representatives of the nationally dominant Golkar Party. In 1976, the school was officially inaugurated by the then-Minister of Religion, Mukti Ali. In 1984, President Soeharto awarded the Hidayatullah a medal for the school's contribution to East Kalimantan development.

The central ambition of the Hidayatullah pesantren was to use schooling to build a broader community in which Islamic values could be implemented in a comprehensive (*kaffah*) manner. This was to be done, not merely through an integrated school curriculum, but by creating "an integrated form of society." Far more than their PKS counterparts, Hidayatullah staffers interpret this principle of social integration in egalitarian and ascetic terms. Students and staff at Hidayatullah boarding schools are supposed to be "willing to let go of all the social attributes that they bring from outside and take on a status that is the same as all others."[8] At Gunung Tembak, students and staff live around the central school campus, in homes that are neat but, by any standard, spartan. Staff and students are also enjoined to avoid ostentatious clothing and luxury goods, as well as Western and hedonistic entertainments.

In 1978, Hidayatullah leaders dispatched their first team of graduates to Java and Sulalwesi to explore the possibility of opening branch schools and businesses. The graduates' first duty was to engage in predication (*da'wa*), in the hope of recruiting a small group of supporters. As its numbers grew, the branch was supposed to erect a boarding school. Staff and students were also expected to move quickly to establish businesses, with the understanding that their operations were to become self-sufficient as soon as possible.

Like their PKS counterparts, Hidayatullah schools use an integrated curriculum that blends religious lessons into all portions of the curriculum. Hidayatullah officials prefer to refer to their curriculum, however, as "integral" (Ind., *integral*) rather than "integrated" (*terpadu*), although they admit that its aims are similar.[9] Notwithstanding the school movement's commitment to the virtues of simplicity and modesty, intellectual activity is greatly prized, and pedagogy makes generous use of discussion groups and outside speakers.

As with PKS schools, Hidayatullah educators also understand their mission of integration as including participation in the affairs of the surrounding community. Hidayatullah officers point out, however, that in three other respects their understanding of integration differs from that of the PKS. First, and in keeping with its emphasis on egalitarianism and asceticism, Hidayatullah gives priority to the poor and lower-middle class, rather than the middle and upper-middle classes drawn to PKS schools. School officials explain that they see their segment of the educational market as the *mustad'afin,* the downtrodden and oppressed. Second, Hidayatullah officials distinguish their schools from those of the PKS in the Hidayatullah's willingness to recruit students from diverse doctrinal backgrounds. In the words of the secretary of the regional Hidayatullah office in Yogyakarta, "We don't fill our schools with just one group [kelompok]. We say 'please enter' to people from all other groups."[10]

This second difference is in turn related to a third. Rather than striving for ideological purity, the leadership speaks of its organization as (in the words again of the above Yogyakarta officer) "just one organization among other Islamic organizations, and we don't want to consider ourselves the only one that is true." There are nonetheless two ideological emphases to which all members are expected to subscribe. First, all associates must agree with the goal of implementing Islamic law in an all-encompassing (*kaffah*) manner. And second, all must reject the "Western" values of secularism, pluralism (here understood to refer to the belief that all religions are in essence equal), and liberalism.

In 2000, the Hidayatullah announced that it was turning itself into a national political movement, while continuing to operate its network of schools. The movement's aims are described in religious rather than explicitly political terms. In particular, the movement is dedicated to the creation of an Islamic civilization with the Qur'an and Sunna as its "blue print."[11] Movement leaders and publications play down any interest in the establishment of a state other than that of the currently existing Indonesian state. At the movement's national meeting in 2005, representatives renounced any association with groups advocating radical change or violence.[12]

In sum, both the PKS and Hidayatullah offer examples of schools instrumentalized as social movements and dedicated to the nonviolent but comprehensive transformation of state and society. The schools aim not only to impart knowledge and piety, but to construct interpretive frames and organizations capable of curing society's ills through the comprehensive realization of God's law. Both movements also agree that, for the time being, the bases of the state can be nationalist. But both movements emphasize the comprehensiveness and purity of the *shari'a*, implying that at some future moment the state will change of its own accord as a result of society's peaceful Islamization.

Not all social movement schools agree with the PKS and Hidayatullah on this last point. Some take strong exception to any accommodation with nationalism. In the post-Soeharto era, a few of these schools even became involved in violent challenges to the Indonesian state.

Education Against Nation

Since the early decades of the twentieth century there have always been Muslim educators who taught that Indonesia's version of multiethnic and multiconfessional nationalism is antithetical to Islam. For most of

Soeharto's New Order, educators who dared to voice sentiments like these were harassed or imprisoned, so people who harbored these views tended to keep them to themselves.

The criticism never stopped entirely, however. Even under Soeharto, a small network of independent schools continued to use classrooms as platforms for opposing the Indonesian nation-state. The most prominent of these schools today is Abu Bakar Ba'asyir's al-Mukmin pesantren outside of Solo, Central Java. With funding from the Saudi-financed Indonesian Council for Islamic Proselytization (DDII), the al-Mukmim school was founded in 1972 by Ba'asyir and the late Abdullah Sungkar. At the time, both were activists in the Central Javanese wing of the DDII. Both also took a radical turn in the late 1980s, joining the underground wing of what had once been Indonesia's most radical Islamist movement, the Darul Islam. Ba'asyir and Sungkar eventually broke with the DI, but only to establish their own, more radical organization, which in the 1990s became the nucleus for a militant group known as the Jemaah Islamiyah.

On matters of educational method and content, Ba'asyir and Sungkar were not radical but conservative modernists, and al-Mukmin implemented a fairly conventional curriculum. On topics like nationalism and relations with non-Muslims, however, al-Mukmin's message was and is still today uncompromising. Textbooks 1A and 1B of the pesantren's *Study Materials on Principles of Doctrine*[13] convey the school founders' views quite clearly:

"To act for reasons of nation is polytheistic idolatry, and polytheism destroys the values of the Islamic profession of the faith. Truly, a Muslim is forbidden to defend his country except if its rules and constitution are based on Islam. If the country is based on Islam and carries out God's law, then a Muslim may act to defend the country, because in this case such an act is the same as defending Islam. However, if one acts to defend a country that clearly refuses God's law then that is polytheism."[14]

Pages 34 to 38 of the same *Aqidah* textbook go further, laying out a program of struggle for the implementation of Islamic law. The program has three stages: 1) building a community of believers in opposition to unbelievers; 2) preparing a well-organized army; and 3) developing a facility in the use of firearms. Others among Ngruki's texts warn students against the dangers of befriending non-Muslims and even mingling with inobservant Muslims.

It is interesting to note that, although the radical intent of passages like these seems apparent enough, some students at al-Mukmin hear the text's message in an accommodating manner. In fact, many of al-Mukmin's students graduate and go on to state universities and otherwise ordinary careers in business and education. Of the seven Ngruki students my research team has interviewed since 2003, five insisted that they had no interest in opposing the nationalist bases of the Indonesian state. Several pointed out that, although some of Ngruki's students are politically radical, the majority are not. Most students, these interviewees explained, are drawn to Ngruki because of the quality of its educational programs and the availability of generous scholarships. They pointed out (and educators at nearby Islamic schools agreed) that Ngruki has a reputation for providing some of the finest instruction in all of Central Java in Arabic, English, and computer software.

In interviews, even some teachers expressed embarrassment at Ngruki's ties to political radicals, such as the perpetrators of the October 2002 Bali bombings. One teacher added that, in the 2004 parliamentary elections most of the staff had turned away from the school's previously favored party, the Crescent and Stars Party (PBB), a conservative Islamist party, and cast their vote instead for the moderately Islamist Prosperous Justice Party (PKS). One teacher pointed to the vote as evidence that a more "moderate" current was in the ascendance at Ngruki.[15]

Whatever the Ngruki staffers' personal views, the school's curriculum makes clear that the directors regard both democracy and nationalism as un-Islamic. In interviews and statements, Abu Bakar Ba'asyir has not backed away from these views. To judge by their behavior, some of Sungkar and Ba'asyir's more radical students—especially those that had the additional experience of participating in the anti-Soviet jihad in Afghanistan (Hasan 2005, 44)—have taken al-Mukmin's curriculum at its word.

Horn Of A Dilemma: Muslim Educators and The Shari'a

The larger question posed by these various social movement schools is: what is the attitude of most educators on democracy, pluralism, non-Muslims, and women? In an effort to answer these questions, in January 2006 I worked with staff at the Center for the Study of Islam and Society (PPIM) at the Hidayatullah National Islamic University in Jakarta to carry out a survey of 940 Muslim educators in 100 madrasas and Islamic boarding schools in eight provinces in Indonesia. The interviews were carried out by senior college students hired and trained by the PPIM in each of the eight provinces. The full survey had 184 questions, the aggregate results of which are too complex to present here. However, the second column of the table below summarizes the data that dealt with Muslim educators' attitudes toward democracy and the shari`a. The first column presents data from a near-identical survey of 1000 members of the general Muslim public in eight regions across Indonesia. This survey, too, was carried out by PPIM researchers, who kindly shared their findings, allowing a comparison of the general Muslim public's views with those of Muslim educators.

These survey data reveal several striking facts regarding the Muslim public's and educators' views on democracy and the *shari`a*. On one hand, an impressive 71.6 percent of the Muslim public and 85.9 percent of Muslim educators agree that democracy is the best form of government for Indonesia. Equally striking, neither the public nor the educators' support is formalistic or based on a crudely majoritarian perspective on democracy. Rather, the public and the educators' views extend to subtle understandings of civil rights, including support for the equality of all citizens before the law (82.8 percent for the general public, 94.2 percent for Muslim educators); citizen freedom to join political organizations (79.5 percent and 82.5 percent respectively); legal protections for the media from arbitrary government action (78.6 percent and 92.8 percent); and the notion that open party competition helps to improve the performance of government (74.7 percent and 80 percent). These figures are comparable to or even higher than survey data on similar issues from Western Europe and the United States (cf. Norris and Inglehart 2004; Fattah 2006). The educators' support for democracy and civil rights should also dispel any impression that the Islamic educational establishment is a reactionary drag on an otherwise pluralist public.

The second row of figures on the public and the educators' support for aspects of the *shari`a* is equally striking. Notwithstanding the strength of their commitment to democracy, 72.2 percent of the public and educators believe the state should be based on the Qur'an and Sunna and guided by religious experts. A full 75.5 percent of the public and 82.8 percent of educators think the state should work to implement the shari`a. Public support for the shari`a wobbles on a few issues. It

Table 7.1   Muslim attitudes on democracy & Islam

Survey 2004 is based on a survey of 1000 members of the general Muslim public in eight provinces across Indonesia. 2006 data are based on a survey of 940 Muslim teachers in secondary-level Islamic schools (madrasas and pesantrens) in eight provinces.

No.	Percentage who Agree with the Following Statement	2004	2006 Survey
Support for Democracy			
1.	Democracy, compared to other forms of governance, is the best form of government for a country like ours	71,6%	85,9%
2.	Democracy is a source of political disorder	7,0%	8,1%
3.	Every citizen is equal before the law regardless of his or her political views	82,8%	94,2%
4.	Every citizen should be allowed to join any political organization	79,5%	82,5%
5.	Mass media should be protected by law from the arbitrary actions of government	78,6%	92,8%
6.	Our economy will be better if the government gives more freedom to each citizen to do as he or she wishes	76,9%	73,4%
7.	Free and fair contestation between political parties improves the performance of government of this country	74,7%	80%
Support for Shari`a and Islamism			
1.	Islamic governance, i.e. governance based on the Qur'an and Sunnah under the leadership of Islamic authorities is the best for this nation.	72,2%	72,2%
2	The state should enforce the obligation to implement Islamic law (shari`a) for all Muslims.	75,5%	82,8%
3	The amputation of the hand of a thief as prescribed in the Qur'an should be enforced by the government.	38,9%	59,1%
4.	In general elections Muslims should only elect candidates who understand and fight for the implementation of Islamic teachings in the polity.	59,5%	63,9%
5.	In general elections voters should only support Islamic parties	29,5%	24,3%
6.	Muslims who do not perform their religious duties should not be allowed to be members of the People's Consultative Assembly or Parliament	45,6%	74,3%
7.	The ideals and practices of Islamic organizations (such as Darul Islam, Negara Islam Indonesia, Front Pembela Islam, Laskar Jihad, etc.) to implement Islamic law (shari`a) in the society and polity should be supported	55,6%	64,4%
8.	The practices of polygyny should be allowed	33,0%	75,7%
9.	Females should not be not allowed to take long trips without being accompanied by a close family member or relative	60,7%	79,6%
10.	The government (police) should engage in surveillance so as to make sure that Muslims perform the Ramadan fast	33,0%	49,9%
11.	The government (police) should close restaurants during Ramadan	69,3%	82,9%
12.	The government (police) should engage in surveillance (mengawasi) to make sure that two persons (male and female) walking together in the street are married or relatives	43,7%	66,6%

drops to 38.9 percent for the general public and 59.1 percent, for educators with regard to the amputation of thieves' hands. Nonetheless, a full 55.6 percent of the public and 64.4 percent of educators agree with campaigns to implement Islamic law.

These findings provide a glimpse into a serious cultural and moral dilemma for Indonesian Muslims. The Muslim public and educators' commitments to democracy are about as strong as anywhere in the democratic world. However, where a democratic principle runs up against an issue on which the shari`a and its interpreters have something important to say, the majority of people feel that piety requires that they defer to conventional understandings of the shari`a. This deference results in judgments that many observers, including most Muslim democrats, would regard as inconsistent with democracy.

These data suggest two broader conclusions. On one hand, the Muslim public's commitment to democracy bears witness to one of the most remarkable changes in Muslim political culture in modern times: the fact that growing numbers of Muslims see democracy as compatible with Islam and as vital for good government. Here is a cultural event of far-reaching political importance, but one often overlooked in discussions of modern Muslim politics (cf. Inglehart and Norris 2003). Second, and more complex, the public's commitment to democracy exists in conflict with an almost equally strong commitment to the shari`a. Most Muslim political theorists of democratic persuasion regard a literalist implementation of the *shari`a* as incompatible with modern democratic citizenship (see Abou El Fadl 2004; An-Na`im 1990). One might be tempted to say that the data point to a clash of cultures between the values of democracy and those of the *shari`a* as conventionally understood.

However, the tension between *shari`a* and democracy may not be as great as the survey data first suggest. The Muslim public's support for the *shari`a* as revealed in opinion surveys does not result in the majority of Muslims voting for parties committed to the implementation of Islamic law. All of the parties that made implementing the *shari`a* a central feature of their political platforms fared poorly in the 1999 and 2004 elections. My in-depth interviews with more than one hundred educators between 2004 and 2007 revealed a similar pattern: Fewer than 30 percent gave their support to Islamist parties advocating the implementation of *shari`a* in any form; fewer than 10 percent of respondents voted for parties advocating the law's immediate implementation.

The discrepancy between the survey data and election choices can be interpreted in several ways, but, based on interviews over the past five years, I think it reflects two primary influences. First, it shows that, like their counterparts in much of the world, most Indonesian Muslims accept that the *shari`a* is God's guidance for humanity and, as such, it must be just and true. Second, and complicating the matter considerably, for most Muslims this generalized understanding does not generate clear and specific procedures for how to act or govern politically, even with regard to Islamic law. Rather than agreeing with radical Islamist claims that the *shari`a* is clear and unchanging and that its implementation will solve all problems, most Muslims are uncertain as to the law's practical entailments. They prefer a pragmatic, "get-the-job-done" approach to political and economic problems, and most are not sure that the *shari`a* is, as the radicals claim, a toolkit rather than a source of inspirational ideals. These findings are consistent with recent scholarship on Islamic law, which has emphasized that for most believers the *shari`a* is more a "vocabulary of morality and justice" than it is an entity akin to Western positive law or, least of all, a set political ideology (Zubaida 2003, 11).

If this conclusion is correct, it means that the educators' and public's commitment to the *shari`a* is real but also, so to speak, procedurally ambiguous. It coexists with an equally important conviction that solving problems of unemployment and corruption requires effective empirical instruments, not just abstract notions of the good. All this means that the effort to balance the *shari`a* with democracy is a work in progress. It also means that, in Indonesia and many other countries, the precise course of that work will depend critically on quality schooling and higher education.

Conclusion

In an article published in 1960, a young anthropologist named Clifford Geertz surveyed the state of Islamic education in Indonesia, directing his gaze toward Islamic boarding schools (*pesantren*) and the figure of their director, known in Java as *kyai*. Geertz observed that the rise of nationalism in Indonesia had created a dangerous gap between the country's secular-nationalist leaders and a citizenry "still largely absorbed" in "a plurality of distinct regional cultures" (Geertz 1960, 227–8). Geertz also speculated that the *kyai* might be able to mediate this divide by serving as a cultural broker between an otherwise distant national leadership and the Muslim masses. However, if the *kyai* was to play this role, Geertz believed, Islamic education was going to have to change:

> "Only through the creation of a school at once as religiously satisfying to the villager as the pesantren, and as instrumentally functional to the growth of the 'new Indonesia' as the state-run secular schools can the kijaji [kyai]... become a man once more competent to stand guard 'over the crucial junctures of synapses of relationships which connect the local system with the larger whole'.... Failing this the kijaji's days as a dominant force in pious Javanese villages are numbered, and the role of Islam in shaping the directions of political evolution in Indonesia is likely to be marginal at best" (Geertz 1960, 249).

Leaping ahead a half century from the time of Geertz's field work, it is startling to realize that much of the educational transformation Geertz envisioned has actually taken place. Indonesia's Islamic schools have taken giant steps to bridge the gap between general and religious education. They have forged ties between Islamic and non-Islamic higher education, in the process creating one of the world's finest Islamic university systems (Azyumardi, Afrianty, and Hefner 2007, 188–91; Hefner 2009).

Much as Geertz had hypothesized (even while hinting its actual achievement was improbable), the reconstruction of Islamic education has also buttressed the "role of Islam in shaping the directions of political evolution in Indonesia." On this last point, however, recent events in Indonesia have proved more complicated than Geertz imagined. Rather than enhancing the role of the *kyai* and creating a neatly unified community of believers, Muslim Indonesia has witnessed a fractious pluralization of schools, movements, and authority. The process has unleashed a creative competition for Muslim hearts and minds, expressed in myriad political parties, a bold Islamic publishing industry, and innovative Islamic schools. Equally impressive, the majority of Muslims have concluded that the way to handle the new pluralism is for everyone to agree to play by the rules of a democratic game. The pluralization has also given rise, however, to a rejectionist minority willing and able to defy the will of the majority. This community rejects democracy, nationalism, and modern citizenship as antithetical to Islam. A fringe among the rejectionists has framed its stance as a clash, not between varied interpretations of Islam, but between godlessness and religion.

It is important, however, to keep the radicalism in perspective. Indonesia has 47,000 Islamic schools. Of these, schools advocating the violent overthrow of the state number only several dozen. For every radical school, there are hundreds operated by the Muhammadiyah, Nahdlatul Ulama, and like-minded organizations committed to multireligious nationalism. The great majority of these latter schools are not "liberal" in the modern American sense of the term; but they are keen on both the idea of Indonesia and democracy. Moreover, whereas in a country like Egypt Islamists have moved into the vacuum created by the state's inability to provide basic services for the poor (see Wickham 2002, 99; Clark 2004), in Indonesia services of this sort have long since been provided by mass organizations of a moderate sort. Although their mettle was tested in the crisis years of 1958–1966, these mainline groups today have reestablished themselves as pillars of civil society.

The varied data discussed in this chapter, then, point to three broad conclusions: that debates over the role of *shari`a* in public life are likely to remain a key feature of Indonesian education and politics for some time; that the public's stated interest in *shari`a* does not preempt other concerns, including support for democracy; and that the public prefers an ethicalized and substantive understanding of the *shari`a* to a formalistic and literalist view.

Of course, this prognosis leaves the precise nature of Muslim politics in Indonesia's future unclear. But it hints at another, no less important trend, this one in the educational field. It is that Muslim schools will remain central to efforts to resolve the tensions of modern Muslim politics and culture in a peaceful and forward looking way. In other words, contrary to what we were told in the modernization theories of a generation ago, Islamic schools will not be pushed to the margins of the modern Muslim experience, but will remain at its heart. The reason for this is that schooling offers a unique platform for addressing the question of how to carry Muslims forward into modernity at once plural and open-minded yet religious.

Notes

1. The social-change orientation of Christian social movements is strikingly apparent in studies like Freston 2001 and Joel Robbins 2004.
2. On al-Faruqi and the Islamization of knowledge debate, see Abaza 2002, 77–87.
3. Interview with teacher Tangerang, West Java, December 6, 2005.
4. Interview with PKS leaders in Jakarta, August 7, 2003.

5. My annual interviews with PKS officials in Jakarta and Yogyakarta from 1999–2003 indicated that there were serious differences among leaders on the question of the *shari`a*. Some members in Makassar, Padang, and Surabaya were inclined to support a more "immediatist" and *étatist* approach to the law.

6. Interview with Hidayatullah spokesperson, Gunung Tembak, December 17, 2005.

7. Anonymous interview with Hidayatullah activist, Yogyakarta, August 12, 2005. See also, International Crisis Group 2002, 3.

8. The quote is from an unpublished study by the Center for the Study of Islam and Society (PPIM) in Jakarta. See PPIM 2004, 63.

9. Interview with Saryo SA, School Principal, Hidayatullah Elementary School, Sleman, Yogyakarta, December 20, 2005.

10. Interview with DPD Secretary for Hidayatullah Office Yogyakarta-Sleman, 13 February 2006.

11. Interview, Gunung Tembak, December 17, 2005.

12. A French colleague, Gwenael Njoto-Feillard, attended the Jakarta conference and kindly provided me with this information on the discussion.

13. See No Author, *Aqidah 1A* and *Materi Pelajaran Aqidah 1b* (Surakarta: Pondok Pesantren Islam al-Mukmin, n.d.). I was discretely given these books in 2005 by a al-Mukmin teacher.

14. *Aqidah 1b*, p. 17.

15. Interview with Ngruki instructor (name withheld at instructor's request), February 7, 2006.

CHAPTER 8

Communitarianism, the Muslim Identity, and Islamic Social Studies in Singapore

CHARLENE TAN AND INTAN A. MOKHTAR

Introduction to Singapore and Singapore Muslims

As a multireligious country with a Muslim minority population in Southeast Asia, Singapore offers a useful case study on the complex issues of religion, citizenship, identity, education, and state control. This chapter critically examines Singapore's conception of citizenship based on a variant of communitarianism and its articulation for Muslim citizens. It focuses on the state's introduction of the Singapore Muslim Identity Project for all Muslim citizens and a new subject "Islamic Social Studies" for full-time madrasah students. First, we will provide some background on Singapore and its Muslim citizens.

Singapore is a "secular state" in the sense that the state mandates that religion should be kept out of the public sphere, especially in politics. The Maintenance of Religious Harmony Act, passed in 1989, stipulates that no religious groups should be involved in politics and that religious organizations are not to stray beyond the bounds of educational, social and charitable work. A city-state with over 4.9 million people, Singapore is comprised of Chinese (74.2 percent), Malays (13.4 percent), Indians (9.2 percent) and other ethnic groups such as Arabs and Eurasians (3.2 percent). Just under half of the population subscribes to Buddhism (42.5 percent), with the rest adhering to Islam (14.9 percent), Christianity (14.6 percent), Taoism (8.5 percent), Hinduism (4 percent), other religions (0.6 percent) and no religion (14.8 percent).

The ancestors of the Malays in Singapore arrived at the Malay Archipelago between 2,000 and 5,000 BC. As the indigenous people of Singapore, the Malays formed the majority even before the arrival of the British in the early nineteenth century. However, they found themselves outnumbered by the Chinese who later migrated in increasingly large numbers from China beginning in the middle of the nineteenth century. Among all of Singapore's racial groups, the Malays, which comprise various ethnic subgroups such as Javanese and Baweanese, are the most homogenous with 99.6 percent of them belonging to the Islamic faith. The remaining Muslim population (about 15 percent) consist of people of South Asian, Chinese, Eurasian, and Arab descent. Due to historical reasons, special administrative policies and initiatives have been put in place for the Malays in Singapore. For instance, only the Malays enjoy free education in the state schools and universities (i.e. they do not have to pay any school or tuition fees).[1] In addition, because the majority of Malays are Muslims, a special ministerial position (Minister in-charge of Muslim Affairs) has been created to see to the administration of Muslim affairs in the country. Only the Muslims have a separate Registry of Marriages and the *Shariah* Court to deal with legal cases according to Muslim laws. Furthermore, the government has reserved locations in public housing estates for the building of mosques.

Muslim children in Singapore can receive a full-time schooling at a secular state school (known as "national school") or a madrasah (Islamic school).[2] Only about 4 percent of the total Muslim students in Singapore opt to study full-time at one of the six madrasahs from the primary to pre-university levels. The mission of the madrasahs is primarily to produce religious elites to lead the community on religious matters. Both academic subjects such as English, Mathematics, Science, and religious subjects such as Qur'anic Study, and Arabic Language are taught, with between 30 percent and 60 percent of the curriculum time devoted to academic subjects across the six madrasahs. As the madrasahs are private institutions and not part of the state school system, they receive very limited state funding. An exception is Madrasah Al-Irsyad that is directly funded by the central statutory Muslim body, Majlis Ugama Islam Singapura (MUIS; Islamic Religious Council of Singapore) that receives a substantial amount of its funds from compulsory monthly salary deductions from Muslims in Singapore, which is on top of the annual *zakat* collected during the fasting month of *Ramadan*.[3] The other madrasahs obtain small capitation grants from MUIS based on the number of students and the level they are in, as well as grants for the audio-visual and library facilities (MUIS, 2009). But the amounts received are insufficient to cover the operational costs of the madrasahs; consequently many madrasahs have to rely on fundraising activities and donations mainly from the Muslim community.

Communitarianism in Singapore

Liberal communitarianism

Before understanding Singapore's state conception of citizenship that is derived from the political ideology of communitarianism, it is instructive to highlight the salient features of communitarianism as a basis for comparison. Although by no means a homogenous group, "liberal communitarians" shared a common rejection of the view of a self that is detached from society and independent of all concrete encumbrances of moral or political obligations (Taylor, 1985, 1989; Sandel, 1981). In other words, they object to "liberal individualism" with its emphasis on abstract and excessive individualism while ignoring the centrality of community for personal identity and moral thinking (Arthur, 1998). Instead, they assert that that the self is always constituted through community that exists in shared social and cultural understandings, traditions and practices; the community provides the interpretive framework within which individuals form their values, view their world and conduct their lives (Walzer, 1983; Taylor, 1985; MacIntyre, 1988). Its main purpose is to say that our conceptions of right and wrong and the good life are derived from cultures/ traditions of which we are a part. It follows that, for the communitarians, individuals need to fulfill their civic obligations and pursue the "common good," by framing that good as a collective determination of a set of goals or values for the community (Bang, Box, Hansen & Neufeld, 2000; Watson, 1999).

However, the communitarians' critique of excessive individualism does not necessarily mean that they are antagonistic towards liberalism in general. In fact, liberal communitarians affirm their commitment to liberal values such as furthering the development of an individual's capacities and supporting the state's role to protect our powers to shape, pursue, and revise our own life-plans (Arthur, 1998; Watson, 1999). It is also important to point out that the communitarian view on the primacy of the community is not at odds with the recognition that some of our communal attachments such as those regarding the traditional role of women can be problematic and may need to be changed (Bell, 2009).

A common criticism of communitarianism is that it runs the risk of making a group's collective identity a matter of imperatives rather than of historical explanation, of telling people who they are or must be regardless of their explicit consent (Winch & Gingell, 2004). Worse, it may assume common interests within communities (when none exists) by relying on an ideal of the "common good" that favors the values and interests of its most articulate and powerful groups (Arthur, 1998). A particular worry among some liberals of communitarianism is with patriarchy and abuse of power (Barry, 2001; Okin, 1998, 2002). When that happens, an undesirable (and unintended) consequence is that communitarianism tends to absorb, assimilate, and finally monopolize all public space (Bang, Box, Hansen & Neufeld, 2000). Against this backdrop of philosophical communitarianism, we now turn to a variant of communitarianism in Asia, with a focus on Singapore.

"Asian communitarianism" in Singapore

An Asian version of communitarianism is evident not only in Singapore but also in other countries such as South Korea, China, Malaysia and Indonesia (e.g. Adler & Sim, 2005; Chua, 1995; Han, 2007; Hill & Lian, 1995; Kennedy, 2004; Lee et al, 2004; Sim & Print, 2005; Tan, 2008a). Chua (2005a) avers that many political leaders in East and Southeast Asia attempted to develop communitarianism into an explicit national ideology for the purpose of rationalising general political governance and specific administrative policies.

What, then, are the key similarities and differences between liberal communitarianism and "Asian communitarianism?" A fundamental commonality is that Asian communitarians, like their counterparts in Anglo-phone societies, highlight the importance of community for the formation and shaping of individual values, behaviour and identity. The chief proponents of Asian communitarians are political leaders who are opposed to what they perceive to be excessive "Western" individualism that disregards the shared history, language, culture and tradition of ethnic and religious groups. Linked to the importance of community is the Asian communitarians' preference for collectivism over individualism. Studies on citizenship values in Asian countries such as Singapore, Malaysia and China show that the accent is on the responsibilities citizens have towards family and the community rather than the rights they enjoy (Kennedy, 2004; Tan, 2008a). In other words, a "good citizen" in Asia is principally one who contributes to society by supporting his or her community and adhering to a set of communitarian values. Here there is a strong overlap between philosophical communitarianism and its Asian variant.

Yet a key difference between "Asian communitarianism" and liberal communitarianism concerns their contrasting views towards liberalism. Liberal communitarianism, while critical of abstract and excessive individualism, is nevertheless generally supportive of liberal values such as the individual's freedom and right to choice and justice. In contrast, many Asian political leaders who champion "Asian communitarianism" have viewed the popular conception of "Western" liberalism negatively as the source of decadent moral values and social problems such as promiscuity, high divorce rates, single parenthood and drug abuse (Chua, 2005a; Thompson, 2004; Barr, 2006). Asian communitarians choose instead to undergird their communitarian ideology with "Asian values"—collectively defined as "moral values, social norms and cultural attitudes" that are said to be derived from Asian philosophical traditions and historical experiences (Han, 2007, p. 386).

But the concept of "Asian values" is an ambiguous and contentious issue. Apart from a lack of consensus on what constitutes "Asian values," it is arguable whether there is anything uniquely "Asian" about these values. For instance, the shared values identified by the Singapore state such as "community support and respect for the individual" are not exclusively Asian and are in fact compatible with liberal ideals in Western contexts (these communitarian values in Singapore will be elaborated later). Also, the justification for Asian values—that "Western" liberalism is responsible for social ills and undesirable moral behavior—is too simplistic and untenable. Such a stark bifurcation of "Asian values" and "Western values" also ignores the strong communitarian traditions in Anglo-phone societies, as highlighted by communitarians such as Sandel (1981), Taylor (1985, 1989) and MacIntyre (1988).

In the case of Singapore, the "Asian values" selected by the Singapore government, known as "Our Shared Values", are as follows:

(1) Nation before community and society before self;
(2) Community support and respect for the individual;
(3) The family as the basic unit of society;
(4) Consensus in place of conflict; and
(5) Racial and religious harmony.

It can be observed that these shared values resemble Confucian teachings; indeed the Singaporean government believes that Confucianism forms a good foundation for propagating Asian values among the younger generation (Chua, 1995; Barr, 2006). Of special relevance to our discussion is the value of "racial and religious harmony" that is premised on the Singapore state's idea of "multiracialism" where all citizens are classified based on four racial identities according to one's paternal line: Chinese, Malay, Indian, and Others (CMIO). A depoliticised definition of "race" is advocated where specific characteristics such as food, attire and religious festivals are ascribed to the "races."[4] The concept of "harmony" in Singapore refers to people of different racial and religious backgrounds coexisting peacefully together without feelings of enmity, ill-will or hostility; rather all citizens are expected to manifest mutual tolerance, respect, and understanding. For instance, Taoists and Buddhists are reminded to burn joss paper and incense in designated bins and not on open grass so as to not risk having the ashes flying around and landing on their neighbors' laundry or in their apartments; Muslim clerics can only read highly scripted sermons that have been approved by MUIS during Friday prayers to eliminate any interreligious ill-feelings that may threaten racial or religious harmony in the country.

Various legislative measures have also been introduced to ensure that racial and religious harmony is preserved all the time. The Penal Code considers the following as offences: injuring or defiling a place of worship, disturbing a religious assembly, and uttering words or sounds to deliberately wound religious feelings. The Sedition Act states that words to promote feelings of ill will and hostility between different races and classes of the population are seditious. The Declaration of Religious Harmony introduced in 2003 serves to remind all people of Singapore that religious harmony is vital for peace, progress and prosperity in their multiracial and multireligious nation and that they should ensure that religions will not be abused to create conflict and disharmony in Singapore.

Another essential difference between "Asian communitarianism" and liberal communitarianism lies in the *origin* of the shared beliefs, values and practices of the constitutive community. Liberal communitarianism generally focuses on the common social and cultural understandings, traditions and practices that *already* exist in the communities. Asian communitarianism, on the other hand, tends to stress the communitarian qualities, thinking and behavior as interpreted or constructed by the political leaders. As such, there is a greater likelihood for Asian communitarianism to be used as a political tool to promote state interests and nation-building. Maintaining that Singapore is a hegemonic state that is based on ideological consensus as defined by the ruling party, People's Action Party (PAP), Sim (2001) explains its relationship between communitarianism and citizenship:

> Communitarianism encourages citizens, as good Asians, to priva-
> tize and subordinate their individualism/difference, and to com-
> munitarianly [sic] put national interests (as defined by the PAP)
> above self. In this way, ideological alternatives are delegitimized
> and ideological fragmentation averted (Sim, 2001, p, 49).

Accordingly, the "shared values" such as "consensus in place of con-flict" and "racial and religious harmony" are upheld by the state as secular supra-racial values; they function as a normative centre or moral consensus to define what is moral/immoral, legitimate/illegitimate or Asian/Western for the goal of "consensual" nation building (Sim, 2001). All ideological alternatives and dissenting views are judged by the state based on these "shared values," and subsequently subordinated or rejected. In other words, rather than removing dissent by coercion, the Singapore state prefers to delegitimize it by appealing to the com-mon good and the citizens' civic obligations within a communitarian framework (Sim, 2001). It is arguable that such a strategy is evident in the two recent state initiatives for the Singapore Muslims: the Singapore Muslim Identity Project, and a new school subject known as Islamic Social Studies.

The Singapore Muslim Identity Project

In 2002 the Singapore state embarked on a "Singapore Muslim Identity project" to be spearheaded by MUIS. Underpinning the Singapore Muslim Identity project is a vision of a "Muslim Community of Excellence" where ten "desired attributes" of Muslims in Singapore are spelt out (MUIS, 2004a). Accordingly, an ideal Muslim is one who

(1) holds strongly to Islamic principles, yet is adaptable to change;
(2) is morally and spiritually strengthened to face the challenges;
(3) is enlightened about Islamic history and civilization;
(4) believes that a good Muslim is also a good citizen;
(5) is well-adjusted in living as full members of secular society;

(6)   is progressive, beyond rituals or form;
(7)   is enlightened and appreciates richness of other civilizations;
(8)   is inclusive and practices pluralism;
(9)   is a blessing to other communities; and
(10) is a model and inspiration for others.

Initiatives to support the Singapore Muslim Identity Project included didactic and counter-ideological materials such as "Muslim, Moderate, Singaporean" that set out the principles of moderation as guidelines for Singapore Muslims (Tan 2007a). Interfaith talks, forums and dialogues between the Muslim and non-Muslim communities were also regularly held. MUIS also rolled out a new curriculum for the madrasahs, including a new subject "Islamic Social Studies" to ensure that full-time madrasah students are not left out in the state's promotion of the "desired attributes" of Muslims (this will be discussed in detail in a later section).

Several observations can be made about the ten "desired attributes" of Muslims in Singapore. First, there are strong communitarian undertones in the project, as evidenced by reference to Muslims collectively as a "Muslim Community of Excellence" and other citizens as "other communities." Additionally the references to "practices pluralism," "appreciates richness of other civilizations" and "a blessing to other communities" clearly point to the principle of "racial and religious harmony" for Muslims. It is also interesting to note that the ten "desired attributes" are rather vague in their description and not unique to Islam; one can easily replace the words "Muslim" and "Islamic" with another religion that exists in Singapore (such as "Christian" or "Hindu") and the attributes will still be applicable to the adherents of that religion. The reason for the interchangeability of religion is that the desired attributes are fundamentally the Singaporean state's communitarian values dressed up in nominal Islamic/religious terms.

But why are Muslims singled out by the state to (re)construct the collective identity of a religious community? Why are Muslims, and not other religious adherents, reminded that "a good Muslim is also a good citizen?" No other religious groups, including the Buddhists who comprise the majority and the Christians who form the third largest religious group in Singapore, have garnered similar attention and faced such intense scrutiny from the state. The state's palpable concern with and resolve in promoting a "Muslim Community of Excellence" has to do its perception that its communitarian ideology (and political hold) has been challenged by counter ideologies from terrorist groups in the aftermath of the September 11 airliner attack in New York. Since 2001, at least thirty members of the terrorist group *Jemaah Islamiah* (JI) have been arrested in Singapore for attempting to commit violent attacks against western embassies and Singapore key installations. With networks in Singapore, Indonesia, Malaysia, Thailand, Philippines and Australia, JI aims to create an Islamic Caliphate (*Daulah Islamiyah*) in Southeast Asia through violent means. JI's teachings, including the beliefs that the Singaporean government is opposed to Islam, that Muslims in Singapore are oppressed, and that Muslims should not mix with non-Muslims, are antithetical to the state communitarian ideology and threaten the very survival of a secular government in Singapore. The ubiquity of the internet also means that the possibility of Muslims in Singapore accessing and being influenced by terrorist websites is high, with Singapore being the fourth most networked country in the world (World Economic Forum, March 26, 2009); a Singaporean Muslim has already been arrested recently for his pro-terrorism plan after he was self-radicalized and indoctrinated by terrorist websites.

In view of the JI arrests since 2001, several senior political leaders in Singapore have publicly voiced their concern about a perceived lack of social integration among Singaporean Muslims and how such insularity attracted some Singapore Muslims to join terrorist groups. For example, then Senior Minister Lee Kuan Yew expressed his concern:

> In keeping with a worldwide trend, over the last three decades many Muslims in Singapore and the region are becoming stricter in their dress, diet, religious observances, and even social interaction, especially with non-Muslims. Increasingly Muslim women will not shake hands with men....My original concern was over the growing separateness of our Muslim community, as Singaporean Muslims tended to congregate for their social and extramural activities in their mosques, instead of in multiracial community clubs. What came as a shock was that this heightened religiosity facilitated Muslim terror groups linked to Al-Qaeda to recruit Singapore Muslims into their network (Lee Kuan Yew, as cited in Tan, 2007, p. 447).

The Singaporean government is also aware that the arrests of JI members in Singapore have led to some level of suspicion and distrust between Muslims and non-Muslims in Singapore. For instance, there also have been reports of non-Muslim Singaporeans avoiding taking the same elevator with Muslims, and parents who insisted that their children not be taught by a *tudung* (headscarf)-wearing teacher (Ismail & Shaw, 2006).

Against a backdrop of the JI arrests and the perceived social exclusivity of the Muslims in Singapore, the Singapore Muslim Identity project, underpinned by a vision of a "Muslim Community of Excellence" and expressed through the prescribed "desired attributes" of Muslims, represents the Singaporean state's attempt to assert its communitarian ideology and delegitimize alternative ideologies. The "desired attributes" of Muslims are used by the state as a normative centre or moral consensus to define and prescribe publicly the qualities of a "good Muslim" and a community of "excellence." Referring to the need for MUIS to spell out the desirable attributes, a MUIS official states that "We must show that we understand and get along with other communities, and that we are not inward-looking" (Chia, 2005). At the same time, the state uses the "desired attributes" to identify and castigate "bad Muslims"—Muslims who are not "inclusive," not "well-adjusted in living as full members of secular society," do not appreciate "richness of other civilizations" and so on. This state agenda was acknowledged by Yaacob Ibrahim, the Minister in-charge of Muslim Affairs who announced that the Singapore Muslim Identity Project aims to debunk "extremist" teachings by certain Muslim groups outside Singapore, such as the teaching that Muslims can only live in a Muslim-majority nation (as cited in Tan, 2008b, p. 37). Adding that these "extremists" are Muslims who "are pushing for a narrow and rigid interpretation of Islam," he encouraged Singaporean Muslims to "reject the path of the extremists" by becoming a "community of excellence" (as cited in Tan, 2008b, pp. 37–38). In other words, the project is a tool used by the state to marginalize and discredit alternative ideologies promoted by terrorist groups such as Al-Qaeda or Jemaah Islamiah by securing the Muslims' cooperation to reject the terrorist ideology and pursue communitarian goals. By highlighting the "desired attributes" of the Muslims and permeating them into all aspects of the Muslims' lives, the Singapore state aims to maintain its secular hegemony in the face of an ideological opposition from terrorist groups.

Crafting identity by erasing difference

In our critique of the state communitarian ideology through the Singapore Muslim Identity Project, two points can be made. First, the communitarian ideology prescribed by the Singaporean state runs the risk of overemphasizing the homogeneity of the community and ignoring the diversity within the community. The differences within the Muslim community centre not so much on doctrinal differences but on the application of these doctrines in the context of a multireligious society under a secular state.

A case in point was the "tudung controversy" when four primary school Muslim girls turned up in their national schools in 2002 with their headscarves and modified school uniforms covering their arms and legs. All national schools in Singapore prohibit Muslim girls from donning the headscarves in school on the ground that the national schools should remain secular. Subsequently three were suspended from school while one was withdrawn to be homeschooled. The Muslim community was divided by the sensitive issue, with the Mufti Syed Isa Semait (the highest authority on Islam in Singapore), Muslim Members of Parliament and some Muslim organizations supporting the state ban on the headscarf, and other parties such as the Singapore Islamic Scholars and Religious Teachers Association (PERGAS) and some Muslim parents arguing for the reverse. It is important to note that the disagreement among Singaporean Muslims is not whether Muslim girls should fulfill the religious obligation of the modest covering of "aurat" (parts of the body that must be covered). Rather, the contention is whether Muslim parents should insist that their daughters don the headscarves at the expense of their schooling in a national school. It is telling that Mufti Syed Isa Semait advised the parents to comply with the state rule on the basis that education was more important than wearing the headscarf (Ariff, 2002). On the other hand, those who argue against the ban contend that they were merely obeying their religious duty for their daughters to don the headscarves; they also argued that Muslim girls should be allowed to don their headscarves with their school uniforms because male Sikh students are allowed to wear turbans in national schools.[5] This incident illustrates that the Muslim community, like the other religious communities in Singapore and elsewhere, is not a homogenous and unified community but a diverse one with differences and conflicts between the community and the state, and within the community itself.

Secondly, the Singapore Muslim Identity Project with its vision of a Muslim Community of Excellence also reveals the inherent tension between treating Muslims as part of a community and emphasizing individual success through thee principle of meritocracy. On the one hand, the need to maintain the "racial" community (as defined by the state) functions as a rationale for downplaying individual rights; individuals are presumed to be represented via the racial group and therefore should express grievances through the group (Chua, 2007). On the other hand, the Singaporean state underscores the value of meritocracy for all Singapore citizens. The Minister-in-Charge of Muslim Affairs explains that meritocracy means "we recognize and reward people not because of who their parents are, or on account of their race or religion, but what they have to offer" (as cited in Tan, 2007b, p. 54). This implies that every individual's interests are extracted from those of his or her racial group, and the individual is solely responsible of his or her success or failure in life.

But this emphasis on meritocracy has inadvertently encouraged competition, individual merit and self-interest in Singapore—values that are at odds with the concomitant emphasis on putting the community before self and championing harmony and consensus in society. Additionally, the rhetoric of meritocracy may deny the public recognition of social systemic structural disadvantages and the historical legacy of structural inequalities of a racial group (Chua, 2007). In the case of Singapore, the Malays (who are predominantly Muslims) have been lagging behind the other ethnic groups in Singapore in their academic performance at the primary, secondary and preuniversity levels. There is also a relatively high attrition rate among the Malay Muslim students enrolled in national schools, with 5–6 percent the primary 1 Malay cohort opting out of the national school system in Singapore every year, compared with 1.5 percent and 4.6 percent of the Chinese and Indian cohorts respectively (Tan, 2007b). In addition, entrance to some good schools in Singapore is contingent on the child taking Mandarin Chinese as a Mother Tongue Language. Hence, there may be bright Malay students who may not be able to gain entry into good primary or secondary schools because they do not have the preferred Mother Tongue Language, even if they have done well in national examinations. The focus on the equality of the individual and meritocracy, coupled with the absence of relevant affirmative action policies, means that the Malay community continues to face great hurdles in closing the gap with other ethnic communities.

Responses from the Singapore Muslims

How then do the Muslim citizens in Singapore respond to the state's intervention in their identity construction? It appears that there have been mixed responses. On the one hand, a number of Muslim community leaders have heeded the government's call to promote greater interreligious understanding and harmony. Mosques such as the Al-Khair Mosque and Muslim scholars from the Singapore Islamic Scholars and Religious Teachers Association (Pergas) have published materials or participated in public talks to inform the public on "moderate" Islam. Madrasahs such as Madrasah Al-Irsyad Al-Islamiah have also organized talks and games with secular schools such as United World College, Anglo-Chinese Junior School and Nanyang Junior College. A national survey conducted in 2002 reports that more Malays (of which 99.6 percent are Muslims) indicated that they have close friends who are not of their own race (from 71 percent in 2001 to 86 percent in 2002). Commenting on the increase, Chan (2003) claims that the spotlight cast on the Malay community as a result of JI arrests between 2001 and 2002 may have led some Malays to reach out more to non-Malay Singaporeans.

On the other hand, the aftermath of the JI arrests has intensified the sense of pressure on Singaporean Muslims to prove their loyalty and trustworthiness (Ismail & Shaw, 2006). Meanwhile, Muslims have started to question the need for them to prove their national allegiance as many do not see any incompatibility between their increased religiosity and social integration in a multireligious society. Compounding the unwanted attention faced by Singaporean Muslims is their discomfort with the state's repeated, and in their view, unnecessary reminder for them to be "inclusive" and be "well-adjusted in living as full members of secular society." It is noteworthy that a national survey on social attitudes of Singaporeans conducted in 2002 by the Ministry of Community, Development and Sports informs us that a majority of Malays (86 percent) indicated that they have close friends who are not of their own race, compared with the national average of 76 percent (Chan, 2003). The fear of social fragmentation appears unfounded as the same survey reports that the vast majority (9 out of 10) of Chinese, Malay, and Indian Singaporeans continued to be satisfied with present race and religious group relations. This is confirmed by another survey conducted by Ooi (2005) who reported that a majority of Malays will invite non-Malays to celebrate their special occasions (70 percent of Malays will invite Indian friends and 84 percent of Malays will invite Chinese friends). A more recent survey conducted by Chin and Vasu (2007) report that 90 percent of Muslims were open to interacting with non-Muslims in the social, economic, political and security domains. In terms of interreligious relations, the same survey shows that Muslims were generally highly receptive to people of other faiths: Muslims were the most receptive to the Freethinkers with a mean of 94 percent, followed by the Buddhist/Taoists, Christians and adherents of minority religions ("Other religion") with a mean of 93 percent each, and then the Hindus with 92 percent. Therefore while it is true that there are Singaporean Muslims who are insular and inclined towards terrorist activities, the majority of the Muslims in Singapore appear to be socially integrated into a multiracial society.

Singaporean Muslims also resist being classified based on the binary terms of moderate/extremist, tudung wearing/not tudung wearing, and good/bad Muslim (Ismail & Shaw, 2006; Kadir, 2004; Azhar, 2006). Apart from the fact that such classifications are too simplistic, it "also does not give room to Muslims who do not support terrorist groups such as Al Qaeda and JI, and are thus not 'extremists,' but are also reluctant to heed the government's call for 'moderates' to speak up against the 'extremists' because they may not want to be perceived as 'liberal' Muslims singing the same tune as the United States" (Tan 2008b, p. 42). Ismail and Shaw (2006) add that the increasing calls for Singaporean Malay-Muslims to join the "mainstream" "are interpreted by some Singapore Malay-Muslims as a call for some form of assimilation within a hegemonic mainstream" (p. 43). This perception is aggravated by the hegemonic nature of communitarianism that is defined by the Singaporean state and tends to monopolize all public space. Rather than prescribing the ideals of a "good Muslim" and "good citizen" for Singaporean Muslims, we believe that it is more effective and sustainable for the state to work more closely with various segments of the Singaporean Muslim community in formulating a Singaporean Muslim identity. The next section continues our discussion on the Singapore state's attempt to promote its communitarian ideology to the Muslim population, this time to full-time madrasah students through a new subject.

Islamic Social Studies

As part of its plan to create "good" Muslim citizens, MUIS initiated a "Curriculum Development Project" to "produce a comprehensive, systematic and integrated educational system for the madrasahs in Singapore that would facilitate the teachings of Religious Knowledge with a cross curricular perspective" (MUIS, 2002, p. v). One example is "Islamic Social Studies." Islamic Social Studies is a new subject for full-time Muslim students studying in the madrasahs. It is modelled after the Ministry of Education-developed "Social Studies" subject that is compulsory for all primary and secondary students in the national schools. Introduced to the primary schools in 1981, the Social Studies syllabus aims to inculcate in all pupils a sense of belonging to the community and country, as well as cultivating the right dispositions for reinforcing social cohesion (MOE, 1999). The premium placed on racial and religious harmony is seen in its goal for students to respect the customs and traditions of the various communities in Singapore (MOE, 1999). The Islamic Social Studies (ISS) syllabus, on the other hand, was developed much later and in stages over a period of 6 years between 2002 and 2007. MUIS managed to bring together a group of established Muslim academics and scholars to develop the ISS syllabus, which was guided by the Social Studies syllabus.

The concept of communitarianism is strongly underlined in the ISS textbooks. For instance, the Primary 1A textbook (MUIS, 2002) introduces the neighbourhood to students and the importance of working together to keep the neighbourhood safe and clean. In the Primary 6B textbook (MUIS, 2008a), the importance of being active and responsible citizens who preserve and protect the environment is supported with a verse from the Chapter of *Al Ahzab* in the Qur'an (p. 36).[6] The value of "racial and religious harmony" is seen through various examples in the ISS textbooks. For instance, the Primary 2B textbook (MUIS, 2004b), students are introduced to the Hindu festival of lights or *Deepavali* (pp. 19–20), and the Chinese lantern or Mid-Autumn festival (pp. 21–22). Reminders are given at the end of the respective sections regarding the strong stand that Islam takes on respecting different cultures and practices. Similarly, in the Primary 6B textbook (MUIS, 2008), an entire chapter or lesson entitled, "We Are Respectful" emphasises the importance of fostering and promoting racial and religious harmony such as celebrating Racial Harmony Day on 21 July each year (pp. 13–14) and promoting inter-faith dialogues (pp. 19–20). Relevant verses from the Qur'an are also included to underscore this importance (pp. 16–17). The students are also cautioned about "many instances of fighting and unrest all over the region" and "aggression by irresponsible groups" (MUIS, 2008a), and taught to eschew violence and promote peace and diplomacy (MUIS, 2006).

Why was ISS curriculum introduced more than 20 years after the Social Studies curriculum? As we have seen, in the climate of continual terrorist threats and the perceived vulnerability of some Singaporean Muslims to terrorist doctrines, the Singapore government felt the need to introduce Social Studies, albeit one that promotes the state ideology from an Islamic perspective, to the full-time madrasah students. The government's scrutiny of full-time madrasah students is due to the fact that these students, as private school students, are exempted from citizenship education that is compulsory in national schools. Known locally as "National Education," it aims to develop in all Singaporeans national cohesion, the instinct for survival, and confidence in the future. The values of National Education are infused into school subjects such as Social Studies, Civics and Moral Education, and History, as well as through sports and various school enrichment programs in all the national schools. Hence the conceptualization and implementation of Islamic Social Studies demonstrates the state's desire for the madrasah students to be inculcated with the same communitarian values as their counterparts in the national schools. Hence the introduction of ISS should be understood as part of the state's defensive strategy to counter the terrorist ideologies as well as a preemptive move to prevent the madrasah students from being influenced by these ideologies.

ISS and the construction of surface identity

In analyzing the content of ISS textbooks, we have identified two key areas of concern. First, we question the classification of Singaporean citizens in the ISS textbooks into various "races" based on the principle of "multiracialism." Such an approach has the danger of essentializing and stereotyping others according to their "races," Although the students learn about other "races" and their customs and festivals in ISS such as *Deepavali* for the Hindus and the Mid-Autumn or lantern festival for the Chinese (MUIS, 2004b), the learning tends to be superficial. This form of learning focuses on "surface culture" that highlights the food, festivals, arts, religions, and other cultural artifacts (Tan, 2009; Bokhorst-Heng 2007). What is neglected is "deep culture" that refers to the often implicit values, assumptions and worldviews embraced by people and transcends the rigid and essentialized classification of "races." Adler and Sim (2005), in their analysis of the Social Studies curriculum, also assert that "there is little in the texts or the curriculum that helps learners move beyond a superficial approach to understanding diverse cultures" (p. 5). Consequently, "racial and religious harmony" in Singapore is essentially "maintained by the passive tolerance of visible and recognisable differences without encouraging cultural exchanges, deep understandings, and cultural boundary-crossings" (Chua, 2007, p. 917). In other words, the concept of "harmony" in the official discourse in Singapore is little more than the scrupulous avoidance of conflict rather than a substantive and meaningful engagement.

Secondly, we argue that the content in the ISS textbooks serves mainly to endorse and entrench a dominant state narrative, rather than for the students to consider alternative perspectives and draw their own conclusions. For example, the students are asked to brainstorm a list of activities for their madrasah to foster interaction and understanding between students and teachers of different madrasahs and those from the national schools (MUIS, 2005). The underlying message is that the madrasah students are insular and need to be integrated into society. Is such a view of the madrasah students warranted? A survey conducted in 2001 on 52 former and current madrasah students in Singapore suggests otherwise. The survey reports that 92.3 percent regarded English as absolutely essential for living in Singapore, linking it to "making money" (98.1 percent), "building a stable career" (96.2 percent) and "networking for contacts" (100 percent) (Rukhaidah, 2001). This research finding implies that rather than being inward-looking and only interested in religious pursuits, the madrasah students and graduates regard English as an economically valuable language for them to integrate and thrive in a secular world. It is also important to point out that none of the JI members arrested for terrorism-related activities was educated in the madrasahs in Singapore. Nevertheless, more up-to-date surveys are needed to ascertain whether madrasah students in Singapore are indeed exclusive and poorly-integrated into a pluralistic society after 2001.

The narrow and prescriptive nature of practicing Islam in the ISS textbooks means that limited opportunities are given to students to examine complex and controversial issues and debate on competing viewpoints. The promotion of the state communitarian ideology may hinder an honest exchange of ideas and possible resolution of controversial interethnic issues such as racial prejudice and discrimination, doctrinal disagreements and the role of religion in terrorist acts. Similar to the case for Social Studies as pointed out by Adler and Sim (2005), issues covered in ISS such as ethnic and religious conflicts are superficially and cursorily covered without the complexities in their causes and consequences. For instance, while the students learn about "many instances of fighting and unrest all over the region" and "aggression by irresponsible groups" (MUIS, 2008), there is little provision to help the students understand what these incidents of fighting and unrest are, who the "irresponsible groups" are, and to what the "irresponsibility" refers. Again, while the students are taught to eschew violence and promote peace and diplomacy (MUIS, 2006), they are not encouraged to consider cases where diplomacy may not be possible and fighting may be justified, such as when one acts out of self-defense. Neither is there any coverage on the real controversies and dilemmas some Singapore Muslims face, such as the concept of jihad or the wearing of headscarf for girls. Avoiding a more indepth exploration of these sensitive but pressing issues does not help Muslim students to grapple with the realities and perplexities surrounding them, especially when they are being confronted with frequent news on the American troops in Afghanistan and the sufferings of the Palestinians. Given that the students are inevitably exposed to these current affairs through the mass media, especially the Internet, there is a need to equip the Muslim students with the wherewithal to critically examine these issues as Muslims *as well as* citizens of Singapore.

Conclusion

This chapter has critiqued Singapore state's conception of communitarianism that underpins the concept of a "good" Muslim citizen in Singapore. It explained how the Singaporean state attempts to assert its communitarian ideology and delegitimize alternative ideologies through the introduction of the Singapore Muslim Identity Project and Islamic Social Studies. We argued that the state communitarian ideology runs the risk of overemphasizing the homogeneity of the Muslim community and imposing the state ideology on the Muslim citizens. There also exists the inherent tension between treating the Muslims as part of a community and emphasizing individual success through the principle of meritocracy. By analysing the content in the Islamic Social Studies textbooks, we maintained that the communitarian ideology embedded in the textbooks tends to limit the students' learning to surface culture. Furthermore, the content in the textbooks is circumscribed by the official state narrative that focuses on national economic progress and political socialization. A consequence is that students are given limited opportunities to consider, discuss and deliberate on complex and controversial issues relating to religion, ethnicity and identity.

What is recommended is for Singapore Muslim citizens to go beyond learning about the state communitarian ideology such as "racial and religious harmony" to explore important cultural differences and to engage with complex issues on society, culture, nationality, ethnicity and religion. Doing so is to acknowledge the multiple and conflicting attachments, identities and tensions that exist within and between

Muslim communities and the larger societies in which they reside. Such an approach towards citizenship education would highlight the autonomy, creative responses and positive contributions of the Muslims in developing richer identities and understandings into a multireligious society.

Notes

1. Since the 1990s, tertiary education is no longer free for Malay students who come from middle-class family background. But the fees they pay are channeled into a Malay community fund, making tertiary education free for the community as a whole. No such provision is given to non-Malay students or communities.

2. Although the national schools in Singapore are officially secular, national schools which are Christian missionary schools are allowed by the state to retain their traditional religious activities such as chapel or Mass in the school curriculum. But student attendance in these religious activities is not compulsory and no proselytisation to the students is permitted by the Ministry of Education even in these schools. For further discussion on how the Ministry of Education publicly censured a Christian school teacher for attempting to evangelise a student in a national school, see Tan (2008a).

3. Majlis Ugama Islam Singapura (MUIS; Islamic Religious Council of Singapore) was established in 1968 as a statutory body to advise the President of Singapore on all matters relating to Islam in the country. Responsible for setting the Islamic agenda, shaping religious life and forging the Singaporean Muslim identity, MUIS's main functions include the construction and administration of mosques development and management, and the administration of Islamic religious schools and Islamic education. Under section 87 and 88 of the Administration of Muslim Law Act, the control of the madrasahs is vested in MUIS. That only Madrasah Al-Irsyad is directly funded by MUIS is due to their traditional close ties. Even so, the funding from MUIS is still insufficient for the madrasah and it has to raise its own funds to meet its operating costs.

4. The Singaporean government's preference for categorizing Singaporeans into *race* over *ethnicity* or *culture* is a reflection of its colonial history. Chua (2005b) points out that the Singaporean government "extended and intensified the British colonial administrative practice, used throughout its extensive colonies in Asia and Africa, of erasing social cultural differences among the immigrant population, and regrouping them into a smaller number of categories with bigger numbers of individuals" (p. 4; also see Purushotam 1998). The categorization according to race means, for instance, that Javanese, Baweanese and Bugis ethnic groups from the Indonesian archipelago are collectively grouped under the race of 'Malay'.

5. For another example of the contestations and struggles between the Muslim community and the state and among the Muslims themselves in Singapore, see Tan (2010).

6. The verse is "We did indeed offer the trust to the Heavens and the Earth and the Mountains; but they refused to undertake it, being afraid thereof: but man undertook it ..." (Al-Ahzab:72), cited in MUIS, 2008, p. 36.

CHAPTER 9

The Challenge of Identity, Education, and Citizenship for Muslims in a Pluralistic Society: A Case Study of Malaysia

Rosnani Hashim

This chapter examines the path the Malay-Muslims in Malaysia have travelled in establishing and maintaining their identity in the modern context. It examines the educational responses of Malaysia, with a predominantly Muslim population, in molding Muslim identity within the context and needs of a pluralistic society. The discussion proceeds within two contexts: the first is the most immediate context of colonization that bequeathed Malaysia an educational system that catered to the needs of a small elite group, and the second is the larger context of Muslim reform movements beginning in the nineteenth century that made education of Muslims an issue. Malaysia is one of the very few countries in the Muslim world and in Asia that has, since gaining independence, tried to overhaul its educational system to make it more responsive to the needs of all its members while maintaining its Muslim identity.

Historical Context

It is a tradition of Muslims to be able to read their holy book, the Qur'an. And wherever there are Muslims there is bound to be a mosque, which functions both as a place of congregational worship and a community center. From the very early days of Islam one of the functions of a mosque as a community center was for it to serve as a place of learning. Later mosques, or *jami' masjid,* served as institutions of higher learning, as in the Al-Azhar University where besides teaching Muslims to read, interpret, and understand the Qur'an, Muslim laws, or *fiqh,* and the articles of faith, or *aqidah,* were discussed and taught. In Malaysia, Qur'an classes for the purpose of learning existed as early as the advent of Islam. The mosque or *pondok,* an educational institution where students resided in small huts surrounding the teacher's house or mosque, was traditional in its methods. Students sat in a *halaqah* (semicircle) facing the teacher who would read a text and elaborate on its meanings. The texts taught and discussed were time honored classics of traditional sciences such as *Kitab al-Hikam,* and *Ihya' Ulumuddin;* however, no studies except *ulum al-shari'ah* (religious sciences) were offered. Subjects such as mathematics, geography, or history never made the list of subjects that were taught.

Thus, Muslim education always revolved around the Qur'an, even though the vast majority of Malays did not understand the Arabic of the Qur'an. Because of the lack of understanding of Arabic, the role of the *ulama* (religious scholars) became significant because they were relied upon to elaborate and explain the traditional religious sciences in Malay, the mother tongue of the people. Among the famous *ulama* in the eighteenth century were Shaikh Daud al-Fatoni, Shaikh Abd al-Samad Palembani, Shaikh Abdul Rashid Banjar, and Tuan Tabal.

Malaya was colonized by the British beginning in 1786. As a result of the British policy of bringing in indentured laborers from China and India, Malaya became a plural society, defined by Furnivall (1944) as a society composed of "two or more elements or social classes who live side by side as parts of a single political unit without merging into each other" (p. xxii). As the British established themselves in Malaya, they opened government English schools, in addition to missionary schools. Later they opened Malay vernacular schools for the Malays, giving Malays a choice between the Malay vernacular or English school on one hand, and the *pondok* on the other. Thus began the dualistic education system in Malaya, a system that ran along ideological lines between the liberal, secular, and traditional religious. This system, set in place by the British, provided opportunities for higher education only to those attending English schools. The system was maintained even after national independence in 1957.

Modern Malaysian Education

Independence has enabled the Malays[1] in Malaya to reflect on and make choices regarding their identity. They have to make a critical ethical choice regarding their identity in relationship to the world they live in, which has serious consequences for their lives. They may choose to remain Muslims by virtue of the fact that they were born within a Muslim family, or they may choose to accept the responsibility of designing themselves in the light of the Qur'an and the Prophetic Tradition. They may choose to be shaped by the events surrounding them, which in this context means to accept secularization and the Western mode of life, or they may choose to design their lives to be consistent with the Qur'anic principles and goals. It is only by adopting and appropriately applying the latter that they will remain true to their faith and attain success in this life and the hereafter.

By the time Malaysia obtained its independence it had already been transformed into a multicultural, multifaith, and multiethnic society. Malaysia's population in 2008 was 27.73 million with 65 percent Malays and other indigenous (*Bumiputera*) groups, 26 percent Chinese, 8 percent Indians, and 1 percent others (Department of Statistics, 2008). It is comprised of 60.4 percent Muslims, 19.2 percent Buddhists, 9.1 percent Christians, 6.3 percent Hindus, 2.6 percent Confucianists/Taoist/other traditional Chinese religion, and 2.4 percent others. This plurality could be considered positively as a factor that encourages Muslims to recreate their Islamic identity, or it could be viewed negatively as a threat to their identity. Hence the challenge for Muslim educationists in Malaysia is to design a system of education that not only helps to regain Muslims' identity but imbues them with a sufficiently robust historical consciousness to be effective historical actors while simultaneously celebrating diversity without surrendering commonality. If this challenge is successfully met, then the issues of identity and citizenship in a plural society can be resolved.

The only guarantees in the Malaysian constitution that the Malay-Muslims obtained from their colonial masters upon independence was the recognition of their right as the original owners of the land, and acknowledgment of Islam as the official religion of the state, the Malay language as the national language, and the special position of the Malay rulers for their sacrifices in giving up the civil administration of their states to pave the way for the birth of the Federation of Malaya in 1948. The Malays were accorded special rights in terms of education and economic opportunities—in view of their socioeconomic backwardness resulting from the British colonial policy—in exchange for citizenship given to the Chinese and Indian communities. This became the unwritten social contract in Malaysian history. History has witnessed the significance of these constitutional articles in the development of the country after independence, especially in interethnic, intercultural, and interfaith matters and the survival of the nation, in particular the Muslim community. Thus, one can truly appreciate the vision and insight of the architects of the constitution, namely Lord Reid (chair), Sir Ivor Jennings (Britain), Sir William McKell (Australia), Judge B Malik (India), and Judge A. Hamid (Pakistan).

Malaysia adopted cultural pluralism on the eve of its independence as the basic approach toward nation building. In this approach the "members of the different groups are permitted to retain many of their cultural ways, as long as they conform to those practices deemed necessary for the survival of the society as a whole" (Bennett, 1995, p. 86). The cultural pluralists argue that minority ethnic cultures generally contribute to and enrich the host society. Thus, the different groups would retain their languages, customs, religions, and artistic expressions. Upon Independence, the educational policy opted for a pluralistic *primary* education system, tolerating what is now called National-Type Chinese and Tamil primary schools having Mandarin and Tamil as the major medium of instruction respectively, alongside the supposedly premier Malay medium National Schools. It was decided in the Rahman Talib Report in 1961 that there should only be a single National *secondary* school system having Malay, the national language, as its medium of instruction as the most important instrument for national unity. However, alongside this national system there are sixty Independent Chinese secondary schools and about 161 *rakyat* religious secondary schools (BPPI Jakim, 2006) that provide school choice for the Chinese and Muslim communities respectively.

Muslim education and the revival of
the integrated Muslim personality

Ever since Muslim countries gained independence there have been various attempts at regenerating Muslims through education. The seeds of Muslims' reform and independence were planted beginning in the second half of the nineteenth century through the efforts of Muslim reformers such as Jamaluddin al-Afghani and Muhammad Abduh in

Egypt, Sayyid Ahmad Khan and Shah Waliyullah in India, and Mahmud Yunus and Sheikh Tahir Jalaluddin in the Malay Archipelago. With the exception of al-Afghani, who had taken the political course for *islah* (reform) and independence, these other reformers desired change through what was perceived as a more gradual but more rooted means, which was education. They wanted to bring back the notion of Muslim education that is transformative and creative rather than just informative and passive. They desired to bring back the dynamism of Islam that had transformed the *ummah Islamiyya* in its glorious period of the ninth to the thirteenth century (Kazmi, 2006). They aspired to revive the learning culture, the spirit of inquiry, and the freedom of expression that were the trademarks of that period.

Thus Afghani and Abduh called for the reopening of the door of interpretation (*ijtihad*) and the end to blind imitation (*taqlid*). They criticized the *ulama* for being the root of the problem of *taqlid*, for not encouraging fresher solutions to contemporary problems, such as the issue of *halal* meat for Muslims living in non-Muslim lands, polygamy, and a woman's right to choose her lifemate. Abduh attempted to reform the administration and curriculum of al-Azhar University, the mother of Islamic educational institutions then, but failed. His aspiration to see al-Azhar teach the *Muqaddimah* of Ibn Khaldun was dashed. Similarly, his hopes to see the teaching of the natural sciences failed, although he succeeded in minor administrative reforms. Despite these difficulties, the seeds of reform had been planted in his students, who subsequently went on to reform Islamic education throughout the Malay-Riau Archipelago, including Malaya (Othman, 2005).

Gradually the *pesantren* and *pondok* in the Malay-Riau Archipelago were transformed into formal *madrasah* or modern *pondok* where learning was more formal with regular schedules for the various subjects and the set up of modern classrooms. Several "modern" subjects such as mathematics, geography, and English language found their way into the curriculum. However, the content of the *madrasah* was still found wanting in terms of empowering Muslims to be able to write their own narratives and thus fortify their identities because it fell back on the old ways of traditional rote learning. What was required was education that not only focused on the form but also on the substance to transform their lives. This was badly needed because the tendency was and is for Islamic education to be taught in the manner of prescribing the rules of the game, rather than learning to be creative, and to construct new moves within the parameters allowed by the Qur'an. This was essential, in view of the fact that the informative mode of learning associated with traditional education resulted in an ossified identity, in taking the Qur'an literally and ignoring the historical context of being a Muslim, which ultimately endangers their own survival in a competitive, diverse social environment.

But the traditional *madrasah* formed only a minor portion of Muslim education toward the end of the century, the major portion being taken up by the national system of education, which in most cases was the continuation of the education system set up by the colonial masters based on Western liberal, secular ideology. This colonial national education system offered only the acquired sciences without any Islamic religious sciences. That deficiency had to be taken up by supplementary classes offered by other agencies after school hours.

The continuing secular nature of the education system even after independence could be traced to the Muslim political leaders' inability or unwillingless to break free from Western influence which, among other things, has had the debilitating effect of compartmentalizing the lives of Muslims into a spiritual life that was becoming privatized and a public life that became secularized. In extreme cases it was reflected in their inability to reconcile what they believed in and what they knew, which rendered them *qua* Muslims intellectually inert. The identity their professions or roles conferred upon them had priority over their identity as Muslims. To put it more starkly, they exercised their intellect when they were not acting as Muslims, and when acting as Muslims they saw no reason to exercise their intellect (Kazmi and Hashim, 2010).

Islamization of education to foster Muslim identity

The 1970s witnessed the resurgence of Islam following the OPEC oil embargo of 1973, educational programs to help the Malays through the New Economic Policy, the Malay urban movement, large scale movement of Malays into higher education, the Iranian revolution, and the role of *dakwah* organizations like ABIM, Darul Arqam and Jama'atul Tabligh (Hashim, 1996; Mutalib, 1990). This new wave saw Islam not only as religion for worship but also as a way of life. Soon after the First World Conference on Muslim Education in 1977 Muslim intellectuals began strategizing for concrete reform, even to the point of making it a national agenda. Thus, as most reformers of the past, such as Abduh and Sayyid Ahmad Khan resorted to schooling for change, a new generation of Muslim intellectuals, in particular Syed Muhammad Naquib

Al-Attas, Ismail Al-Faruqi and Syed Ali Ashraf, called for changes in the education system, in particular the school curriculum, which was seen as the breeding ground for the secularization of Muslim minds. It was believed that Muslim minds were fed with knowledge that had lost its sacredness and had been secularized and Westernized.

Syed Muhammad Naquib Al-Attas, a Malay scholar, concerned himself with trying to explain his diagnosis of the disease plaguing the *ummah Islamiyya* to the Muslim intellectuals (Al-Attas, 1978). Al-Attas saw the need to fortify Muslims with the proper Islamic worldview that emanates from the Qur'an, whose prescriptions and proscriptions define and express one's identity as a Muslim. It can be viewed as describing a circle where Muslims are to create their respective narratives, that is, to be creative in the ways sanctioned by the Qur'an. Any transgression of the circle would make their narratives as Muslims incoherent. This reflects the importance of the Qur'an for proper action; it helps to transform their minds and see themselves as Muslims before all other things, even their professions.

Al-Attas also argued that those who held political power in Muslim nations were themselves corrupted and confused, and propagated this confusion or "loss of *adab*," that is the confusion in the hierarchy of knowledge and values, through the use of their power and the national education system. He emphasized the need to de-Westernize or Islamize contemporary knowledge in a curriculum where the *fard 'ayn,* or the *shari'ah sciences,* form the core while the *fard kifayah,* or the philosophical-intellectual sciences, form the parts of the whole (Al-Attas, 1978). In this context, Al-Attas elaborated the needs and nature of the Islamic university, which would have this integrated curriculum as its unifying principle. This was a contrast to the views of the days in which the Islamic university only dealt with the religious, or *fard 'ayn* sciences. He was ultimately able to translate his ideas into The International Institute of Islamic Thought and Civilization (ISTAC), which he founded in 1993.

Ismail Al-Faruqi, an American scholar of Palestinian origin, identified the problems of the *ummah Islamiyya* in an education that is dualistic between religious, traditional education and secular, public education. It lacked, he argued, a clear vision. He called for reform toward integrating the Islamic and secular sciences to end the duality, thus creating an integrated knowledge and curriculum (Al-Faruqi, 1982). He also pointed out the inadequacy of the traditional methods of *ijtihad*[2], which was either restricted to legalistic reasoning or eliminated all rational criteria and standards. But what was most significant about al-Faruqi's work was his clarion call for the Islamization of knowledge, which he delineated in a flowchart designed to attain this end, including the production of Islamicized textbooks in various intellectual disciplines. This effort became the mission of the International Institute of Islamic Thought (IIIT), established in the United States in Virginia in 1981, and later, the International Islamic University Malaysia (IIUM), established in 1983. One prominent scholar of the period, however—Fazlur Rahman—disagreed with both al-Attas and al-Faruqi regarding Islamizing knowledge *('ilm)* because he believed that *'ilm* is neutral (Rahman, 1988). He argued that one has to use knowledge with responsibility and that abandoning that responsibility has resulted in its misuse. He argued that one cannot map knowledge. For him what was more important was the creativity of Muslim minds in constructing knowledge, which he viewed as anything new to those minds.

In the context of Malaysia, however, Al-Attas' and Al-Faruqi's diagnoses of the problem and their remedies in the form of Islamization of contemporary knowledge and an integrated education have been more widely accepted than Fazlur Rahman's. Al-Attas seems to be more rooted in the Malay psyche, history, culture and tradition. In addition, he seems to be more rooted in al-Ghazali, whose influence in the Malay world is deep, especially in *tasawwuf.*[3] In fact, Al-Attas' effort has been described by certain scholars as a neo-Ghazalian Attasian project that:

> represents a blueprint for a philosophical dimension of not only *tahafut*—deconstruction, but also *tajdid*—renaissance. This renaissance does not surrender to modernity or reject it utterly but understands it, confirms its positive aspects and rejects its excesses—just as al-Ghazali did in his engagement with the philosophical foundations of the Avicennian/Aristotelian worldview. With that paradigm well and truly established, change in the Muslim world need not be negotiated by means of western notions of modernity—but in a way that ultimately transcends them (Al-Akiti and Hellyer, 2010, p. 134).

Among the Muslim countries, Malaysia was at the forefront of educational reform in response to the deliberations of the First World Conference on Muslim Education, first by addressing the proper Islamic concept of education, which resulted in the change in the name of the Ministry of Education from *Kementerian Pelajaran* to *Kementerian Pendidikan.* This was in accordance with Al-Attas' concept of *ta'dib,* instead of *tarbiyah,* to mean education in the true sense of *adab,* that is the discipline of the mind and the soul rather than just the body (Al-Attas, 1990). A second key reform involved the formulation, in 1987, of a National Philosophy of Education that is integrated and holistic, and which includes the development of moral and spiritual potential consistent with the spirit of Islamic and universal education and appropriate for a plural society. Yet another reform transformed the basic education curriculum by integrating Islamic and universal moral values beginning in 1989. Other reforms also experimented with transforming university curricula to encompass the perennial and acquired knowledge in all disciplines of studies through the establishment of the IIUM and ISTAC. This move inspired local existing universities to follow suit in some ways, for example in offering a compulsory course on Islamic civilization that has now been changed to Islamic and Asian civilizations.

In this fashion, the Muslims in Malaysia have made their choice of identity. This can be clearly discerned in the mission and vision of IIUM[4] that attempts to integrate Islamic Revealed Knowledge and values in all academic disciplines and educational activities and restore the leading role of the Muslim *ummah* in all branches of knowledge, thereby contributing to the improvement and upgrading of the qualities of human life and civilization. Islamicization of contemporary human knowledge, which proponents of Islamization argue has been tainted with a secular worldview to the point of losing its sacredness, has become the next important mission. Another significant mission of the university is the cultivation of an *ummatic* vision in representatives of the *ummah islamiyya* studying together and thus potentially exemplifying an international community of dedicated intellectuals, scholars, professionals, officers and workers who are motivated by the Islamic world view and code of ethics as an integral part of their work culture (S.A. Idid, 2009).

Education reform and non–Muslim Malaysians

But being a plural society, the Malay community's reassertion of its Muslim identity has raised some tensions with other ethnic communities. Its attempt, since 1987, to put in place an integrated system of education where Islamic values permeate the knowledge and educational ambience faced some complications. Earlier, in 1961, when Islamic Religious Knowledge was seriously introduced into the system for the first time after independence, it did not meet any opposition from the other communities because it was treated as just any other subject. Religion was viewed from the secular perspective as worship and thus, a private matter. The nature of the system, which was still secular and compartmentalized knowledge easily allowed for this arrangement. Thus, in a sense, although religious knowledge was taught, it was not comprehensive and the system was still secular.

However, the reform that began in 1987 was of a different nature. It was a stronger challenge to the secular nature of the school. It moved toward a system based on a philosophy rooted in the people's tradition and thus would dethrone secularization completely. Tensions were, perhaps, inevitable for, as Amy Gutmann (1987) has argued, "we cannot make good educational policy by avoiding political controversy; nor can we make principled educational policy without exposing our principles and investigating their implications" (p. 6). Thus the formulation of the National Philosophy of Education itself deliberately involved representatives of all faiths.[5] It is worded in such a manner that the phrase "based on a firm belief in and devotion to God" is acceptable to all faiths and reaffirms the *Rukun Negara*, that is the nation's ideology drawn up in 1970, the first pillar of which is Belief in God.[6] Due to the differences in their conceptions of God, for the benefit of all Malaysians, the phrase "belief in and devotion to God" had to be interpreted with some latitude to refer to each citizen's conception of god.

Implementation and practical challenges

The next issue confronted by educational reformers in Malaysia was how to translate this integrated curriculum within the National school system. What were the elements that needed to change? In general, the translation of the philosophy into the Integrated Curriculum for Secondary School intended the permeation of sixteen universal values recognized by all the religious faiths. From the Islamic perspective, the integrated curriculum would mean the integration of revealed knowledge with acquired knowledge. This means that faith in Allah ought to be one of the learning outcomes because, as Muslims believe, He is the source of all the sciences—whether revealed or acquired. His signs are manifest in the natural world and also in the Holy Book. Studying these sciences, Muslims believe, provides a means to recognize and consequently obey His Way. Therefore, integrated education and an integrated curriculum from the Islamic perspective would also mean that the Qur'an and the Prophetic Traditions are relevant in all sciences—including acquired sciences such as natural science, mathematics, social studies, and the humanities—and thus should be spelled out in the textbooks. This would be consistent with the effort of Islamicization of knowledge propounded by Muslim scholars. This would be one of the important ways for Muslim students to see the relationship between knowledge and faith, which is one of the major goals of Islamic education. But in practice this has been avoided because the textbooks are meant for all children regardless of faith. Thus the textbook remains faith neutral, emphasizing the concept of a universal God and universal values. It is left to Muslim teachers' personal efforts, and the informal and hidden curricula, to do the job of instilling Islamic values in other subjects besides Islamic Education (Islamic Studies). Thus, in a sense, the mission of Islamicization and integration of knowledge has been left hanging due to the plural nature of the society.

In its moral aspects, the integrated curriculum was also interpreted as acknowledging good universal values across all subject matter, not only in the Islamic education or moral education classes, in order to promote the internalization of these values in students' lives. On the practical side, the integrated curriculum also means the consistency between theory and practice. This means translating the theoretical understanding of Islam into practice: simply knowing that a Muslim prays five times a day is not adequate. It is important that schools also facilitate its practice. Thus, it became important for a school to have *musalla* (prayer rooms) or a prayer hall. Supplication or Qur'anic verses are sometimes recited in school assemblies or functions. Consequently, the ambience of the National Malay medium schools, especially the primary schools that are populated mostly by Muslim children, was transformed to absorb the Islamic ethos, just as the National-Type primary Chinese and Tamil schools absorbed theirs.

The integrated curriculum also allows for complete compliance with the modest Islamic dress code, which is more obvious for the girls than the boys, whose attires are already in keeping with it. The female dress code now allows female students to cover their heads with the *tudung* (head cover), in contrast to the earlier period when it was shunned by the schools. Consequently, as a natural course, sports attire has also changed from shorts to slacks for both boys and girls. But in all these changes students are given the right to choose. Thus, in a sense, the integrated curriculum has succeeded in laying the foundation of a

Muslim identity that had been diluted almost to the point of nonexistence during the colonial period.

Even more significant was the establishment of National Religious Secondary Schools (*Sekolah Menengah Kebangsaaan Agama*), which offer foundations for specialization in both the acquired and Islamic sciences for higher education and Arabic language. Unlike the other national schools, teachers in these schools are more free to integrate Islamic religious principles with the other sciences. Thus, the system succeeded in producing professionals who are Muslims first and professionals second rather than the other way around, as it was in the past.

The integrated curriculum is not only confined to basic schooling, however, but is also implemented at the university level, especially at the IIUM, which has adopted it as one of its missions. Thus, many of the courses taught in the various disciplines such as Medicine, Natural Sciences, and Engineering offer Islamic and Western perspectives, especially in the social sciences. The Qur'an, the Prophet's Tradition and classic works of Muslim scholars of the past are included in the readings as part of the effort to reclaim the conversation with the Islamic tradition. Arabic and English are the media of instruction and students are required to be competent in at least one language. The university is open to all Malaysian students—Muslims and non-Muslims alike.

Revitalizing and empowering the Islamic Education curriculum

In line with the education reform of the 1980s, the Islamic education syllabus was revised and empowered. The Islamic worldview that forms the core of Al-Attas' ideas was introduced in the curriculum so that Muslim students would better appreciate Islam as a way of life and not just go through the physical motion of worship thoughtlessly as mute performers of rites and rituals. With the proper *weltanschaaung*, they would be able to understand Islam as a whole, understand the concept of God, the Prophet, knowledge, the universe, the Qur'an, man himself, and also the human–God, human–Creation, and human–human relationship. The history of Muslim scholars such as al-Ghazali, Ibn Sina and the four *Imam* of the schools of jurisprudence, and reformers such as Jamaluddin Afghani and Muhammad Abduh, became part of the curriculum in order to acquaint students with the greater Islamic heritage and civilization.

The Qur'anic verses that form the content of the syllabus were also revised so that those that call for Muslims to be transformative rather than passive recipients were selected. The spirit of the Qur'an that elevates the possessor of knowledge and exhorts Muslims to think creatively and be of service to mankind were disemminated. The idea is to inform students of the role of the Qur'an in spurring Muslims to seek knowledge. The importance of spirituality in Islamic education was also given consideration when the practice of prayers was incorporated in schools along with the the recitation and understanding of the Qur'an. *Jawi* (Malay language written in the Arabic alphabets), *al-Qur'an*, Arabic and *Fard 'Ayn* or J-QAF was introduced in primary schools to ensure that pupils really grasp the fundamentals of the religion.

Despite the curricular changes noted above, there has been no emphasis on pedagogical changes. Teaching is still subject-centered, especially among graduates from Middle Eastern universities such as al-Azhar in Cairo. Information and communication technologies that could make teaching more interesting through the use of materials such as video clips of real phenomena and also the internet have not been attempted. More importantly, the pedagogy of philosophical inquiry, which involves examination of central and common concepts, especially those found in the Qur'an, such as *halal* (allowable), *haram* (forbidden), *fikr* (contemplation) and *iqra'* (read) through deliberation and discussion have not been been applied. This important pedagogical tool, which is based on wondering and questioning, a legacy of Islamic learning of the past and also consistent with the spirit of the Qur'an, ought to be revived (Hashim, 2009). This is crucial if Muslims are to create their own narratives that are relevant to their own historical context in the future.

Non-Muslims' response to the reassertion of Muslim identity in education

What are the non-Muslims' response to these gradual changes in the education curriculum? At the level of basic education, due to the universal nature of the moral values to be inculcated in the curriculum, the integrated curriculum did not face much criticism. Moral education is offered to the non-Muslims. In fact, the National-Type primary schools—Chinese and Tamil—have more freedom to inculcate their cultural values in addition to the moral values prescribed in the curriculum than the National Malay Medium primary schools because of the homogeneity of their student population. This is a unique aspect of Malaysian education with regard to transmission of values. Each ethnic group has the right to inculcate its culture and values among its children during primary education due to the plural and segregated primary education system.

However, the secondary school is more heterogenous and thus the reassertion of Muslim identity can only be done within a certain limitation so as not to offend non-Muslim communities. The nature of discussion and inculcation of values is quite dependent on the context—whether it is an all Muslim or a mixed class. But being in a Muslim society and being in schools with Muslim children has sensitized most non-Muslim students to the activities and requirements of Muslims, such as their five daily prayers, and manner of greeting and dress codes and this is evident in adult social lives.

We rarely hear of cases where Islamic norms are imposed on non-Muslim students. At most it would be having to maintain silence as the short supplication (*doa*) is being recited in the school assembly or at the beginning of the class. However, we do hear of Muslim students being compelled by school regulations to adhere to the Islamic dress code and perform other duties. The curtailment of Muslim students' rights is sometimes much worse, such as forbidding Muslim male students from putting on the *serban* (headgear) or *jubah* (long flowing garment) in emulation of the tradition of the Prophet, which is allowable in the private or *rakyat* (community) religious schools. Though parents did take the MoE to court on this matter, they lost the case.

Some non-Muslim parents could not tolerate the Islamic ethos of the National Malay medium primary schools, especially recitation of the *doa* and the Qur'an and the lack of the use of Mandarin and thus prefer to send their children to the National-Type Primary schools, Independent Chinese or private secondary schools. But it is also equally true that many prefer the National Type Primary schools because they are assured that these schools will instill their own cultural ethos, rather than any antagonism to the Islamic ethos (Ye, 2003).

At the tertiary level, with the existence of many private and public universities and colleges since the Private Higher Education Institution Act of 1996, Malaysians do not face a problem in acquiring higher education. Thus, there is no longer a problem related to the reassertion of Muslim identity as, there was in the past when a quota system was applied for admission into public universities. Ethnic rather than religious groupings are still distinct, probably due to differences of cultural, language and school background as well as racial prejudices.

However, Malay and Chinese students do mix freely and easily with other international students in the campuses.

Reassertion of Muslim identity in
the larger Malaysian society

School mirrors society; therefore, it is important to examine the reassertion of Muslim identity in the larger Malaysian social context. Living in a plural society is not, theoretically, a problem for Muslims because Islam is by nature plural, that is Muslims are comprised of people of different nationalities, languages and races. The annual assembly in Makkah for the pilgrimage is a true manifestation of the plurality of Islam as is also manifested in the Qur'an.[7] Islam has also taught Muslims to live among people of various faiths with an attitude of mutual respect and tolerance, and to respect all houses of worship, even those belonging to other faiths, just as it expects others to respect the Muslim's house of worship.

However in practice, living together with people of different races, languages, and faiths is bound to cause conflict. This certainly is true for Malaysia, where many intricate and complex cases involving both parties—Muslims and non-Muslims—have been brought to court in an attempt to find a fair resolution. Among them are cases of *khalwat*, that is close proximity between unwed men and women one of whom is a Muslim, where only the Muslim is charged because the court has no jurisdiction over non-Muslims. Others involve interfaith marriages where problems arise when the marriage does not work and the partner who converts desires to return to his or her original faith. Non-Muslim civil marriages in which the husband converts to Islam but his wife decided otherwise have also wound up in court. Cases involving the death of converts who did not inform spouses, parents, or children of their conversion for fear of threats to their lives have resulted in a commotion when their burials are claimed by two parties, as have cases of Muslim women who would like to apostate in order to marry non-Muslim men as in the famous case of Azlina Jailani (Lina Joy).[8] One of the most recent and most explosive controversies involves the use of the word "Allah" for God by the *Herald*, a Borneo Catholic Church publication, despite several prior prohibitions of its use by the Ministry of Home Affairs.[9] These cases drew a lot of sentiment from the general public, each side giving arguments and debates and had there been no self-restraints, it could have developed into serious conflicts.

However, there are also religion-related cases involving only Muslims such as moral policing done by officials from the Islamic Religious Department to prevent social ills and moral crimes that have been rising by policing certain premises such as hotels and nightclubs, based on tips given by members of the public who are upset by immoral behaviors, *khalwat,* adultery, and illicit premarital sex. Even recently, the Shari'ah court has implemented the Islamic law of *hudud,* that is caning, for adultery. These cases drew criticisms and debates especially, between the moderate and liberal Muslims, to the extent that the latter are often regarded as anti-Islam, as in the case of Dr M. Asri, the former *Mufti* of Perlis, Farish Noor, and the Sisters-in-Islam. Instead of using such opportunities for dialogue, Muslim authorities often prefer to appeal to the authority of the law or the King, violating the spirit of freedom of expression in Islam. Sometimes non-Muslim organizations, such as Woman's Aid Organization (WAO) and non-Muslim political parties such as Malayan/Malaysian Chinese Association (MCA) and the Democratic Action Party (DAP) criticized these issues as infringing on individuals' rights despite the actor being a Muslim. In such cases these organizations are often put off by asking them not to interfere in Muslims' affairs. One consequence therefore of the reassertion of Muslim identity seems to heighten the fear of non-Muslims toward Islam and affirm their perceptions, which have been influenced by the already biased and prejudiced Western media, especially after September 11, 2001.

Discussion on Malaysian citizenship and communal identity

Despite the good intentions and efforts of the Ministry of Education, several weaknesses were evident from the reforms for an integrated and holistic education. The role of the National Philosophy of Education (NPE) would be to provide direction for the National Education system based on the type of citizens envisaged. It is clear that the NPE desires to produce a Malaysian citizen who is knowledgeable, competent and possess excellent moral character and is of service to him/herself, society and humanity at large. However, the NPE fails to give any attention to the goal of national unity as has been emphasized in the Razak Report of 1956 and the Education Act of 1961 that formed the foundation of the Malaysian system of education. Not much has been done in this area, except for the Vision primary schools where the three types of National schools are built in adjoining areas and share the same canteen, sports field and some school activities. But this does not look like a practical solution because learning is still segregated and one cannot find a multiple of three such schools in every locality. Even the spirit of the Vision school seems to be waning.

There have been debates in the mass media for a single national school system, but so far there has been no action, strategy, or development. We have to heed Gutmann (1987)'s advice that sometimes the interest of the state precedes the interest of parents and educators. The state has the right to plan for a long term solution even if it is controversial instead of sweeping it under the carpet. Ethnic relations, especially prejudice and mistrust in Malaysia, do not seem to improve despite the fifty years of Independence and improved economic conditions. In this context, the authoritarian Lee Kuan Yew of Singapore was probably more successful than the Malay leaders in his firmness. This also reveals how tolerant or weak the Malay-Muslim leaders have been.

In 2005 Civics and Citizenship education was reintroduced as a core school subject for all so that it provides the space for discussing "sensitive" yet crucial matters, such as the social contract, Malay special rights, and citizenship. However, the way this subject is taught defeats its purpose because there is little meaningful discusssion on the pretext of fear of being misconstrued. Ethnic relations are also being introduced in the university as a compulsory course, but the sensitivity to the content is evident when the textbook used in Universiti Putra Malaysia had to be withdrawn upon the denial of the Chinese community of certain historical facts.

What is evident from the discussion above is that a common Malaysian identity has not yet been formed despite fifty years of independence, but what has developed is a form of a hypenated ethnic-national identity (Hashim and C. Tan, 2009). The education system has not been able to forge a national identity due to many factors. Basically, due to historical reasons, the political parties in Malaysia are communal-based where each major party represents an ethnic community and loosely unites in an alliance. The concept of power-sharing has been successful in the past due to its ability to bargain and contain its members.

In addition, the pluralistic primary school system strengthens communal allegiance, racial stereotypes and prejudices, especially communal identities that weaken national identity. The idea of a single school system failed because the bulk of the Chinese community has a very strong affiliation to their language and cultural identity, and from the perspective of many Malays, harbors feelings of cultural superiority. Ye (2003) argues that many in the Chinese community look down upon the National Malay-medium schools and the Malays in general asserting that, "in Malaysia, Chinese superiority also rests on the notion that the Malays are culturally inferior, but this is an unfounded belief based on ignorance of Malay History.... They consistently underestimate Malay capability" (p. 111).

Furthermore, the affirmative actions taken under the New Economic Policy in the aftermath of the May 13, 1969 racial conflicts, has sharpened the wedge between these two major ethnic groups.[10] The NEP was to improve the social and economic conditions of the Malay-Muslims through eradicating rural poverty and restructuring society by breaking job identification according to ethnic group. To achieve this the government established the Malay-medium Universiti Kebangsaan Malaysia for students from the Malay-medium secondary schools, science colleges and schools, university matriculation programs, awarded scholarships to deserving Malay students to pursue their studies overseas and set up a quota system based on population ratio for admission into the local universities and colleges. Economically, all private companies were required to have at least 30 percent Bumiputra participation. The Chinese felt that asserting the Malay special rights as assured in the constitution has made them now the second class citizens. The generation that experienced these policies definitely felt bitter.

In actual fact, the affirmative actions have been more successful in Malaysia than in many other countries, including the United States. Statistically, these policies did not deprive the Chinese of their economic share, and it also helped in giving upward mobility to the Malays, which also resulted in an increase in their self-confidence (Hashim, 2005; Ye Lin-Sheng, 2003). However, as Ye (2003) argues, many Chinese reject these positive views of affirmative action policies.

Conclusion

Malaysia has come a long way in dismantling the educational system it inherited from the colonial rulers, a system that preeminently served the social, political, and economic needs of an elite group, and putting in place a system that is more responsive to the socioeconomic and religious needs of the masses. Aside from the tensions that arise due to its plural nature, and with the exception of the May 13, 1969 Crisis, the Malaysian communities have been able to live in relative harmony ever since their independence. The relatively harmonious coexistence of Muslims and non-Muslims in Malaysia is testament to Malaysia's successful Muslim leadership and principles of tolerance and mutual respect guided by its *Rukun Negara*. The existence of a plural system of Chinese and Tamil National-Type vernacular schools[11], the freedom of worship, the freedom to acquire economic wealth, freedom to establish private schools, colleges and universities have all helped to stabilize this spirit of co-existence. In this regard the Malay-Muslims have most conspicuously shown an attitude of accommodation and tolerance that is actually embedded in their Islamic culture and world-view. It is hoped that non-Muslim citizens will take notice of the positive effect Islam has on the Malays and thus reject efforts to equate them with the actions of other Muslims in other parts of the world, for Islam is not monolithic. Nonetheless, the rise of Muslim identity has triggered two kinds of responses from among the non-Muslim citizens. For some there is a feeling of optimism because it means the Malays have set a higher Islamic standard of performance, behaviour and tolerance in order to become a model Islamic country . For others, however, it has triggered pessimism due to the bad press Islam has been getting, especially post September 11. Widespread Western prejudice against Islam lessens its appeal to the Chinese community (Ye 2003, 145).

The effects of the educational reform that began in the late 1980s to address Muslim identity through an integrated curriculum are beginning to bear fruit. Muslims have a better understanding of their faith, the language of the Qur'an, their identity and thus, their responsibility. This is important, especially for their progress in this world and to help avoid blind indoctrination, religious deviation and blind imitation. Progress has also been made in the economic field with the introduction of Islamic banking, insurance and other investment tools that have also benefited non-Muslims. The duality that still bothers Muslims in their aspiration to realize Islam as a way of life in Malaysia lies in the dualistic legal system—having shari'ah and civil courts—which has resulted in inter-faith problems such as those mentioned earlier. Justice is a very important virtue in Islam, which it equates to piety. Peace is another important attribute of Islam as indicated by the meaning of the word *aslam*, from the same root as *Islam*. In this sense the shari'ah courts have yet to transform themselves to be non-Muslims friendly and win their confidence as a better system. In living in a diverse community, "what it is to be a Muslim" should be emphasized more than "who is a Muslim" so that Muslims are cognizant of others around them and the social context. Despite the progress that has been made in this regard many Chinese continue to feel that their opportunities are restricted, while many Malay-Muslims feel that they have given so much.

Clearly, Malaysia has yet a long way to go in developing an educational system that would be responsive and speak to the cultural diversity of the Malaysian people by helping to create a national consciousness that primes cultural communities to see each other as neighbors, and although different, not aliens. An educational system that is inspired by the Islamic culture of learning encourages learning from and about each other to knit a unitary nation out of multicultural strands in order to be true to its celebrated advertisement, "Malaysia, truly Asia." It also encourages *husn al-zann* (good thoughts) instead of *su'u al-zann* (bad thoughts) regarding others' actions.[12] Malaysia has progressed well in economic prosperity and its people do live a relatively comfortable life. Thus, this should be the right time for the government to really foster a Malaysian identity. In this context, it should think of educational reform for fostering the concept of "1Malaysia," which is the slogan of the present administration, instead of merely economics and physical development which, if based on greed alone, will never succeed in forging a national identity. The government should continue social restructuring so that more non–Malays can participate in the public sector while more Malays should participate in the private sector to allow for interethnic interaction and the breakdown of stereotypes. It is thus imperative for the diverse communities to look to moral, spiritual and religious values that transcend racialistic and materialistic values in the aspiration to achieve lasting good, justice and peace.

Notes

1. In the context of Malaysia, the Malays are synonymous with Muslims. The member of the race is defined as one who professes Islam and adopts the Malay language and customs in his or her daily life. There are of course a growing number of Muslims of Chinese and Indian origins.
2. *Ijtihad* is interpretation of the Qur'an through exerting one's reason.
3. *Tasawwuf* is the Arabic term for the inner, mystical dimension of Islam, also known as sufism. It is a science whose objective is the purification of the heart and turning it away from all else but God through *dhikir* or remembrance and asceticism.
4. The mission is well known as IIICE or Triple ICE, that is Islamization, Integration, Internationalization and Comprehensive Excellence.

5. The National Philosophy of Education states: Education in Malaysia is an on-going effort toward further developing the potential of individuals in a holistic and integrated manner, so as to produce individuals who are intellectually, spiritually, emotionally and physically balanced and harmonious, based on a firm belief in and devotion to God. Such an effort is designed to produce Malaysian citizens who are knowledgeable and competent, who possess high moral standards, and who are responsible and capable of achieving a high level of personal well being as well as being able to contribute to the harmony and betterment of the society and the nation at large. See Rosnani Hashim, *Educational Dualism in Malaysia,* 159.

6. The other four pillars of *Rukun Negara* are (2) Loyalty to King and Nation; (3) Upholding the Constitution; (4) Rule of Law; and (5) Good behavior and morality.

7. See al-Qur'an 49:13 states: "O mankind! We created you from a single (pair) of a male and a female, and made you into nations and tribes, that you may know each other. Verily the most honored of you in the sight of Allah is (he who is) the most righteous of you."

8. Her case was brought to civil court instead of the Shari'ah court but was rejected by the civil judges since it was determined to be under the jurisdiction of the Shari'ah court. Questions of intention were raised because of the international attention it drew, including that of the US Congress.

9. This drew objections from Muslim Religious Departments and NGOs who desire to maintain the purity of Allah and the faith, arguing that Allah is not the Malay term for God, *Tuhan* is. In the view of Muslims, Allah is reserved for the One God. Many Muslims were not happy with the court decision allowing *Herald* to use the term on the ground that it does not pose a problem to national security. Consequently, several youth who cannot restraint themselves attacked three churches and have been arrested. Probably, that was enough evidence on national security and the decision has been suspended.

10. The May 13, 1969 racial conflict occurred after the May 10 general election during which the DAP won more seats than the MCA which has traditionally been representing the Chinese constituencies due to Chinese chauvinistic issue. The Malay had suppressed their grievances against the government especially the lack of opportunity for higher education in the national language and this incident provided an avenue to vent out their anger especially after being provoked by the DAP victory procession which turned into a bloodshed killing approximately 190. An emergency was declared, the parliament was suspended and democracy was only restored in 1971.

11. According to the Minority Rights Group Report on the Chinese in South-East Asia (1992), "Malaysia has Southeast Asia's most comprehensive Chinese-language system of education" (p. 2). Tan (1997) argues that the Chinese schools in Malaysia are unique because "Even in Singapore, where the Chinese constitute more than 75 percent of the population and where Mandarin as a language is taught more extensively than before, schools teaching entirely in Chinese no longer exist" (p. 1).

12. Refer to the Qur'an 49:12 which states: "O ye who believe! Avoid suspicion as much (as possible), for suspicion in some cases is a sin; and spy not on each other, nor speak ill of each other behind their back..."

AFTERWORD

Education, Islam, and the Secular State in Turkey

AHMET T. KURU

The editors and contributors of this book made a wise decision in attaching importance to education in their analysis of Muslims' identities and citizenship status. In many countries, schools have a central position in public debates on religion and politics given their importance for shaping identities, mindsets, and behaviors of the next generation. My brief essay engages with two main themes of this book: (a) the theoretical analysis of Muslims' relations with and integration to non-Muslim sociopolitical contexts, and (b) the empirical examination of school systems inspired by Islamic faith and practice. I aim to contribute to the exploration of these themes by the theoretical discussion of the two types of secularism and the empirical analysis of the Turkish case.

Theoretical and empirical analyses of this book successfully bring together cases where Muslims are either a majority (Pakistan, Malaysia, and Indonesia) or a minority (Britain and Singapore). In fact, particular state ideologies are generally more important than being a majority or minority in a country, in terms of Muslims' freedoms of religious expression, education, and association. I wish to focus on secular state ideologies, of which there are two types. "Passive secularism" requires the state to play a passive role by allowing public visibility of religion. "Assertive secularism," however, demands that the state play an assertive role in excluding religion from the public sphere (Kuru 2009). Muslim minority groups often have more liberties in countries where passive secularism is dominant, such as the United States and Canada, than the Muslim majorities under assertive secularism such as those in

Uzbekistan and Tunisia. Thus the classical terms of *dar al-harb* (adobe of war) and *dar al-Islam* (adobe of Islam) are no longer relevant to Muslims' daily lives and sociopolitical conditions.

Schools are contested institutions under both passive and assertive secularism. In the United States, for example, although passive secularism is dominant, its various interpretations are struggling to shape schooling as seen in recent debates over the reference to God in the pledge of allegiance or school vouchers providing public money to parents for religious schools' tuition. But schools are perhaps even more contested spaces under assertive secularism, such as in France and Turkey where this model is dominant. In both countries passive secularists are challenging state policies toward religion in schools.

In France, Muslims constitute the largest minority (8 percent) with a population of five million, but they have experienced many obstacles in constructing mosques and opening schools due to historical and financial reasons, as well as bureaucratic restrictions (Conseil d'Etat 2004:318–9). In French politics, right wing parties have generally supported pro-Catholic views against the assertive secularist leftist politicians. Public funding of Catholic schools was a major controversial issue between these two groups from 1984 to 1994. Yet in the headscarf debate, which took place over a longer period of time (1989–2004), right wing Islamophobes allied with left wing assertive secularists to support a general ban. In contrast, multiculturalists among both rightists and leftists largely opposed the headscarf ban and defended passive secularism. Eventually, the alliance between Islamophobes and assertive secularists dominated public opinion and led to the ban on religious symbols, especially Muslim headscarves, in public schools.

Turkey, despite the dominance of assertive secularism, is still the prime example of inconsistent and even contradictory state policies toward religion in schools. On the one hand, the Turkish state funds religious education through obligatory religious instruction in public schools, the public Islamic (Imam-Hatip) schools, and the state run Qur'an courses. On the other hand, the Turkish state has exclusionary policies toward religious education. Private Islamic education is forbidden and the educational institutions of Christians and Jews have faced bureaucratic obstacles. For example, the only seminary of the Greek Orthodox Church, Halkalı Seminary, was closed down in the 1970s for reasons having to do with the Greco-Turkish conflict over Cyprus and it never reopened. Wearing the headscarf also is banned in all educational institutions; so is teaching the Qur'an to children under fifteen (it is only permitted for those between the ages of twelve and fifteen in summer courses). Graduates of the Imam-Hatip schools are given a lower coefficient to calculate their scores in the nationwide university admission exam, which makes their enrollment in any university extremely difficult.

The Janus-faced image of state policies toward religious education is associated with two opposing tendencies in Turkey. Assertive secularism, which aims to exclude religion from the public sphere and confine it to the private sphere, is the official ideology of the Turkish state. Yet at the same time Turkish society is highly religious. Ninety-nine percent of the people in Turkey are Muslim and about seventy percent of them observe Muslim worship at least once a week (Friday prayer in mosque for men and daily prayer for women). Accordingly, the interaction between the assertive secularist state and religious society has resulted in the contradictory state policies toward religion.

Given its aim to confine religion to the private domain, the Turkish state has tried to control Islam, instead of establishing a true state-religion separation. Thus the framers of the assertive secularist republic in the 1920s founded the Directorate of Religious Affairs (Diyanet) to control all mosques. Because the state confiscated all Islamic foundations, it was necessary to pay imams' salaries with public funds. Similarly, the Turkish state opened Imam-Hatip schools because it had closed down all public and private madrasas. Later, however, it even closed down the Imam-Hatip schools. The "golden era" of assertive secularism was the period from 1933 to 1949 when there were no legal institutions to teach Islam except for few Qur'an courses in some villages.

The transition from single-party rule to multi-party democracy in 1950 played an important role in the moderation of assertive secularism in Turkey. Right wing parties with a passive secularist background and friendly policies toward Muslims have received overwhelming popular support in parliamentary elections from the 1950s to present. Although they could not abolish assertive secularist state ideology protected by the military and the judiciary, these politicians have still been able to improve the conditions of Muslims (and recently non-Muslims) in Turkey, particularly in terms of their demands for religious education.

The transformation from the "Islamic" Ottoman Empire to the assertive secularist Turkish Republic had a deep impact on the Islamic actors' relationship toward the state. Said Nursi (1876–1960) was an Islamic thinker and activist who sought to open a university in Eastern Anatolia that would teach various scientific disciplines together with Islamic sciences. For him, "The light of conscience is religious sciences and that of mind is modern sciences. Their combination reveals the truth. Equipped with both, the student flourishes. If these two are separated, the former produces bigotry, while the latter gives birth to deceit and skepticism" (1996:1956). For founding such a synthesizing university—namely Medresetü'z-Zehra, as the sister of Al-Azhar—Nursi asked for funding from two Ottoman sultans and then the Republic's founding parliament. Although the second sultan and parliament promised him financial support, this did not come to fruition for several reasons including the First World War and later the secularization of the republic. Nursi realized that the assertive secularist state would never fund an Islamic university. Therefore, during the last thirty-six years of his life Nursi disassociated himself from the statesmen while focusing on the writing of his 6,000-page collection of pamphlets (*Risale-i Nur Külliyatı*) and its dissemination among the masses with the help of villagers and a few university students (Kuru and Kuru 2008).

Fethullah Gülen (1938–) may be regarded as an intellectual successor of Nursi. In the late 1960s, Gülen initiated a social movement that currently runs more than 1,000 schools and 10 universities in about 100 countries around the world.[1] The movement is also affiliated with media outlets, business associations, intercultural dialogue institutes, and charity organizations worldwide.[2] Unlike Nursi's approach during his early years, Gülen did not seek public funding for his movement's schools; instead, the Gülen movement depended on private donors from various segments of society in Turkey and abroad. In other words, the secularization of the Turkish state structure instigated the "privatization" of Turkish Islamic actors' educational activities. Facing state oppression, or at least the lack of state patronage, these actors strengthened their ties with society, where they have found a reliable source of support. As another impact of the secular state in Turkey and other countries, the Gülen movement's schools and universities pursue exclusively secular curricula, unlike Nursi's Medresetü'z-Zehra, which was designed to synthesize modern and Islamic sciences (Kuru 2003).

The Gülen movement is a rare example of a transnational educational movement. Conversely, other school systems discussed in this volume are largely bound by state borders. While several chapters of the volume examine philosophical and societal dimensions of Islam and education, this essay has analyzed its more explicitly political aspects. While doing so, I have largely emphasized the controversial relations between the secularist state, Islam, and education. Though I have highlighted various ways that secular states may utilize schools as instruments of ideological domination, education can, in fact, be used for conflict resolution. Education, for example, can play a crucial role in hindering the mutual reproduction of Islamophobia and anti-Westernism. Analyzing citizenship, identity, and integration, this book rightly combines studies on Muslim majorities and Muslim minorities, because we live in an increasingly globalized world where problems of ethnoreligious conflict and xenophobia are spreading internationally. Successful educational systems, which may aid in providing solutions to these problems, can promote toleration and integration in both Muslim-majority and non-Muslim-majority societies.

Notes

1. See Pelin Turgut, "Muslim Missionary: The Preacher and His Teachers," *Time*, April 26, 2010; Sabrina Tavernise, "Turkish Schools Offer Pakistan a Gentler Vision of Islam," *New York Times*, May 4, 2008.
2. In this volume Andrew March discusses some Islamic legal opinions about Muslims' residence in non-Muslim-majority countries. Gülen, who has lived in the United States since 1999 and encouraged his sympathizers to open institutions in non-Muslim-majority countries, would constitute an interesting case for March's analysis.

Postscript

MICHAEL S. MERRY AND
JEFFREY AYALA MILLIGAN

As this book goes to print, the city of New York is wrestling anew with what it means to be a free and open society. Plans to build an Islamic cultural center only blocks from Ground Zero have unleashed powerful emotions not only from families of victims but also from ordinary citizens throughout the United States and elsewhere. These emotions give the lie to the idea that anti-Muslim or anti-Islamic sentiment in the United States is the monopoly of the far right or a lunatic fringe. Rather, Ground Zero has become the epicenter of the search for the ever-elusive overlapping consensus between democratic principles and Islamic beliefs.

The controversy occasioned by talk of an Islamic cultural center illustrates both the distance we have yet to travel to achieve such a consensus and the heartfelt desire of so many to reach that goal. The debate in New York, however, resonates far beyond the confines of that city, testing not only whether Islam and Muslim communities can embrace democracy—a theme of several of the contributions in this book—but also whether liberal democracy, as understood and practiced by majorities in the United States and Europe, can embrace Muslims.

The hopes and tensions manifested in this controversy are powerfully expressed in two recent speeches in response to the plans to build the Islamic cultural center in lower Manhattan. On August 3, 2010, New York Mayor Michael Bloomberg, flanked by religious leaders of various faiths, delivered an impassioned defense of the plans to build the Islamic cultural center as an expression of the religious tolerance enshrined in the traditions of American democracy. In his speech he invoked the history of immigration to the United States, symbolized in the background by the Statue of Liberty; the rich cultural and religious diversity of contemporary New York; the common experience of religious intolerance shared by Jews, Catholics, and Muslims; and the slow evolution of principles of religious tolerance that gradually came to embrace Jews and Catholics as fellow citizens. This common experience, he argued, should embrace Muslims as well. The need to defend this right only a short time ago would have seemed odd, perhaps even unnecessary, in New York City, where persons of myriad cultural and religious backgrounds have blended for four hundred years. But something had changed. "Muslims are as much a part of our city and our country as the people of any faith," Bloomberg reminded his audience. "And they are as welcome to worship in lower Manhattan as any other group." He concluded his speech with an explicit invocation of American democratic tradition, saying "political controversies come and go, but our values and traditions endure, and there is no neighborhood in this city that is off-limits to God's love and mercy."

Five weeks later, on the ninth anniversary of the 9/11 attacks, a very different kind of speaker, this time arriving from Europe, stepped to the platform at Ground Zero with a different purpose: to draw a line. For Geert Wilders, Islam is not a religion but rather a totalitarian ideology, one whose encroaching menace he warned his angry public against. "A tolerant society," he charged, "is not a suicidal society...it must defend itself against the powers of darkness." Invoking references to ancient Middle Eastern conquests, Wilders elicited enthusiastic approval from the audience when he declared, "we must never give a free hand to those who want to subjugate us."

Of course polemicists like Wilders are curiously tone deaf to the incongruities of their belief in freedom and tolerance. In the place of reasoned discussion and debate there is talk of us and them. Rather than acknowledging the perils of extremism wherever they are to be found, he offers the facile belief in Western civilization as the very bastion of broad thinking and mutual respect. "The West has never harmed Islam," he asserted without irony, while in the Netherlands he routinely calls for the closure of all Islamic schools, an immediate cessation to immigration from majority Muslim countries, and a banning of the Qur'an. All references to exclusion, fascism, repression, intolerance, and violence are simply attributed to Islam.

Both Bloomberg and Wilders have their equivalents in countries around the world. Yet these recent events in New York, along with the threat by an obscure Christian pastor in Florida to burn copies of the Qur'an, protests against the construction of mosques in other U.S.

states, and the demonstrations and threats these acts have elicited in Afghanistan, Indonesia, and other parts of the Muslim world, suggest that we all, Muslim and non-Muslim alike, have a lot to learn about the tensions and affinities between religious identity and democratic citizenship. This fact is both an indictment of and a challenge to education in the Muslim world *and* the secular West. Muslim educators must convey an understanding of Islam to their students that foregrounds doctrinally plausible interpretations of religious ideals consistent with democratic principles if democratic citizenship is to take root and flourish throughout the Muslim world.

At the same time, U.S. and European educators must do a better job of teaching their students about Islam and Muslims, about the dreadful history of religious intolerance, and the hard-won principles of religious liberty enshrined in their founding documents if they are to avoid the pitfalls of ethnocentrism and make good on the promise of democratic citizenship for future generations. The imperative is all the more urgent in a world in which lies, misunderstandings, and half-truths circle the globe in an instant. In such a world, ignorance is dangerous. The dissemination of knowledge through education is painfully slow by comparison. But it is the only antidote we've got. It is our fervent hope that the essays brought together in this volume make some modest contribution to the effort.

REFERENCES

Abaza, M. (2002). *Debates on Islam and knowledge in Malaysia and Egypt: Shifting worlds*. London, England: Routledge Curzon.

'Abd al-Qadir, K. (1998). *Fiqh al-aqalliyat al-Muslima*. Tripoli, Libya: Dar al-Iman.

Abdo, G. (2006). *Mecca and main street: Muslim life in America after 9/11*. New York, NY: Oxford University Press.

Abou El Fadl, K. (1994). "Islamic law and Muslim minorities: The juristic discourse on Muslim minorities from the second/eighth to the eleventh/seventeenth centuries." *Islamic Law and Society 1*(2), 141–187.

Abou El Fadl, K. (2004). *Islam and the challenge of democracy*. Princeton, NJ: Princeton University Press.

Abu Dawud, Sulayman ibn al-Ash'ath al-Sijistani. (1997). *Sunan Abi Dawud*. Beirut, Lebanon: Dar Ibn Hazm.

Abuza, Z. *Militant Islam in Southeast Asia: Crucible of terror*. Boulder, CO: Lynne Rienner, 2003.

Adler, S. & Sim, J. B. (2005, June). *Social studies in Singapore: Contradiction and control*. Paper presented at the Redesigning Pedagogy: Research, Policy, Practice Conference, Singapore.

Al-Akti, M. A. & Hellyer, H. A. (2010). The negotiation of modernity through tradition in Contemporary Muslim intellectual discourse. In W.M.N. Daud & Z. Uthman (Eds.), *Knowledge, language, thought and the civilization of Islam*. Skudai, Malaysia: Universiti Teknologi Malaysia.

Al-Attas, S. M. N. (Ed.). (1979). *Aims and objectives of Islamic education*. London, UK: Hodder & Stoughton.

Al-Attas, S. M. N. (1990). *The concept of education in Islam*. Kuala Lumpur, Malaysia: ISTAC.

Al-Faruqi, I. R. (1982). *Islamization of knowledge*. Herndon, VA: IIIT.

Ali, A. Y. (1999). *The meaning of the holy Koran*. (10th ed.). Beltsville, MD: Amana Publications.

An-Na'im, A. A. (1990). *Toward an Islamic reformation: Civil liberties, human rights, and international law*. Syracuse, NY: Syracuse University Press.

An-Na'im, A. A. (2008). *Islam and the secular state: Negotiating the future of shari'a*. Cambridge, MA: Harvard University Press.

Ariff, S. (2002, February 12). Third tudung girl suspended. *The Straits Times*. Retrieved from LexisNexis Scholastic Edition database.

Arthur, J. (1998). Communitarianism: What are implications for education? *Educational Studies 24*(3), 353–368.

Asad, T. (2003). *Formations of the secular: Christianity, Islam, modernity*. Palo Alto, CA: Stanford University Press.

Aspinall, E. (2005). Elections and the normalization of politics in Indonesia. *South East Asia Research 13*(2), 117–156.

Azhar, I. A. (2006, April). *Critical perspectives on contemporary Islamic thought.* Paper presented at conference on Philosophy in Schools: Developing a Community of Inquiry, Singapore.

Azra, A., Afrianty, D., & Hefner, R. W. (2007). Pesantren and madrasa: Muslim schools and national ideals in Indonesia. In R. W. Hefner and M. Q. Zaman, (Eds.), *Schooling Islam: The culture and politics of modern Muslim education.* (pp. 172–198). Princeton, NJ: Princeton University Press.

Bader, V. (Ed.). (2005). Multicultural futures? International approaches to pluralism [Special issue]. *Canadian Diversity, 4*(1).

Bang, H. P., Box, R. C., Hansen, A. P. & Neufeld, J. J. (2000). The state and the citizen: Communitarianism in the United States and Denmark. *Administrative Theory & Praxis 2*(2), 369–390.

Barr, M. D. (2000). Lee Kuan Yew and the Asian values debate. *Asian Studies Review 24*(3), 309–334.

Barry, B. (2001). *Culture and equality.* Cambridge, MA: Polity Press.

Bawer, B. (2006). *While Europe slept: How radical Islam is destroying the west from within.* New York, NY: Doubleday.

Bell, Daniel. (2009). Communitarianism. In E.N. Zalta (Ed.), *The Stanford encyclopedia of philosophy.* Retrieved from http://plato.stanford.edu/entries/communitarianism/

Benford, R. D. and Snow, D. A. (2000). Framing processes and social movements: An overview and assessment. *Annual Review of Sociology 26*, 611–39.

Benhabib, S. (1992). *Situating the self.* New York, NY: Routledge.

Bennett, C. I. (1995). *Multicultural education: Teaching and practices.* Boston, MA: Allyn & Bacon.

Bi, F. (2006, July 3). Re: Alienation, the London bombs, one year on. *openDemocracy.* Retrieved from http://www.opendemocracy.net/articles/ViewPopUpArticle.jsp?id=3&articleId=3704.

Bohman, J. (1996). *Public deliberation: Pluralism, complexity, and democracy.* Cambridge, MA: MIT Press.

Bokhorst-Heng, W. D. (2007). Multiculturalism's narratives in Singapore and Canada: Exploring a model for comparative multiculturalism and multicultural education. *Journal of Curriculum Studies 39*(6), 629–658.

Bowen, J. R. (2007). *Why the French don't like headscarves: Islam, the state, and public space.* Princeton, NJ: Princeton University Press.

Bowen, J. R. (2009). *Can Islam be French? Pluralism and pragmatism in a secularist state.* Princeton, NJ: Princeton University Press.

BPPI, Jakim. (2006). *Data dan Maklumat Sekolah Agama 2006.* Retrieved from http://www.islam.gov.my/lepai/sekolah.html

Brown, G. (2005, April 20–25). Roundtable: Britain rediscovered. *Prospect 109.*

Brown, G. (2006, January). *The future of Britishness.* Keynote speech presented at the Fabian Conference on The Future of Britishness. London. Retrieved from http://www.fabiansociety.org.uk/press_office/news_latest_all.asp?pressid=520.

Bukhari, Muhammad ibn Ismail. (1997). *Sahih al-Bukhari.* al-Riyadh, Saudi Arabia: Dar al-salam.

Cannon, B. (2006, May 4). Britishness, multiculturalism and globalization. *Rising East Online.* Retrieved from http://www.uel.ac.uk/risingeast/currentissue/academic/cannon.htm

Chan, D. (2003). *Attitudes on race and religion survey on social attitudes of Singaporeans (SAS).* Singapore: Ministry of Community Development and Sports.

Chapireau, F. & Colvez, A. (1998). Social disadvantage in the international classification of impairments, disabilities and handicaps. *Soc Sci Med. 47*(1), 59–66.

Chia, S. A. (2005, February 5). Bid to enhance identity of Singapore Muslim: Muis project to help Muslims excel as Muslims and citizens. *The Straits Times.*

Chin, Y. & Vasu, N. (2007). *The ties that bind and blind: A report on inter-racial and inter-religious relations in Singapore.* Singapore: Centre of Excellence for National Security, S. Rajaratnam School of International Studies, Nanyang Technological University.

Chua, B. H. (1995). *Communitarian ideology and democracy in Singapore.* New York, NY: Routledge.

Chua, B. H. (2005a). The cost of membership in ascribed community. In W. Kymlicka & B. He, (Eds.), *Multiculturalism in Asia* (pp. 170–195). Oxford, England: Oxford University Press.

Chua, B. H. (2005b). *Taking group rights seriously: Multiracialism in Singapore.* (Working Paper No.124). Asia Research Centre, Murdoch University.

Chua, B. H. (2007). Political culturalism, representation and the People's Action Party of Singapore. *Democratisation 14*(5), 911–927.

Clark, J. A. (2004). *Islam, charity, and activism: Middle-class networks and social welfare in Egypt, Jordan, and Yemen.* Bloomington, IN: Indiana University Press

Commission on the Future of Multi-Ethnic Britain (CMEB). (2000). *The future of multiethnic Britain.* London: Profile Books.

Conseil d'Etat. (2004). "Rapport public: Réflexions sur la laïcité." http://lesrapports.ladocu-mentationfrancaise.fr/BRP/044000121/0000.pdf, accessed on March 20, 2010.

Cook, D. (2005). *Understanding jihad.* Berkeley, CA: University of California Press.

Dahl, R. (1989). *Democracy and its critics.* New Haven, CT: Yale University Press.

Daniels, N. (1999). Enabling democratic deliberation: How managed care organizations ought to make decisions about coverage for new technologies. In S. Macedo (Ed.), *Deliberative politics: Essays on democracy and disagreement.* New York, NY: Oxford University Press.

Department of Statistics Malaysia. (2008). Retrieved from http://www.statistics.gov.my/eng/index.php?option=com_content&view=article&id=50:population&catid=38:kaystts&Itemid=11

Dewey, J. (1927). *The public and its problems.* New York, NY: H. Holt and Co.

Dhami, R. S., Squires, J. & Modood, T. (2006). *Developing positive action policies: Learning from the experiences of Europe and north America.* London, England: Department of Works and Pensions.

Doomernik, J. (2005). The state of multiculturalism in the Netherlands. *Canadian Diversity, 4*(1), 32–35.

Du Bois, W. E. B. (1999/1903). *The souls of black folk centenary edition.* London, England: Norton Critical Edition.

Elshtain, J. B. (1995). *Democracy on trial.* New York, NY: Basic Books.

European Council for Fatwa and Research. (1999). *Fatawa al-majmu'a al-ula.* Cairo, Egypt: Islamic Publishing.

Fadl Allah, M. H. (1999). *al-Hijra wa al-ightirab: ta'sis fiqhi li mushkilat al-luju' wa al-hijra.* Beirut, Lebanon: Mu'assasat al-'Arif li-al-Matbu'at.

Fattah, M. A. (2006). *Democratic values in the Muslim world.* Boulder, CO: Lynne Rienner. al-Fawzan, S. F. A. A. *Muhadarat fi al-'aqida wa al-da'wa.* Riyadh, Saudi Arabia: Dar al 'Asima.

Fearon, J. D. (1998). Deliberation as discussion. In J. Elster (Ed.), *Deliberative Democracy.* (pp. 44–68). New York, NY: Cambridge University Press.

Feillard, A. & Madinier, R. (2006). *La fin de l'innocence? L'Islam Indonésien face à la tentation radicale de 1967 à nos jours.* Paris, France: IRASEC.

Fetzer, J. S., & Soper, J. C. (2005). *Muslims and the state in Britain, France, and Germany.* New York, NY: Cambridge University Press.

Fish, M. S. (2002). Islam and authoritarianism. *World Politics 55*, 4–37.

Fraser, N. (1992). Rethinking the public sphere. In C. Calhoun (Ed.), *Habermas and the public sphere*, Cambridge, MA: MIT Press.

Freston, P. (2001). *Evangelicals and politics in Asia, Africa and Latin America.* Cambridge, England: Cambridge University Press.

Fromm, E. (1991). *The fear of freedom.* London, England: Routledge.

Furnivall, J. S. (1944). *Netherlands India: A study of a plural economy.* London, UK: Cambridge University Press.

Gadamer, H. G. (1975). *Truth and method.* (G. Barden & J. Cumming, Trans./Eds.). New York, NY: Seabury Press.

Geertz, C. (1965). *The social history of an Indonesian town.* Cambridge, MA: MIT Press.

Geertz, C. (1960, January). The Javanese kijaji: The changing role of a cultural broker. *Comparative Studies in Society and History 2*(2), 228–49.

Gilroy, P. (1987). *There ain't no black in the union jack: The cultural politics of race and nation.* London, England: Heinemann.

Gilroy, P. (2004). *After empire: Melancholia or convivia culture?* Abingdon, England: Routledge.

Guillaume, A. (1955). *The life of Muhammad: A translation of Ishâq's Sîrat rasûl Allâh.* London: Oxford University Press, 1955.

Gutmann, A. (1987). *Democratic education.* Princeton, NJ: Princeton University Press.

Gutmann, A. & Thompson, D. (1996). *Democracy and disagreement.* Cambridge, MA: Harvard University Press.

Gutmann, A. & Thompson, D. (2004). *Why deliberative democracy?* Princeton, NJ: Princeton University Press.

Habermas, J. (1992). Citizenship and national identity: Some reflections on the future of Europe. *Praxis International 12*(1), 1–19.

Habermas, J. (1996). *Between facts and norms: Contributions to a discourse theory of law and democracy.* Cambridge, MA: MIT Press.

Haddad, Y. & Lummis, A. (1987). *Islamic values in the United States.* New York, NY: Oxford University Press.

Haidar, G. (1985, June). Promising exile. *Afkar inquiry 54*, 47–62.

Hall, S. (2000). Conclusion: Multi-cultural questions. In B. Hesse (Ed.), *Un/settled multiculturalisms: diasporas, entanglements, transruptions.* London, England: Zed Books.

Hampshire, S. (2000). *Justice is conflict.* Princeton, NJ: Princeton University Press.

Han, C. (2007). History education and 'Asian' values for an 'Asian' democracy: The case of Singapore. *Compare 37*(3), 383–398.

Hasan, N. (2000). In search of identity: The contemporary Islamic communities in Southeast Asia. *Studia Islamika 7*(3), 57–89.

Hasan, N. (2005). *Laskar Jihad: Islam, militancy and the quest for identity in post-New Order Indonesia* (Unpublished Doctoral Dissertation). University of Utrecht: Utrecht, Netherlands.

Hashim, R. (2004/1996). *Educational dualism in Malaysia: Implications for theory and practice.* Kuala Lumpur, Malaysia: The Other Press.

Hashim, R. (2005). Balancing cultural plurality and national unity through education: The case study of Malaysia. *Educational Awakening 2*(1), 1–26.

Hashim, R. (2009). Philosophy in the Islamic tradition. In E. Marsal, T. Dobashi & B. Weber (Eds.), *Children philosophize worldwide.* Frankfurt, Germany: Peter Lang.

Hashim, R. & Tan, C. (2009). A hyphenated identity: Fostering national unity through education in Malaysia and Singapore. *International Journal of Citizenship Teaching and Learning 5*(1), 46–59.

Hefner, R. W. (2005). Muslim democrats and Islamist violence in post-Soeharto Indonesia. In R. W. Hefner (Ed.), *Remaking Muslim politics: Pluralism, contestation, democratization.* (pp. 273–301). Princeton, NJ: Princeton University Press.

Hefner, R. W. (2009). Introduction: The politics and cultures of Islamic education in Southeast Asia. In R. W. Hefner (Ed.), *Making modern Muslims: The politics of Islamic education in Southeast Asia* (pp. 1–54). Honolulu, HI: University of Hawaii Press.

Heidegger, M. (1968). *Being and time.* New York: Harper and Row.

Hill, M. & Lian, K. F. (1995). *The politics of nation building and citizenship in Singapore.* New York, NY: Routledge.

Holmes, S. (1995). *Passions and constraint: On the theory of liberal democracy.* Chicago, IL: University of Chicago Press.

Huntington, S. P. (1996). *The clash of civilizations and the remaking of world order.* New York, NY: Simon & Schuster.

Ibn 'Abidin, Muhammad Amin ibn 'Umar. (1994). *Radd al-Muhtar ala al-Durr al-mukhtar sharh Tanwir al-absar.* Beirut, Lebanon: Dar al-Kutub al-'Ilmiyya.

Ibn al-Humam, Muhammad ibn 'Abd al-Wahid al-Siwasi. (n.d.). *Sharh fath al-qadir.* Beirut, Lebanon: Dar al-Fikr.

Ibn Kathir, Isma'il ibn 'Umar. (1998). *Tafsir al-Qur'an al-'Azim.* Beirut, Lebanon: Dar al-Kutub al-'Ilmiyya.

Ibn Qudama, Muwaffaq al-Din. (1990). *al-Mughni.* Cairo, Egypt: Hajar.

Ibn Rushd, Abu al-Walid ibn Muhammad ibn Ahmad. (1996). *Bidayat al-mujtahid wa nihayat al-muqtasid.* Beirut, Lebanon: Dar al-kutub al-'ilmiyya.

Ibn Taymiyya, Ahmad ibn 'Abd al-Halim. (1980). *Majmu' fatawa Sheikh al-Islam Ahmad Ibn Taymiyya.* Rabat, Morocco: Maktabat al-Ma'arif.

Idid, S. A. (Ed.). (2009). *IIUM at 25: The path travelled and the way forward.* Kuala Lumpur, Malaysia: IIUM Press.

Inglehart, R. & Norris, P. (2003). The true clash of civilizations. *Foreign Policy.* (March/April) 62–70.

International Crisis Group. (2002). *Indonesia: The search for peace in Maluku.* (Asia Report No. 31). Jakarta & Brussels: ICG.

Ismail, R. & Shaw, B. J. (2006). Singapore's Malay-Muslim minority: Social identification in a Post-'9/11 world'. *Asian Ethnicity* 7(1), 37–51.

Jakubowicz, A. (2005). Pluralism in crisis—challenges to multicultural agendas in the UK, the USA, Canada, and Australia. *Ideas in Action: Social Inquiry Seminar Series*, September.

Jedwab, J. (2005). Muslims and multicultural futures in western democracies: Is Kymlicka's pessimism warranted? *Canadian Diversity* 4(3), 92–96.

Jelen, T. G., & Wilcox, C. (2002). Religion and politics in an open market: Religious mobilization in the United States. In T. G. Jelen & C. Wilcox (Eds.), *Religion and politics in comparative perspective: The one, the few, and the many* (pp. 1–26), New York, NY: Cambridge University Press.

Joppke, C. (2004). The retreat of multiculturalism in the liberal state: theory and policy. *The British Journal of Sociology* 55(2), 237–257.

Kadir, S. (2004). Islam, state and society in Singapore. *Inter-Asia Cultural Studies* 5(3), 357–371.

Kamali, M. H. (1997). *Freedom of expression in Islam.* Cambridge, U.K.: Islamic Texts Society.

Kant, I. (1983). An answer to the question: What is enlightenment? In T. Humphrey (Trans.), *Perpetual peace and other essays* (pp. 41–48). Indianapolis, IN: Hackett Publishers.

Kastoryano, R. (2006). French secularism and Islam: France's headscarf affair. In T. Modood, A.Triandafyllidou, & R. Zapata-Barrero (Eds.). *Multiculturalism, Muslims and citizenship* (pp. 57–69). New York, NY: Routledge.

Kazmi, Y. (2000). Historical consciousness and the notion of an authentic self in the Qur'an: Towards an Islamic critical theory. *Islamic studies 39*(3), 27–42.

Kazmi, Y. (2006). Rise and learning of Islamic culture. *Occasional paper no. 63*. Islamabad, Pakistan: Islamic Research Institute.

Kazmi, Y. & Hashim, Y. (2010). Is being Muslim a fact or a challenge? A perspective of Muslim identity, citizenship and Islamic education. In M.S. Merry & J.A. Milligan (Eds.) New York, NY: Palgrave Macmillan.

Kedourie, E.(1992). *Democracy and Arab political culture*. Washington, D.C.: Washington Institute for Near-East Policy.

Kennedy, K. J. (2004). Searching for citizenship values in an uncertain global environment. In W. O. Lee, D. L. Grossman, K. J. Kennedy & G. P. Fairbrother (Eds.), *Citizenship education in Asia and the Pacific: Concepts and issues.* (pp. 9–24). Hong Kong: Comparative Education Research Centre, The University of Hong Kong.

Keppel, G. (2005, August 24). Europe's answer to Londonistan. *openDemocracy*. Retrieved from http://www.opendemocracy.net/conflict-terrorism/londonistan_2775.jsp#

Klausen, J. (2005). *The Islamic challenge: Politics and religion in western Europe*. New York, NY: Oxford University Press.

Knight, J. & Johnson, J. (1994). Aggregation and deliberation: On the possibility of democratic legitimacy. *Political Theory 22*), 277–96.

Kabbani, R. (1989). *Letter to Christendom*. London, UK: Virago Press.

Kraince, R. G. (2003). *The Role of Islamic Student Activists in Divergent Movements for Reform During Indonesia's Transition from Authoritarian Rule, 1998–2001.* (Unpublished doctoral dissertation). Ohio University, Athens, Ohio.

Kuru, A. T. (2003). Fethullah Gülen's search for a middle way between modernity and Muslim tradition, in M. H. Yavuz and J. L. Esposito (Eds.), *Turkish Islam and the secular state: The Gülen movement*. Syracuse: Syracuse University Press.

Kuru, A. T. (2009). *Secularism and state policies toward religion: The United States, France, and Turkey.* New York: Cambridge University Press.

Kuru, Z. A. and A. T. Kuru. (2008). Apolitical interpretation of Islam: Said Nursi's faith-based activism in comparison with political Islamism and Sufism. *Islam and Christian-Muslim Relations 19*(1): 99–111.

Kymlicka, W. (2005). The uncertain futures of multiculturalism. *Canadian Diversity 4*(1), 82–85.

Lewis, B. (1992). Legal and historical reflections on the position of Muslim populations under non-Muslim rule. *Journal of the Institute of Muslim Minority Affairs 13*.

Maalouf, A. (2000). *On identity*. London: Harvill Press.

Machmudi, Y. (2006). *Islamising Indonesia: The rise of Jemaah Tarbiyah and the Prosperous Justice Party (PKS)*. (Unpublished doctoral dissertation). Australian National University, Canberra, Australia.

MacIntyre, A. (1998). *Whose justice? Which rationality?* Notre Dame, IN: University of Notre Dame Press.

Madrid, R. (1999). Islamic students in the Indonesian student movement, 1998–1999: Forces for moderation. *Bulletin of Concerned Asian Scholars 31*(3), 17–32.

Mahmoud, S. (2005). *Politics of piety: The Islamic revival and the feminist subject*. Princeton, NJ: Princeton University Press.

Majlis Ugama Islam Singapura (MUIS). (2002). *Our home, our world: Islamic Social Studies. Primary level 1A*. Singapore: MUIS.

Majlis Ugama Islam Singapura (MUIS). (2004a). *Singapore Islamic education system: A conceptual framework*. Singapore: MUIS, Islamic Education Strategic Unit.

Majlis Ugama Islam Singapura (MUIS). (2004b). *Our neighbourhood, our world: Islamic social studies. primary level 2B*. Singapore: MUIS.

Majlis Ugama Islam Singapura (MUIS). (2005). *Our society, our world. Islamic social studies. primary level 4A*. Singapore: MUIS.

Majlis Ugama Islam Singapura (MUIS). (2006). *Our society, our world. Islamic social studies. primary level 4B*. Singapore: MUIS.

Majlis Ugama Islam Singapura (MUIS). (2008). *Our ummah, our world. Islamic social studies. Primary level 6B*. Singapore: MUIS.

Majlis Ugama Islam Singapura (MUIS). (2009). *Our madrasah*. Retrieved from http://www.muis.gov.sg/cms/services/Madrasahs.aspx?id=204

Manin, B. (1987). On legitimacy and political deliberation. *Political Theory 15*, 338–68.

Mansbridge, J. (1999). Everyday talk in the deliberative system. In S. Macedo (Ed.), *Deliberative politics: Essays on democracy and disagreement*. New York, NY: Oxford University Press.

March, A. F. (2006). Liberal citizenship and the search for an overlapping consensus: The case of Muslim minorities. *Philosophy & Public Affairs 34*(4), 373–421.

Maududi, S. A. (1979). *Purdah and the status of women in Islam*. Lahore, Pakistan: Islamic Publications.

Maududi, S. A. (1980). *Human rights in Islam*. Leicester, U.K.: Islamic Foundation.

Maududi, S. A. (1990). *Toward understanding Islam*. Salimiah, Kuwait: IIFSO.

Mawdudi, S. A. (1990). *Towards understanding the Qur'an*. Leicester, UK: The Islamic Foundation.

Mawlawi, F. (1990). al-Mafahim al-asasiyya li-al-da'wa al-islamiyya fi bilad al-gharb. In M.A. Shamala (Ed.), *Risalat al-muslimin fi bilad al-gharb*. Irbid, Jordan: Dar al-Amal.

Mawlawi, F. (2003). How should Muslims in the west deal with the Iraqi crisis? Retrieved from http://www.islamonline.net/fatwa/english/FatwaDisplay.asp?hFatwaID=97351

McPherson, M. (1983). Want formation, morality, and some interpretive aspects of economic inquiry. In N. Haan, R.N. Bellah, P. Rabinow & W.M. Sullivan (Eds.), *Social science as moral inquiry*. (pp. 96–124). New York, NY: Columbia University Press.

Meer, N. (2008). The politics of voluntary and involuntary identities: Are Muslims in Britain an ethnic, racial or religious minority? *Patterns of Prejudice 42*(1), 61–81.

Meer, N. & Modood, T. (2010). The multicultural state we're in: Muslims, 'multiculture' and the 'civic rebalancing' of British multiculturalism, *Political Studies, 57*(3): 473–97.

Miller, D. (1995). *On nationality*. Oxford, UK: Oxford University Press.

Miller, J. (1996). *God has ninety-nine names: Reporting from a militant Middle East*. New York: Simon & Schuster.

Ministry of Education (MOE). (1999). *Social studies syllabus primary*. Singapore: MOE.

Minority Rights Group Report on the Chinese in Southeast Asia. (1992). Minority rights group report on the Chinese in Southeast Asia. In T.L. Ee. (1997). *The politics of Chinese education in Malaya 1945–1961*. Kuala Lumpur, Malaysia: Oxford University Press.

Modood, T. (1992) *Not easy being British: Colour, culture and citizenship*. London, UK: Runnymede Trust/Trentham Books.

Modood, T. (1998). Anti-essentialism, multiculturalism and the "recognition" of religious Minorities. *Journal of Political Philosophy 6*(4), 378–399.

Modood, T. (2005). *Multicultural politics: Racism, ethnicity and Muslims in Britain*. Minneapolis, MN: University of Minnesota Press.

Modood, T. (2007). *Multiculturalism: A civic idea*. Polity Press.

Modood, T. (2008). Multiculturalism and groups. *Social and Legal Studies 17*(4).

Modood, T. (2010). Moderate secularism, religion as identity and respect for religion. *Political Quarterly 81*(1): 4–14.

Modood, T. & F. Ahmad. (2007). British Muslim perspectives on multiculturalism. *Theory, Culture and Society 24*(1), 187–213.

Monsma, S. V., & Soper, J. C. (2009). *The challenge of pluralism: Church and state in five Democracies.* Lanham, MD: Rowman & Littlefield.

Moussalli, A. S. (1992). *Radical Islamic fundamentalism: The ideological and political discourse of Sayyid Qutb.* Beirut, Lebanon: American University of Beirut.

Mutalib, H. (1990). *Islam and ethnicity in Malay politics.* Singapore: Oxford University Press.

Muslim, Abu al-Husayn. (1998). *Sahih Muslim.* Beirut, Lebanon: Dar Ibn Hazm.

Nadwi, S. A. H. (1983). *Muslims in the west: The message and mission.* Leicester, UK: The Islamic Foundation. al-Nawawi, A. Z. (2000). *al-Majmu' Sharh al-Muhadhdhab.* Beirut, Lebanon: Dar al-Fikr.

Norris, P. (Ed.). (1999). *Critical citizens: Global support for democratic governance.* Oxford, U.K.: Oxford University Press.

Norris, P. & Inglehart, R. (2004). *Sacred and secular: Religion and politics worldwide.* Cambridge, UK: Cambridge University Press.

Nursi, Bediüzzaman Said. (1996 [1909]). *Münazarat in Risale-i Nur Külliyatı.* Istanbul: Nesil.

Oakeshott, M. (1962). *Rationalism in politics.* London, UK: Methuen & Co. Ltd.

O'Donnell, M. (2007). 'We' need human rights not nationalism 'lite': Globalisation and British Solidarity. *Ethnicities 27*(2), 248–269.

Okin, S. M. (1998). Feminism and multiculturalism: Some tensions. *Ethics 108*, 661–684.

Okin, S. M. (2002). 'Mistresses of their own destiny': Group rights, gender, and realistic rights of exit. *Ethics 112*, 205–230.

Ooi, G. L. (1998). The role of the developmental state and interethnic relations in Singapore. *Asian Ethnicity 6*(2), 109–120.

Othman, M. R. (2005). Egypt's religious and intellectual influence on Malay society. *Katha-Journal of the Centre for Civilizational Dialogue 1*, 1–18.

Owen, D. & Tully, J. (2007). Redistribution and recognition: Two approaches. In A. S. Laden & David Owen (Eds.) *Multiculturalism and political theory* (pp. 265–291). New York, NY: Cambridge University Press.

Parekh, B. (1991). British citizenship and cultural difference. In G. Andrews (Ed.) *Citizenship: The remaking of a progressive politics.* London, UK: Lawrence & Wishart.

Parekh, B. (2000). *Rethinking multiculturalism: Cultural diversity and political theory.* Basingstoke, UK: Macmillan.

Pharr, S. J. & Putnam, R.D. (Eds.). (2000). *Disaffected democracies: What's troubling the trilateral countries?* Princeton, NJ: Princeton University Press.

Phillips, A. (2007). *Multiculturalism without culture.* Princeton, NJ: Princeton University Press.

Pipes, D. (1983). *In the path of God: Islam and political power.* New York, NY: Basic Books.

PPIM. *Pesantren Indepen: Profil dan Prospek* [Independent Pesantrens: Profiles and Prospects]. Jakarta: PPIM, UIN, Jakarta, 2004.

Preston, P. (2007). Freedom from Britain: A comment on recent elite-sponsored political cultural identities. *British Journal of Politics and International Relations 9*, 158–164.

Purushotam, N. (1998). *Negotiating language, constructing race: Disciplining difference in Singapore.* Berlin, Germany: Mouton de Gruyter.

al-Qurtubi, Muhammad ibn Ahmad. (1996). *al-Jami' li ahkam al-Qur'an.* Beirut, Lebanon: Dar al-Kutub al-'Ilmiyya, 1996.

al-Qaradawi, Y. (2001a). *Fi fiqh al-aqalliyyat al-muslima.* Cairo, Egypt: Dar al-Shuruq.

al-Qaradawi, Y. (2001b). Ulama's fatwas on American Muslim participating in US military campaign. Retrieved from www.islamonline.net/fatwa/english/FatwaDisplay.asp?hFatwaID=52014

al-Qaradawi, Y. (2003). Backing the wronged Afghans. Retrieved from www.islamonline.net/fatwa/english/FatwaDisplay.asp?hFatwaID=51564

Qutb, S. (2001). *In the shade of the Qur'an.* A. Salahi & A. Shamis (Eds./Trans.). Leicester, UK: The Islamic Foundation.

Qutb, S. (n.d.) *Milestones.* Damascus, Egypt: Dar Al-Ilm.

Ramadan, T. (1999). *To be a European Muslim.* Leicester, UK: The Islamic Foundation.

Rawls, J. (1993). *Political liberalism.* New York, NY: Columbia University Press.

Raz, J. (1998). Disagreement in politics. *American Journal of Jurisprudence 43,* 25–52.

Rida, M. R.(1980). *Fatawa al-Imam Muhammad Rashid Rida.* S.D. al Munajjid & Y. Q. Khuri (Eds.). Beirut, Lebanon: Dar al-Kitab al-Jadid.

Robbins, J. (2004). The globalization of Pentecostal and Charismatic Christianity. *Annual Review of Anthropology 33,* 117–43.

Rukhaidah S. (2001). *Language and identity among Singapore madrasah students.* (Unpublished honors thesis). Singapore: National University of Singapore.

Saeed, A. & Saeed, H.(2004). *Freedom of religion, apostasy and Islam.* Burlington, VT: Ashgate Publishing.

Safi, L. (2003). *Tensions and transitions in the Muslim world.* Lanham, MD: University Press of America.

al-Sarakhsi, M. A. (2001). *Kitab al-Mabsut.* Beirut, Lebanon: Dar al-Kutub al 'Ilmiyya.

Shaltut, M. (1983). *al-Qur'an wa al-qital.* Beirut, Lebanon: Dar al-Fath.

al-Shaybani, M.H. (1966). *The Islamic law of nations: Shaybani's Siyar.* M. Khadduri (Trans.). Baltimore, MD: Johns Hopkins Press.

al-Shirazi, A. I. (n.d.). *al-Muhadhdhab fi fiqh al-Imam al-Shafi'i.* Beirut, Lebanon: Dar al-Fikr.

al-Shithri, S. M. (n.d.). *Hukm al-luju' wa al-iqama fi bilad al-kuffar.* Riyad, Saudi Arabia: Dar al Habib.

Sandel, M. (1981). *Liberalism and the limits of justice.* Cambridge, UK: Cambridge University Press.

Sanders, L. M. (1997). Against deliberation. *Political Theory 25,* 347–76.

Savage, T. (2004). Europe and Islam: Crescent waxing, cultures clashing. *The Washington Quarterly 27*(3), 25–50.

Sayyid, S. (2000). Beyond Westphalia: Nations and diasporas: The case of the Muslim *Umma* and diasporic logics. In B. Hesse (Ed.). *Un/settled multiculturalisms.* New York: Zed Books Ltd.

Sayyid, S. (2007). Secularism, multiculturalism and the postcolonial. In G. B. Levey & T. Modood (Eds.). *Secularism, religion and multicultural citizenship.* Cambridge, UK: Cambridge University Press.

Schauer, F. (1999). Talking as a decision procedure. In S. Macedo (Ed.). *Deliberative politics: essays on democracy and disagreement.* (pp. 17–27). New York, NY: Oxford University Press.

Schmidt, G. (2004). *Islam in urban America: Sunni Muslims in Chicago.* Philadelphia, PA: Temple University Press.

Schiffauer, W. (2006). Enemies within the gates: The debate about the citizenship of Muslims in Germany. In T. Modood, A. Triandafyllidou, & R. Zapata-Barrero (Eds.) *Multiculturalism, Muslims and citizenship.* (pp. 94–116). Abingdon, UK: Routledge.

Shapiro, I. (1999). Enough of deliberation: Politics is about interests and power. In S. Macedo, (Ed.). *Deliberative politics: essays on democracy and disagreement.* (pp. 28–38). New York, NY: Oxford University Press.

Sim, J. B. Y. & Print, M. (2005). Citizenship education and social studies in Singapore: A national agenda. *International Journal of Citizenship and Teacher Education 1*(1), 58–73.

Sim, S. F. (2001). Asian values, authoritarianism and capitalism in Singapore. *The Public 8*(2), 45–66.

Snow, D. A., Rochford, E. B., Worden, S. K. Worden & Benford, R.W. (1986). Frame align-ment process, micromobilization, and movement participation. *American Sociological Review* 51, 461–81.

Soroush, 'A. (2000). *Reason, freedom, and democracy in Islam: Essential writings of 'Abdolkarim Soroush*. New York, NY: Oxford University Press.

Swaine, L. (2006). *The liberal conscience: Politics and principle in a world of religious pluralism*. New York, NY: Columbia University Press.

Swaine, L. (2009). Deliberate and free: Heteronomy in the public sphere. *Philosophy & Social Criticism* 35(1–2), 183–213.

Swaine, L. (2010). Heteronomous citizenship: Civic virtue and the chains of autonomy. *Educational Philosophy and Theory* 42(1), 73–93.

al-Tabari, A. J. (1999). *Jami' al-bayan fi ta'wil al-Qur'an*. Beirut, Lebanon: Dar al-Kutub al 'Ilmiyya.

Tan, C. (2007a). Islam and citizenship education in Singapore: Challenges and implications. *Education, Citizenship and Social Justice* 2(1), 23–39.

Tan, C. (2007b). Narrowing the gap: The educational achievements of the Malay community in Singapore. *Intercultural Education* 18(1), 71–82.

Tan, C. (2008a). Creating "good citizens" and maintaining religious harmony in Singapore. *British Journal of Religious Education* 30(2), 133–142.

Tan, C. (2008b). (Re)imagining the Muslim identity in Singapore. *Studies in Ethnicity and Nationalism* 8(1), 31–43.

Tan, C. (2009). Maximising the overlapping area: Multiculturalism and the Muslim identity for madrasahs in Singapore. *Journal of Beliefs and Values* 30(1), 41–48.

Tan, C. (2010). Contesting reform: Bernstein's pedagogic device and madrasah education in Singapore. *Journal of Curriculum Studies* 1, 1–18.

Tan, E. K. B. (2007). Norming "moderation" in an "iconic target": Public policy and the regu-lation of religious anxieties in Singapore. *Terrorism and Political Violence* 19(4), 443–462.

Tan L. E. (1997). *The politics of Chinese education in Malaya 1945–1961*. Kuala Lumpur, Malaysia: Oxford University Press.

Tarrow, S. (1998). *Power in movement: Social movements and contentious politics*. Cambridge, UK: Cambridge University Press.

Taylor, C. (1985). *Philosophy and the human sciences: Philosophical papers 2*. Cambridge, UK: Cambridge University Press.

Taylor, C. (1989). *Sources of the self: The making of modern identity*. Cambridge, MA: Harvard University Press.

Taylor, C. (1991). *The ethics of authenticity*. Cambridge, MA: Harvard University Press.

Taylor, C. (1994). Multiculturalism and the politics of recognition. In A. Gutmann (Ed.) *Multiculturalism and 'the politics of recognition.'* Princeton, NJ: Princeton University Press.

Thompson, M. R. (2004). Pacific Asia after 'Asian values': Authoritarianism, democracy, and 'good governance.' *Third World Quarterly* 25(6), 1079–1095.

Topoljak, S. (1997). *Al-Ahkam al-siyasiyya li-al-aqalliyat al-muslima fi al-fiqh al-Islami*. Beirut, Lebanon: Dar al-Nafa'is.

Van Bruinessesn, M. (2002). Genealogies of Islamic radicalism in post-Suharto Indonesia. *South East Asia Research* 10(2), 117–54.

Verba, S., Schlozman, K. L. & Brady, H. E. Brady. (1995). *Voice and equality: Civic voluntarism in American politics*. Cambridge, MA: Harvard University Press.

Voll, J. O. (1991). Islamic issues for Muslims in the United States. In Yvonne Haddad (Ed.), *The Muslims of America*. New York: Oxford University Press.

Walzer, M. (1970). *Obligations: Essays on disobedience, war, and citizenship*. Cambridge, MA: Harvard University Press.

Walzer, M. (1983). *Spheres of justice*. Oxford, UK: Blackwell.

al-Wansharisi, A. Y. (1981). *al-Mi'yar al-Mu'rib wa al jami' al-mughrib 'an fatawa ahl Ifiiqiya wa'l-Andalus wa'l-Maghrib*. M. Hajji (Ed.). Rabat, Morocco: Ministry of Religious Endowments and Islamic Affairs.

Watson, B. C. S. (1999). Liberal communitarianism as political theory. *Perspectives on Political Science 28*(4), 211–217.

Wertheimer, A. (1999). Internal disagreements: Deliberation and abortion. In S. Macedo (Ed.), *Deliberative politics: Essays on democracy and disagreement*. (pp. 170–183). New York, NY: Oxford University Press.

Wickham, C. R. (2002). *Mobilizing Islam: Religion, activism, and political change in Egypt*. New York, NY: Columbia University Press.

Wiktorowicz, Q. (2004). *Islamic activism: A social movement approach*. Bloomington, IN: Indiana University Press.

Winch, C. & Gingell, J. (2004). *Philosophy & educational policy: A critical introduction*. Oxfordshire, UK: RoutledgeFalmer.

Wolf, M. (2005, August 31). When multiculturalism is nonsense. *Financial Times*. Retrieved From http://news.ft.com/cms/s/4c751acc-19bc-11da-804e-00000e2511c8.html

World Economic Forum. (2003). *The global information technology report 2008–2009*. Retrieved from http://www.weforum.org/en/initiatives/gcp/Global%20Information%20Technology%20Report/index.htm

Ye, L. S. (2003). *The Chinese dilemma*. Kingsford, NSW: East West Publishing Ltd.

Young, I. M. (1990). *Justice and the politics of difference*. Princeton, NJ: Princeton University Press.

Young, I. M. (2000). *Inclusion and democracy*. New York, NY: Oxford University Press.

Zubaida, S. (2003). *Law and power in the Islamic world*. London, UK: I.B. Tauris.

al-Zuhayli, W. (1981). *al-'Alaqat al-duwaliyya fi al-Islam*. Beirut, Lebanon: Mu'assasat al-risala.

CONTRIBUTORS

Rosnani Hashim is Professor of Educational Foundations and Associate Director of the Centre for Philosophical Inquiry in Education, Institute of Education, International Islamic University of Malaysia. Her areas of research interest are curriculum of Islamic education, Moral and Citizenship education, Malaysian educational policies, and the pedagogy of philosophical inquiry for schools. She has collaborated on international research projects on moral, religious, and citizenship education. Her publications include *Educational Dualism in Malaysia: Implications for Theory and Practice* (Oxford University Press 1996), *Economics of Education from an Islamic Perspective* (KL: DBP, 2000, in Malay), and *The Teaching of Thinking in Malaysia* (2003). She is presently editor of *Jurnal Pendidikan Islam* (Journal of Islamic Education, Malaysia).

Robert W. Hefner is Director of the Institute on Culture, Religion, and World Affairs at Boston University and the author or editor of some fifteen books on Islam, modern politics, and citizenship. His most recent book is the edited sixth volume of the *New Cambridge History of Islam, Muslims and Modernity: Society and Culture since 1800.*

H. A. Hellyer is Fellow of the Centre for Research in Ethnic Relations at the University of Warwick, and Founding Director of Muslim world-West relations research consultancy, the Visionary Consultants Group. A public commentator in various media in the West and the Muslim world, he is widely published in academic journals on subjects ranging from political philosophy, the interplay between religion and modernity, to the dynamics of the Western Muslim presence. He has taught and researched in various countries in the West and the Muslim world, and is frequently consulted by different governments in his subject areas. Dr. Hellyer's most recent book is *Muslims of Europe: the "Other" Europeans* (Edinburgh University Press, 2009).

Yedullah Kazmi is Associate Professor at the Institute of Education, International Islamic University Malaysia. His general interests include philosophy of education, with specific interests in philosophy of Islamic education. His work has appeared in such journals as *Studies in Philosophy and Education*, *Philosophy and Social Criticism* and *Islamic Studies*.

Ahmet T. Kuru is Assistant Professor of Political Science at San Diego State University. He was the Postdoctoral Scholar and Assistant Director of the Center for the Study of Democracy, Toleration, and Religion at Columbia University. Kuru received his PhD from the University of Washington, Seattle. He is the author of *Secularism and State Policies toward Religion: The United States, France, and Turkey* (Cambridge University Press, 2009). This book is based on his dissertation that was given the Wildavsky Best Dissertation Award by Religion and Politics Section of the American Political Science Association. Kuru is also the author of numerous articles published in journals including *World Politics*, *Comparative Politics*, and *Political Science Quarterly*.

Andrew F. March teaches political theory and Islamic political thought at Yale University. He is the author of *Islam and Liberal Citizenship: The Search for an Overlapping Consensus* (OUP, 2009), which won the Award for Excellence from the American Academy of Religion. He has published articles on Islamic law and Muslim minorities in *American Political Science Review*, *Philosophy & Public Affairs*, *Journal of Political Philosophy*, *European Journal of Political Theory*, *Ethics & International Affairs* and the *Cardozo Law Review*.

Michael S. Merry is professor of philosophy of education in the faculty of social and behavioural sciences at the University of Amsterdam. His writing covers a wide range of topics, though he engages primarily in minority studies, applied philosophy and ethics in the field of education. He is the author of *Culture, Identity and Islamic Schooling: a philosophical approach* (Palgrave, 2007).

Jeffrey Ayala Milligan is an associate professor of philosophy of education and international development education in the Department of Educational Leadership and Policy Studies at Florida State University. His research focuses on relations between religious communities and education in the U.S. and the Muslim societies of Southeast

Asia. He is the author of *Islamic Identity, Postcoloniality and Educational Policy: Schooling and Ethno-Religious Conflict in the Southern Philippines* (Palgrave, 2005).

Tariq Modood is the founding Director of the Centre for the Study of Ethnicity and Citizenship at the University of Bristol. He is a regular contributor to media and policy debates in Britain, was awarded a MBE for services to social sciences and ethnic relations in 2001, and elected a member of the Academy of Social Sciences in 2004. His latest books are *Multiculturalism: A Civic Idea* (Polity, 2007) and as co-editor with G. B. Levey, *Secularism, Religion and Multicultural Citizenship* (CUP, 2009).

Intan A. Mokhtar is an Assistant Professor in the Policy and Leadership Studies Academic Group in the National Institute of Education (NIE), Nanyang Technological University (NTU), Singapore. Prior to joining the NIE, she was an Assistant Professor of Educational Technology in the Department of Education, College of Arts and Sciences (CAS), Abu Dhabi University (ADU) in the United Arab Emirates. Her research interests are in information literacy, ICT and new media in teaching and learning, and school media libraries.

Matthew J. Nelson teaches in the Department of Politics at SOAS (University of London). His work on the politics of Islamic law has been published by Columbia University Press (*In the Shadow of Shari'ah: Islam, Islamic Law, and Democracy in Pakistan*, 2010); his work on the politics of Islamic education has appeared in several journals, including *Asian Survey, Modern Asian Studies*, and *Commonwealth and Comparative Politics*. In 2009 and 2010, while preparing his chapter for this volume, Dr. Nelson held the Wolfensohn Family Membership in the School of Social Science at the Institute for Advanced Study in Princeton.

Lucas Swaine is Associate Professor of Government at Dartmouth College. He works chiefly in political theory and philosophy, with associated interests in religion and politics, history of political thought, constitutional law, and ethics. He is the author of *The Liberal Conscience: Politics and Principle in a World of Religious Pluralism* (New York: Columbia University Press, 2006), and has published articles in a wide range of journals, including *Journal of Political Philosophy, Ethics, Philosophy & Social Criticism, Contemporary Political Theory, Journal of Church and State*, and *Critical Review*. He is currently pursuing a book length project on heteronomy and heteronomous citizenship in liberal democratic life.

Charlene Tan is an Associate Professor at the National Institute of Education, Nanyang Technological University, Singapore. She has been a Visiting Research Associate at the Oxford Centre for Islamic Studies and a Visiting Scholar at the Prince Alwaleed Bin Talal Centre of Islamic Studies, University of Cambridge. Her research and teaching areas are located in the fields of Islamic/Muslim education, philosophy of education, education policy, and comparative education.

INDEX